Inside the caring services

David Tossell, MSc, BSc (Soc.) (Hons), CQSW, PGCE
Lecturer in social studies,
Department of Community Care,
Kilburn College, London

and

Richard Webb, MA, BSc (Soc.) (Hons), CQSW, PGCE
Lecturer in sociology and social work,
Health, Community and Social Care,
Parkwood College, Sheffield

Edward Arnold

A division of Hodder & Stoughton

LONDON   MELBOURNE   AUCKLAND

© 1986 David Tossell, Richard Webb

First published in Great Britain 1986
  Second impression 1987
  Third impression 1988
  Fourth impression 1989

British Library Cataloguing in Publication Data

Tossell, David
  Inside the caring services.
  1. Public welfare — Great Britain
  I. Title   II. Webb, Richard
  361′.941   HV245

  ISBN 0-7131-3562-X

Typeset in 10/11 pt Compugraphic English Times by Colset Private
Ltd, Singapore.
Printed and bound in Great Britain for Edward Arnold, the
educational, academic and medical publishing division of Hodder
and Stoughton Limited, 41 Bedford Square, London WC1B 3DQ by
Richard Clay Ltd, Bungay, Suffolk

Contents

hostels for offenders. Therapeutic communities. Conclusion. Appendix. Exercises. Questions for essays or discussion. Further reading.

Introduction

What this book sets out to do

A number of books already exist which describe the organisation of the caring services, but such texts can be academic and rather dull. They give little insight into what those engaged in working for the various caring services actually *do* in their daily working lives. This book takes a different and new approach – it looks at the caring services from the viewpoint of the practitioners and clearly outlines their roles, tasks, and responsibilities. Other books on social work describe the problems that clients face in terms of separate client categories – for example, the elderly, the handicapped, offenders, etc. In this book, the problems are viewed from the perspective of the practitioners – for example, social workers, teachers, doctors, or nursery nurses – and how they deal with them. The needs of clients are still highlighted, but from a different viewpoint.

Who the book is written for

The book is aimed at helping anyone who wants to work in the caring services to understand the roles of those already doing so and to grasp the relationship between the various agencies involved, both statutory and voluntary. As a source of reference, it will be useful for anyone currently engaged in the caring services. Primarily, however, the book is designed as a course book for students undergoing preliminary or in-service social-work training, on such courses as the CCETSW-accredited Preliminary Certificate in Social Care (PCSC) course and the In-service Course in Social Care (ICSC). Medical and nursery nurses will find it of benefit for the social-studies components of their courses. For older students on CSS and CQSW courses it will clarify a great deal, and younger students on YTS and CPVE programmes and those doing vocational studies in schools will find it of value. We are confident that the adult interested in, but with no relevant work experience of, the caring services will also find it helpful. Finally, we think that the general reader, on picking it up out of interest or curiosity, will find it a good read.

The structure of the book

After an introductory chapter which deals with some 'key concepts' which often cause confusion, the major statutory agencies are dealt with. The voluntary sector and residential social work are then examined. The next chapter explores the theory and practice of social work, and this is followed by a discussion of the qualities needed by the carer. After a review of current developments in the caring services, the final chapter outlines the economic and political constraints within which the caring services operate. Two annexes to the main text discuss the training courses available to those wishing to work in the caring services and offer advice on the practical work placements which form a part of most of these courses. The index is as comprehensive as possible and includes a good deal of cross-referencing.

Sources of information in the book

In addition to the expository text, the book contains other types of material:

a) *Illustrations*   These are intended to focus the reader's attention on the textual material, and hopefully to lighten it.

b) *Diagrams*   These interpret complex material pictorially in a precise and easily accessible way. Many are deliberately simplified in order to facilitate understanding.

c) *Appendices*   Found at the end of some chapters, these contain case material from practitioners' working experience. These 'flesh out' and expand on the text and so enhance the reader's understanding of what carers actually do. The names quoted are fictitious. In some cases, a 'typical day's work' is presented to enhance the reader's knowledge of what particular jobs involve.

d) *Exercises*   Almost all chapters include practical or role-play exercises for students to undertake in a small or large group setting. Some roles are prescribed, others are more open, thus leaving interpretation to those involved.   The role-play settings are based on 'real-work' situations – again, the names are fictitious. The non-student reader will find the exercises informative, and they will highlight dilemmas frequently faced by carers.

e) *Questions for essays or discussion*   Most chapters contain six of these. Decide yourself on how best to use them. Some build on the text; others introduce topics not mentioned in the text. Many are included for their controversial nature.

f) *Further reading*   We have resisted the temptation to include academically acclaimed texts. Rather we have recommended reading which is informative, interesting, and 'readable'. We have in addition provided the reader with a short indication as to what the material covers. We suggest that readers keep in touch with developments in the caring services by reading weekly journals such as *Community care*, *Social work today*, and *New statesman and society*, as well as 'quality' daily and weekly newspapers.

A note on gender-specific language

In this book we wanted to avoid reinforcing stereotyped sex roles and the traditional general use of the pronoun 'he', which would imply that caring roles are normally undertaken by males. All jobs in the caring services can be, and are, performed equally well by both males and females, and we wanted the text to reflect this.

We rejected the idea of using 's/he' as being too clumsy. Using 'he or she' and 'his or her' we considered cumbersome. We therefore decided to alternate gender so that in chapter 1 the carer is male and the client is female, in chapter 2 the carer is female and the client male, and so on throughout the book. We have made an exception when describing the work of the police – they are referred to as male, as this accurately reflects the predominant composition of the force.

And finally . . .

Much of the material in the book has been drawn from our own experience as a practising social worker or probation officer and as teachers of social work in further education. In order to obtain authentic information about areas of work with which we are less familiar, we have sought the help of a wide range of fellow-professionals who have provided up-to-date useful material concerning their own field (details will be found in our acknowledgements). Any inaccuracies or shortcomings are, of course, our own responsibility.

We hope that you will enjoy this book and that it will help you to build on and extend your own knowledge and personal resources and assist in your intention to become a more effective carer.

David Tossell
Richard Webb

Acknowledgements

We would like to thank the following people for the insight they have given us into the nature of their work within the caring services.

We are particularly indebted to Alan Berry (senior social worker), Stuart Kemp (assistant chief probation officer), Jan Kemp (senior lecturer, social work), Dr Timothy Lambert (psychiatrist), and Howard Millerman (head of year, secondary school).

We are also grateful to Inspector Philip Carman (police community contact), Rod Chambers (study supervisor, social services), Graham Chapman (housing research officer), Alma Cohen (senior social worker, child guidance), John Diamond (lecturer, access) Jim Donoghue (community worker), Ron Eade (NSPCC inspector), Malcolm Freeman (officer-in-charge), Liz George (educational psychologist), Suzanne Kegin (nursery nurse), Catherine Loftus (lecturer, residential social work), Christine Mullaley (lecturer, health), Ann Mycock (social worker), Shelagh Norton (nursery nurse), Brenda O'Driscoll (principal social worker), Dorothy Phillips (social worker), Mary Singer (careers officer), Caroline Staines (officer-in-charge), Michael Tossell (senior clinical psychologist), Phil Williams (social-work training officer), Dr Stephen Waldman (general practitioner), Mark Walker (officer-in-charge), and Stephen Ward (lecturer, health).

We are also very appreciative of the help, advice, and hard work of Bob Davenport at Edward Arnold (Publishers) Ltd.

The diagram of system-induced old age on page 214 is reproduced by kind permission of Bob Browne, and the diagrams on pages 268–9, showing routes to the CQSW, are reproduced by courtesy of the Central Council for Education and Training in Social Work.

Finally, we wish to thank Joyce Tossell for the hard work and long hours she devoted to deciphering the sense of the original manuscript.

David Tossell
Richard Webb

1 Concepts used in this book

There are a number of terms and descriptions which need to be clarified before a discussion of the work of the caring services can begin. What, for example, do people mean when they say they are going down to 'the social'. Are they going to claim welfare benefits at the Department of Health and Social Security (DHSS), or are they going to see a social worker at the social-services department (SSD)? Could they even mean that they are on their way to an activity being held at the local community centre? What if they had said they were going to 'the welfare' – would this have given a clearer indication of their destination?

Part of the reason for the ambiguity of certain terms is that, at different times over the years, different government departments have had responsibility for providing services, and often the areas of responsibility overlapped.

The picture today is much clearer, but it is necessary now to distinguish between the roles of individuals and differing organisations so that the range and work of the caring services can be fully understood.

The Welfare State

This refers to all the provisions made by the government, or State, for people's needs. ('The State' basically means central and local government, along with the Civil Service.) It should ensure *minimum standards* of income, health, housing, and education. With the development of the Welfare State, these services ceased to be provided by charities, and it became the right of everyone in our society to receive them. The Welfare State includes all the services provided by the social-services department (SSD), the Department of Health and Social Security (DHSS), the National Health Service (NHS), and the Probation Service.

The Welfare State came into being over a period of many years – its roots can be said to go back even further than the nineteenth century. The most important laws which established the Welfare State were, however, made during or soon after the end of the Second World War – these are the Education Act 1944 (which introduced compulsory secondary education up to age 15 for all children), the National Health Service Act 1946 (which established the National Health Service), the National Assistance Act 1948 (which abolished the Poor Law and, in providing financial assistance to the unemployed, ill, elderly, and disabled, formed the basis of our social-security system), and the Children Act 1948 (which created local-authority 'children's departments').

The social services

This concept can have three different meanings in common use:

i) At its most general, it refers to all services provided for our society by the State. These would include road maintenance, street lighting, public parks and gardens, libraries, the police force, and a whole multitude of other services that we take for granted most of the time. It also includes all the services that were referred to in the previous section.

ii) A narrower definition of the social services refers to the five particular services of health, housing, education, the personal social services, and the income-maintenance services provided by the DHSS. By the 'personal social services' we mean largely those facilities provided by the SSD for various groups of people in need – for example, the elderly, children at risk, and the physically or mentally handicapped.

iii) The most specific meaning refers to the social-services department itself. The work of this department is dealt with in detail in the next chapter. Large State social-work departments were created in 1970, after the Seebohm Committee's report on local-authority organisation and services.

Social work

This is a very nebulous concept and is very difficult to define exactly. It basically has two separate meanings:

i) It refers to all that we consider to be social-work *provision*. This includes advice and counselling by social workers and probation officers and also the more practical facilities for people in need – for example, residential homes for elderly people and children. The youth service can also be a part of social work, as can those activities we normally refer to as 'community work'.

ii) A narrower definition refers to the theories, methods, and practical ways of working used by social workers. Chapter 7 of this book will deal in some detail with the different methods employed by social workers in achieving their aims.

Client
The term 'client' refers to the person who receives the services of a social worker from any organisation and in any setting. Although the term may be considered imprecise – implying passive acceptance – it is the most convenient term to use and the one constantly used in discussion about social work.

Statutory and voluntary agencies

Again, these terms can be very confusing, as the work of statutory and voluntary agencies sometimes overlaps. Briefly, *statutory agencies* are those run and financed by the State – by either local or central government.

Voluntary agencies are those run and financed by charitable or non-profit-making organisations. They are independent of the State. This independence can, however, be affected because the State often provides financial help, in the form of grants, to a large number of voluntary agencies. Sometimes this assistance has various 'strings attached', which means that the State has a say in what kind of provision is offered, or how it is organised. For example, in return for Home Office funding, voluntary hostels for offenders have to take a certain number of residents referred to them by the Probation Service. The voluntary hostel may also have to accept a liaison probation officer as a member of its running committee.

We refer to all the voluntary agencies in total as the *'voluntary sector'*. This encompasses a very large area of work and involves many thousands of people in the country as a whole.

It is a mistake to imagine that everybody working in the voluntary sector is an unpaid volunteer. There are a large number of paid employees, and the title 'voluntary' refers to its being a non-statutory concern, rather than to the status of people working within it. Both voluntary and statutory organisations employ qualified social workers.

The diagram on page 4 is a deliberate oversimplification of the administration of the statutory caring services – it aims to demonstrate the relationship between the services and the level at which they are administered.

It can be seen that all statutory agencies are ultimately responsible to their respective departments of central government, but the actual range and standard of provision varies from area to area, depending on various factors. For example, the quality of education and social services provided by a local authority reflects the political priorities and financial resources of that authority (and population size determines whether the service is run at county or district level).

Not all services are run by the local authority. Some (the NHS and DHSS, for example) are administered at a regional level as well as locally, and their boundaries do not necessarily coincide with those of the local authorities. Other services (for example, probation and police) are also administered regionally, but their local boundaries are the same as those of the local authorities.

The dotted line in the diagram indicates that, although their services are provided at a local level which has the same boundaries as the local authority, major directives and funding for both the police and the Probation Service derive from the Home Office.

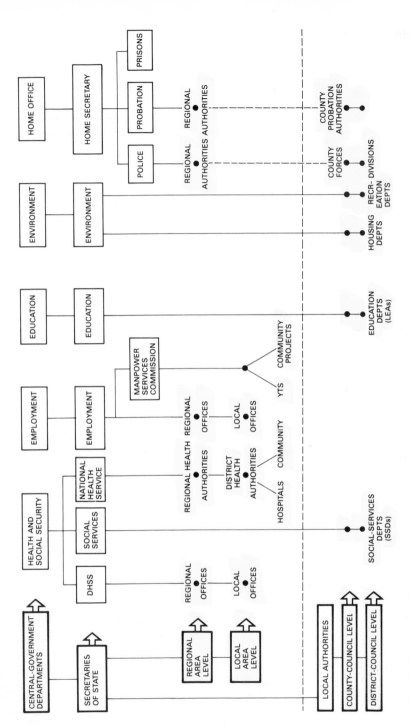

The administration of the statutory agencies

Field-work and residential work

These two can be contrasted with one another. 'Field-work' refers to a social worker who, although having an office base, moves in and about the local community in order to carry out his work. The office base provides secretarial and support services, the mutual support of a team of social workers, and space to store records and to interview clients or others seeking assistance. The working style of field-workers varies a great deal. Some may base their activities more in their office than outside, while others will feel that being out in the community, i.e. 'the field', or visiting clients at home should take precedence.

Residential work, or, as it is becoming more commonly known, residential social work, takes place in a particular residential setting, which will usually be a hostel or a home. Particular client groups who are catered for by residential provision are children at risk, disturbed and difficult children, offenders, the elderly, the physically handicapped, the mentally handicapped, and the mentally ill.

A great deal of residential care is provided by the voluntary sector, and many of the largest national charitable organisations are involved – for example, the Church of England Children's Society, Dr Barnardo's, and the National Children's Home.

Residential social work has traditionally been a 'poor relation' in that it has had a lower status than field-work, but this situation is changing. Even professional training has, in the past, reflected this unequal relationship, with field-workers possessing the more prestigious Certificate of Qualification in Social Work (CQSW), and residential workers the less well accepted Certificate in Social Service (CSS). The Central Council for Education and Training in Social Work, which awards both qualifications, is currently reviewing the arrangements for these qualifications. The Council has expressed its intention to merge the two awards, and this would probably give a long-deserved boost to the residential sector.

Community care

Over the past twenty years it has become fashionable and popular to talk about 'community care'. Much confusion surrounds this, and the phrase is often used inaccurately or too generally, to encompass a wider field of activity than in fact it does.

We can distinguish two different uses:

i) A wide-ranging definition, signifying the care that society, or the community, provides for those in need. This definition is not particularly useful and its use should perhaps be discouraged.

ii) A specific definition which reflects a change of policy in social work. This is the transferring of the care of those in need from residential settings back into the community. Two examples will illustrate what is meant:

a) Many large hospitals for the mentally ill or handicapped, often occupying old and unsuitable buildings, have been closed altogether. Inmates have been found alternative accommodation in smaller-scale ventures in the community – e.g. the group home, where three or four clients might live and be provided with social care or medical support.

b) Some large homes for the elderly have been closed or re-organised and different ways of caring for the elderly have been developed. These include smaller residential units which may have a warden to provide support and security. (These are often referred to as 'sheltered housing' schemes.) At the same time, domiciliary services to the elderly (those services delivered direct to a person's home – for example, home helps and 'meals-on-wheels') have been increased in strength, and this has meant that more old people have been able to go on living in their own or their relatives' homes, without having to resort to residential care. The Government has also made financial help available to families who have elderly relatives living with them.

It is more natural and healthy for people to live ordinary lives, as far as possible, in the community. Large institutions for the elderly tend to generate a 'closed-community' atmosphere, and this in turn creates in the residents a sense of isolation. This sometimes has the effect of stultifying previously active-minded people – their self-respect and personal initiative gradually diminish. It has been found, for example, that old people in large residential homes are more prone to early senility and tend to suffer from it more severely than those who live in their own homes. Being constantly provided for in residential care leads to a person becoming 'institutionalised': it gradually saps the person's ability to make decisions and to assert herself – the institution 'takes over', as it were. This in turn leads to dependency and a premature lessening in personal capability.

To sum up, the main aim of community care is to encourage independence.

Community work

As with 'community care' much confusion exists as to the meaning of 'community work'. The two concepts are different and quite separate.

Community work involves a wide range of skills, and a wide range of resources. It is not necessarily a part of social work, as it does not cater for a particular need or a particular client group. Few community workers would think of themselves as social workers, and training for community work is quite different from that for social work. Many people we might think of as community workers would not actually bear the title – they would be called something else altogether. Examples are wardens of community centres and 'detached' youth workers who do not work from an office base but instead go out into the community to contact young

6

people where they meet – in clubs, cafés, and bars, for example.
There are, generally speaking, two kinds of community worker:

  i) Those, as mentioned above, who are based in a particular location
     (say a community centre) and who work from this base to plan and
     provide facilities, for the area – for example clubs, special events,
     leisure and entertainment activities, day trips, etc.
 ii) Those who have a geographical area for which they are responsible,
     and in which they move about a great deal to help groups of local
     people. This way of working often carries with it a high political moti-
     vation, and its aim is to help local people organise themselves. The
     focus of the work will often be dealing with the quality of social
     provision to a local area or estate – housing issues might be a concern,
     or delinquency, or the lack of facilities for the elderly or the under-
     fives.

The youth service is usually considered a part of community work and,
as far as statutory agencies are concerned, local authorities often run both
provisions from a 'youth and community services department'. It is a
mistake, however, to think that only the statutory agencies employ
community workers. Voluntary organisations are appointing more of this
kind of worker – one example is the Church of England Children's
Society.

2 The personal social services

Local-authority social work – a brief history

The development of the personal social services was gradual, and it was not until the passing of the Social Services Act in 1970 that a uniform and integrated service was finally established. Before this, services to the elderly, the physically and mentally handicapped, children, and the mentally ill were provided by different local-authority departments. Consequently, it was possible for both a child-care officer and a welfare officer to visit the same family – one of these social workers being concerned with the child, the other focusing on the parent – without there necessarily being any liaison between them.

The nineteenth century

Social work had its origins in the Poor Law and the voluntary organisations of the nineteenth century. The Poor Law Act 1834 was based on the idea that people were poor largely through their own fault and that to help them would only encourage idleness and intemperance. The Poor Law stated that those capable of work were no longer to receive any financial assistance in their own homes – instead, support was to be provided only in the *workhouse*. Proof of a person's destitution was that he was prepared to leave home, together with members of his family, to live and work in the workhouse. Conditions were made deliberately harsh – families were split up, labour was long and tedious, and the rules were uncompromising. As a further deterrent, the wages received by inmates were always set lower than those of the lowest paid agricultural labourer outside. Thus it was hoped that only the truly needy would be assisted by the State; the others would be encouraged to help themselves.

What the moral attitude of the Poor Law administrators failed to appreciate was the contribution made to poverty by such factors as low earnings, irregular employment, large families, sickness, widowhood, and old age. Individual inadequacy was hardly relevant in such circumstances.

It could be said that the Poor Law guardians were the first State social workers in that they were responsible for providing very basic welfare. Professional care, however, was a long way off!

Alongside the State provision there existed various voluntary and charitable societies, the foremost of which was the Charity Organisation Society (COS) founded in 1869. Toynbee Hall, in London's East End, saw the establishment of the first *university settlement* in 1884, providing scholars with the opportunity of living and working with the poor so that they would understand their needs better. Together with these organisations, Octavia Hill and other socially aware people helped shape early social work – they introduced group work and community work and developed casework as a method of helping families (see chapter 7). Despite this practical and theoretical foundation being laid, however, much of the early social work was viewed as being of the 'Lady Bountiful' variety where wealthy ladies of independent means distributed monies to the less fortunate. There was a strong moral blame levelled at those who were destitute, so charity was mainly granted only to the 'deserving poor'.

From 1900 to 1945

Early social work was inextricably bound up with poverty, and it was from Toynbee Hall that Charles Booth's enquiry into 'the conditions of the labouring poor of London' was conducted. So too was William Beveridge's early work on unemployment, which shifted the blame from the worker to the organisation of industry. Another late-nineteenth-century social investigation, carried out on the inhabitants of York by Seebohm Rowntree, helped further to expose the extent of poverty and some of its social causes.

At the beginning of the twentieth century, the results of this research began to put pressure on the Government to take collective responsibility for social problems. Reforms and innovations in the field of pensions, employment, and health insurance did follow shortly – in spite of objections made by the COS, who, in response to the proposals of the minority report of the Royal Commission on the Poor Laws 1905–9, argued that increased support for families would encourage dependence and discourage individuals from being responsible for themselves.

Social work was developing in other areas from the early part of the twentieth century. In hospitals, social workers – or *almoners* as they were known – were being employed in the London region. Initially, their main concern was with the financial assessment of patients, since there was not yet any universal free medical service. Charges were made unless it could be established that a person was 'without means'. The Institute of Almoners was formed in 1920, although training courses had been started shortly before. The first *child-guidance clinic* was founded in 1927, but it was not until the 1930s that the *psychiatric social-work* service began in this country. The *Probation Service*, never to be part of the local-authority set-up in England and Wales, had also become established, having its roots in the work carried out by the police-court missionaries of the Church of England Temperance Society.

For the local authorities, the statutory obligations regarding welfare were few but began to increase from the time when they took over the administration of the Poor Law in 1929. However, most social workers at this time, whether trained or untrained, were working with voluntary organisations outside the local authority. It was not until the years immediately following the Second World War, with the *creation of the*

Welfare State, that the local authorities were called upon to provide more extensive social services.

From 1945 to 1970

Following many of the recommendations of the *Beveridge Report* of 1942, the Welfare State aimed to eliminate want, squalor, ignorance, ill health, and unemployment and to provide instead basic security 'from the cradle to the grave'. In support of this, local authorities were to establish a range of personal and caring services. The Poor Law was officially at an end!

Under the Poor Law, old people had been neglected and humiliated, but now appropriate accommodation was to be made available in cases where they could not look after themselves or be looked after by their families. The sad experiences of deprived children kept in huge institutions, including those who had been evacuated during the war, had been observed. A series of correspondence published by *The Times* newspaper brought their plight to public attention, and in 1948 *children's departments* were set up following the death of a child left unsupervised in local-authority care. The emphasis was now on professional care in smaller and more personal establishments. *Welfare* departments were set up to take responsibility for the physically handicapped and to provide social training and day centres for them to attend. Families made homeless by unforeseen circumstances now had a right to be accommodated by the local authority. Initiatives in community work were taking place, and mental-health and mental-handicap services were developing under the new National Health Service.

Despite the wider social provisions introduced after the war, it was clear by the 1970s that the Welfare State had failed to eradicate poverty and its related social problems. The work of the Child Poverty Action Group (CPAG), 'Mind', and 'Shelter' all pointed to the vulnerability of certain social groups – such as the disabled, families in poverty, the homeless, and the mentally ill – and the need for greater equality in the distribution of limited resources. Social-work provision was seen as cumbersome and disjointed. The children's department was the most professional and resourceful: other clients' needs were not being met. Rises in the juvenile crime rate, increasing numbers of the elderly, more frequent breakdown of marriage, and the growing awareness of poverty and family problems called for the creation of a unified social service.

In 1970, following the report of the *Seebohm Committee*, the new local-authority social-services departments were created. They aimed to provide an 'effective, family-orientated, community-based service, available and accessible to all'. This new expanded service would need a larger and more professional personnel. Social workers were to be 'generically' trained, in order to avoid the duplication of attention brought about by the narrow specialist training of the past, and so work with their clients within a family and community framework.

At last a universal and integrated social service had been set up with the opportunity of providing standard professional care. This would be 'a supportive service for individuals and their families within a community setting'.

From 1970 to the present day

Initially, not all the authorities had the buildings or resources to provide localised social services and were somewhat restricted by having to operate from a centralised point. Other authorities established *area offices*, which made the services more accessible to everyone and enhanced the departments' community involvement. Today most authorities have area offices from which the social services are run, although some have gone further and operate an even more localised *patch system*, largely owing to the encouragement expressed by the Barclay Committee.

The Barclay Report   In 1980, a working party set up at the request of the Government by the National Institute for Social Work, chaired by Peter Barclay, examined the workings of the SSDs. Although no legislation followed its publication, this report made several recommendations, some of which some authorities began to put into practice. In recommending a *community approach*, the Barclay Report was repeating the message of the Seebohm Committee, adding that this development had not gone far enough.

According to the Barclay working party, most social care is provided not by *statutory* and *voluntary* social services but by ordinary people (i.e. relatives and neighbours), and it was recommended that this informal caring network should be supported and strengthened. In order to do this, and to make social-work departments even more accessible to the community, the report recommended that area divisions be divided still further. This has led to the creation of *patch*, or neighbourhood, teams within some authorities. Where this situation exists, social workers operate from offices (Portakabins, council houses, shops, etc.) established within the community. Each office is responsible for working in a defined neighbourhood, with the aim of developing local initiative and providing service to that patch.

Whether they run a decentralised patch-based service or operate from traditional area-office bases, most SSDs will include the following personnel and encompass the following areas of work.

The work of local-authority social-services departments

General administrative responsibilities

Every local authority in the country is obliged by law to provide a social-services department. Under the two-tier structure of local government, the population size of an area determines whether the services are organised at county or district level.

Throughout England and Wales there are 115 councils with responsibility for administering the social services, and there are a further

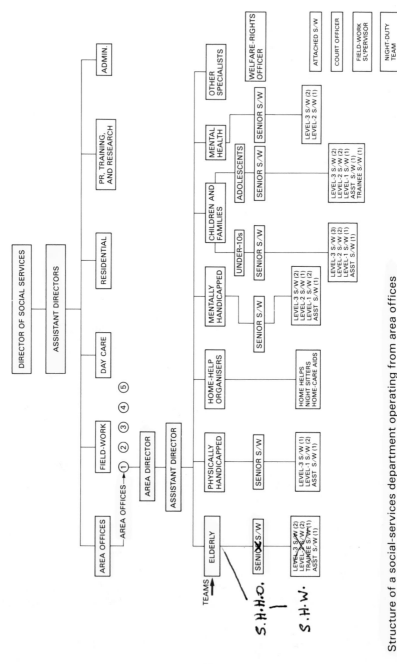

Structure of a social-services department operating from area offices

(*Note* This is only an example – local authorities differ in their organisation of social workers.)

12

eight regional authorities in Scotland and four health and social-services boards with 16 management units for personal social services in Northern Ireland.

Each council has a *social-services committee* made up of local councillors. This committee appoints a *director* of social services from outside the council to run the service on its behalf. The director in turn selects and appoints staff to carry out the workings of the department; however, it is the councillors who are ultimately responsible for the actions of social workers.

As each local authority runs its social-services departments independently, according to its own priorities, there exists a variety in the standards of provision. Some local authorities pride themselves on a comprehensive caring service, while others offer a less extensive range of resources with a correspondingly lower rates charge to the local electorate.

Field social workers
Field social workers receive a *generic* training, which means that they study all aspects of social work, including the needs of many different client groups. Early in their careers, social workers may work with a wide range of people but later they may *specialise* in an area of their own interest, still viewing their client within a family and community perspective. The Seebohm Committee recommended that all social workers in the field should work generically, but the subsequent volume of complex legislation – for example, that introduced by the Mental Health Act 1983 – and the increasing expertise required to do the job properly have meant that a certain degree of specialisation has become necessary.

Broadly, the aim of field social workers is to clarify problems for their clients and assist them to develop ways of coping. They have access to a range of resources, which includes the provision of a place for a child in a day nursery or a nursery centre. In addition to obtaining residential places, social workers may enlist the support of a whole range of domiciliary services which are aimed at helping people function better in their own homes.

Legislation has increasingly extended the role of field social workers, granting them various *statutory rights* with regard to all client groups – for example, the right to work with families before the crisis of reception into care (section 1 of the Child Care Act 1980). Among other statutory duties, social workers have the right, in certain circumstances, to remove a child from his home.

Most field social workers operate from area offices, but some are based in other settings including day centres and hospitals, or they may be attached to general practitioners' (GPs') practices.

Field social workers are paid at three different rates – level one, level two, and level three – according to the responsibility they carry, the complexity of their case-loads, and the decisions they are expected to make. The Barclay Report defined these levels as follows:

Everyone who comes into the office for the first time will see the duty officer.

'*Level one*' – Social workers under close and regular supervision are expected to manage a case-load which may include all client groups and all but the more vulnerable individuals or those with complex problems. Such social workers are not expected to make decisions affecting the liberty of clients or in relation to place-of-safety orders.

'*Level two*' – With supervision and advice are expected to manage a case-load which may include the more vulnerable clients or those with complex problems and may be expected to accept responsibility for action in relation to the liberty or safety of clients in emergency situations. They may be expected to concentrate on specific areas of work where such concentration arises primarily from organisational needs and to supervise trainees or staff other than social workers.

'*Level three*' – With access to advice and within normal arrangements for professional accountability are expected to accept full responsibility for managing a case-load which will include the more vulnerable clients or those with particularly complex problems in situations where personal liberty or safety is at stake. Such officers are expected to contribute to the development of other social workers. They may be expected to concentrate on specific areas of work requiring more developed skills. They may be expected to contribute to the development of new forms of work or service.

Residential social workers

As the name implies, residential social workers are employed by the local-authority social-services department specifically to work in one of the authority's homes. Their chief function is to provide day-to-day care for the residents of the home, be they elderly, physically handicapped, mentally ill, mentally handicapped, or children.

14

In the past, residential social workers were concerned only with what happened in their particular establishments, but nowadays they are becoming increasingly involved in the community. This is particularly true for, say, a residential social worker of a pre-adoption children's home who not only needs to establish a trusting relationship with the child requiring adoption but must also get to know the prospective adoptive parents. This will obviously require visits outside the home, and so the role of the residential social worker overlaps that of the field-worker.

The types of problem

SSDs are faced with a variety of different social problems presented by individuals and families. These may include:

a) *Relationships* – difficulties between husband and wife, or between children and their parents.
b) *Housing* – inadequate housing, overcrowding, or isolation.
c) *Children* – behaviour problems, offences against the law, non-attendance at school, or theft.
d) *Absence of parent* – single-parent families where one parent is permanently absent or where one is temporarily away (in prison, for example).
e) *Parents unable to cope* – they may have several children of a similar age and have difficulty in managing.
f) *Financial* – families may have rent arrears, debts, and/or a basic lack of amenities.
g) *Illness* – one parent may be permanently or temporarily ill and be unable to care for the children.
h) *Mental illness* – one family member may suffer from periods of various forms of mental illness (depression, for example).
i) *Age* – difficulties increase with old age, particularly for those living on their own.
j) *Mental or physical handicap* of any family member may involve difficulties for the whole family.
k) *Ethnic-minority families* are more likely than most to experience social disadvantage in addition to any special problem they may have (language barriers and isolation, for example).

The above examples by no means exhaust the range of problems presented to SSDs. Further, many of those listed are interrelated and are experienced by some families at the same time.

Referrals

Before it can be helped, a family has to become known to the SSD, and this is done by means of one of the following types of referral:

a) *Self-referral* – a family member contacts social services himself, by phone, by letter, or by visiting the area office.
b) *Health-service referral* – via health visitors, district nurses, GPs, or

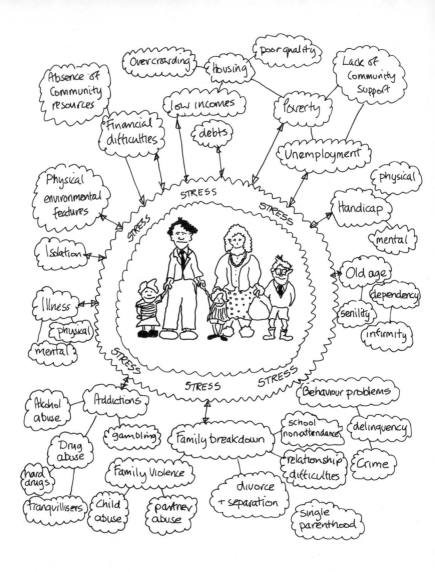

Environmental factors contributing to stress

the community psychiatric nurse when it is felt that the SSD is the appropriate agency to help (with a request for a place in an elderly persons' home (EPH), for example).

c) *School referral* – either directly from the teaching staff or the head of year, or through the education welfare department following behaviour problems at school.

16

d) *The police* may refer children to whom they have given a 'warning' and have taken no further action, if they feel that social services may be able to help.

e) *A magistrate* could refer children under 14, following an appearance in court (there is normally a social worker present in a juvenile court).

f) *Neighbours* could contact the department because of their concern about an elderly person next door, or children being left on their own further down the street.

g) *Other agencies* – the Probation Service, solicitors, or citizens advice bureaux may also refer.

Response

Depending on the problem, the SSD may be able to help in a number of different ways. First of all the situation has to be *assessed*. This can be done through the information on the referral form completed by the duty social worker when the case was first referred to the department, or by a home visit, or by discussion with the family members who arrive at the office.

A social worker will visit people in their homes.

The initial assessment will be carried out by the *intake team*, who, depending on the area of difficulty, may be able to find a solution quite quickly. If not, then the case will be allocated to one of the long-term teams with the appropriate specialism. Very often the presenting problem may be relatively easily sorted out, but the family may go on to reveal more profound and complex difficulties.

SSDs throughout the country organise their staff in different ways, but most area offices have at least one team dealing exclusively with families and their children and another team concerned with the elderly. Another team may concentrate on handicap – physical or mental. In addition, there will be social workers who specialise in other areas – fostering, the under-fives, mental health, intermediate treatment, etc. These specialisations will be commented on after we have discussed more broadly the services offered by the SSDs.

Regardless of how they are organised, SSDs will where possible concentrate their resources on undertaking *preventive social work*. This is aimed at enabling individuals and families to manage their lives more easily and avoid the occurrence of a breakdown or crisis. However, it is often the very experience of a crisis in itself which leads a family to first seek help from the social-services department. In such a case, it is the task of the social worker to help resolve the immediate situation and thereafter to employ the various preventive resources at the disposal of the department.

The diagram below illustrates the different services which can be described as being preventive. They will be described more fully throughout this chapter.

Preventive social work

Note It has been mentioned that most local-authority social-services departments run their services from area offices where social-work staff are divided into teams specialising in the needs of certain client groups. Where local authorities have decentralised their services and operate from smaller patch-based offices, this kind of specialisation is not possible. Here, social workers are more 'generic' in their work, but specialists may be attached to a number of neighbourhood offices, or the small team of social workers may be part-specialist/part-generic. The following sections outline the help given by social-services departments organised on traditional *area*-based lines.

Types of help provided

Social-services departments have a number of statutory responsibilities, and to some extent these govern the deployment of resources within the department. Most of these legal obligations relate to children and their families, and for this reason there is normally at least one team concentrating on this client group. There is usually another team working exclusively with the elderly, reflecting the high number of cases within this category. Specialist teams may similarly exist to work with the physically handicapped, the mentally handicapped, and the mentally ill – although in less populated areas these teams may be combined or the work be dealt with by single specialist social workers.

The children-and-families team
As part of a team, a social worker may work with a family on a regular basis in an attempt to help overcome their difficulties which may be of long standing. She will have a number of *cases* on her *case-load* and will apportion her time according to their urgency and importance. Employing whichever forms of intervention she considers appropriate (see chapter 7), the social worker may be able to assist in a number of ways, ranging from the provision of practical help (the installation of handrails in the home of a handicapped person, for example) to giving sustained emotional support.

A place in a day nursery for one of the children in the family may help alleviate family stress and provide the child with the care and attention he requires, and this may be arranged by the social worker. She will not allocate the place herself; rather she will recommend the position of the family to the under-fives specialist who, in liaison with the officer in charge of the local day nursery, will consider the case in the light of those already waiting. Sometimes it is possible for social workers to arrange holidays for families with the help of voluntary organisations, or to obtain special financial help, say for a family with a mentally handicapped child, again through the voluntary bodies concerned (the Rowntree Trust, for example).

Since the Children and Young Persons Act 1963, social services have been allowed to distribute a certain amount of money, but only in special circumstances. A fund exists (under Section-1 of the Child Care Act 1980 – known as 'section-1 money') to provide direct financial help to families in order to '. . . diminish the need to receive a child into care'. A SSD could, therefore, use this money to help a family forestall a possible cut-off of gas or electricity supplies and the consequent likelihood of a child needing to come into care. This provision can be interpreted widely by the SSD, but the budget is limited and it is still the only legal way in which the department may financially assist its clients.

It may be that the social worker can do nothing to alter the family's immediate circumstances in a practical way, but, by encouraging the members of the family to express and recognise their difficulties, she may facilitate a better understanding of the situation and point to an improved way of coping.

Reception of a child into care is sometimes necessary, but this is done only when all alternatives have been explored, and such action must be in the best interests of the child. Reception into care is not usually an end in itself – most children return home after a short period of time.

A combination of statutory obligations and regulations requiring a minimum number of visits and the preparation of reports for reviews held regularly on children in care are part of a social worker's responsibility and account for some of her time. Accurate record-keeping of involvement with families is maintained on *case files* for the purpose of reference and information. Additionally, social workers may be called upon to write reports for the courts or for reviews (for children in care) or for meetings with workers from other agencies concerned with the same family (case conferences). Regular supervision by a senior officer gives the social worker time to discuss and plan her involvement with families and provides valuable support in this.

Work with the elderly   *Unit 5.*

The emphasis of the work carried out by social workers with the elderly is on encouraging and enabling their independence. The elderly form an increasing proportion of our population as the birth rate decreases and improvements in health care increase life expectancy. Although some people manage an active and self-contained existence well into their eighties, many people experience incapacity and hardship with the onset of old age.

Isolation is often a problem in old age, and this may be offset in a number of ways. The social worker may be in touch with volunteers willing to visit old people; she may know of a luncheon club or elderly persons' group which meets locally, and by arranging transport she may help someone to become involved in such a community resource. She could arrange day care in a local elderly persons' home (EPH) on some days of the week and so cater for some of the needs of an elderly person.

In cases where the physical incapacity of a person makes him unable to cope in his own home, various *aids* and *adaptations* can be supplied to make life easier. Bathrails, non-slip mats, and automatic gas fires can be installed to reduce the possibility of accidents within the home. The social worker may recommend the services of a *home help* for a few hours a week, or arrange for the delivery of *'meals-on-wheels'* on certain days of the week. These provisions are aimed at helping an elderly person remain in the familiar surroundings of his own home.

The residential establishments can be used to help people stay in the community longer, not only through *day-care* provision but also by the use of a short-stay bed to give the elderly person a break from the normal routine and allow time for him to recover strength to return home. At the same time, a short stay can provide a respite for those involved with caring for an elderly person, be they the husband, the wife, or other relatives.

Social work with the elderly does not simply involve allocating resources: the elderly are vulnerable and have the same intellectual and emotional needs we all have, and they often need help to adjust to their changing circumstances – the loss of a loved one or their increasing dependence, for example.

It sometimes becomes necessary to admit to an EPH an elderly person who, through various circumstances (neglect or deterioration), is no longer able to manage in his own home. It is part of the field-worker's task to make this potentially traumatic transition as gradual and familiar as possible. Introductory visits, day care in the same home, and involvement with the family are a means to this end.

Under section 47 of the National Assistance Act 1948, local-authority social workers have a duty to compulsorily admit to residential accommodation any elderly person who is unable to cope for himself and is considered to be in need of care and attention owing to his infirmity and that he is living in insanitary conditions. If this is the opinion of the specially appointed doctor – the medical officer of environmental health – and the social worker concerned, then a compulsory admission will be carried out. Before this can be implemented, the elderly person will have to have refused all domiciliary services offered. This rarely used provision is a safeguard to protect an individual whose confused mental state is life-threatening. (The medical officer of environmental health is appointed by the local authority after being nominated by the district health authority. A deputy will also be appointed and, depending on the size of the area covered, may take geographical responsibility for some of that area. In Scotland there is no formal title for the post, but a community physician will be designated and approved in the same way to undertake duties under section 47 of the Act).

Work with the physically handicapped
Although physical and mental handicap sometimes occur simultaneously, some social workers will work mainly with the physically handicapped, whose needs differ from those of the mentally handicapped. They will help to arrange alterations to a person's home in order to maximise his mobility and independence. They may also contact the housing department with regard to grants available for any structural changes to the home which

might be made. Other domiciliary services families could use are the laundry service, 'meals-on-wheels', and the use of volunteer help. Handicapped people and their families need also to be made aware of the range of social-security benefits to which they may be entitled, including details of the attendance allowance and mobility allowance (for which they may qualify).

Physical handicap is often present from birth, but can happen to any one of us at any time – often in a traumatic way (in a car crash or sports accident, for example). Part of a social worker's task is to help handicapped people to come to terms with their limitations and enable them to live as normal a life as possible.

Not every area office will have a social worker who specialises in the needs of the visually handicapped, but there is usually one worker within the division with expertise in this field. Similarly, there is normally a social worker who is responsible for people who have impaired hearing – among other forms of assistance, she may help by putting the relatives of such people in touch with locally held lip-reading classes so that communication between the handicapped person and his relatives might improve.

Work with the mentally handicapped

Over the past ten years, more awareness has been generated about the needs of the mentally handicapped, and the emphasis is now on integration within the community and support of the family at home, in line with the policy of 'normalisation'.

The discovery that a child is mentally or physically handicapped is distressing and may take a long time for parents to accept. It could lead to a breakdown of the family. The stress may be exacerbated by the withdrawal of friends or relatives who feel awkward when faced with handicap. It is therefore important that social workers provide skilled emotional and practical support. One way they can do this is to arrange periodic short stays for the handicapped child in residential establishments or, if possible, with foster parents. This *respite care* reduces some of the strain of permanently caring for somebody who is mentally handicapped and gives the parents an opportunity to be together, free from their normal responsibility.

Another way in which social workers can be of help is by putting parents of mentally handicapped children in touch with each other or by arranging for groups to meet to discuss and share their difficulties and so reduce the isolation which so often occurs.

When a handicapped person is ready for work, contact is made with either the careers officers (education) or the disablement rehabilitation officers (DROs – employment) who will try to find appropriate work. Social services provide day centres where simple work tasks are carried out in return for modest payments. Depending on the severity of handicap, a whole range of jobs may be appropriate; but, in extreme cases where disability is severe and there is no-one to look after the person, residential care may be the only option.

Work with the mentally ill
SSDs have certain responsibilities towards mentally ill people and their families within the community and will normally have a number of social workers who specialise in this field of work.

Mental illness, like physical illness, is something to which we are all susceptible, and when it occurs it can limit a person's ability to function properly and may consequently affect those around him.

Common forms of mental illness include depression and anxiety, and range to the more serious behaviour disorders. There is often a social component to the illness – breakdown can occur following a family crisis, long periods of unemployment, or time spent in inadequate housing. In some cases the sufferers have no insight into their illness and display behaviours which are threatening. Such people are unlikely to accept help from a doctor and may need to be compulsorily admitted to a psychiatric hospital.

Compulsory admission to hospital   Not all sections of the Mental Health Act 1983 relate to social workers' powers. Section 1, for example, relates to conditions of illness. Only the relevant sections will be dealt with here.

Under section 2 of the Mental Health Act 1983, any person suffering mental illness who is considered to be either a danger to himself or a danger to other people can be compulsorily admitted to hospital (or 'sectioned', as it is known) for *assessment* or *assessment and treatment* for a maximum period of 28 days.

For a compulsory admission to take place, the hospital administrators require three forms. Two of these are medical recommendations – one signed by the person's GP and the other signed by an approved doctor (usually the hospital consultant). The third form, requesting admission, is supplied by either a social worker or the person's 'nearest relative'. Normally it is the social worker who completes the 'section' form, since compulsory admission can be personally distressing to the nearest relative, who may prefer to leave matters to the detached professionalism of the social worker.

In emergency situations, section 4 of the Mental Health Act 1983 can be used to compulsorily admit somebody suffering mental illness, under the same grounds as under section 2. This order needs to be signed by only one doctor and a social worker or nearest relative, but the person can only be legally detained for up to 48 hours. A section-4 order is carried out only when it is not possible to obtain the person's own GP.

The role of the social worker with regard to compulsory admission is basically to safeguard the rights of the person to be 'sectioned'. Before signing the order, she must be sure that such action is necessary and that the person is unwilling to go to hospital voluntarily. She is also responsible for transporting the committed person to the hospital, and this often requires patience and understanding. Sometimes resistance and violence occur, and the social worker may need to call upon the assistance of the ambulance service or, in extreme cases, the police. It is also important for the social worker to spend time with relatives, who may feel devastated that a family member's illness has developed to such an extent that he needs to be forcibly taken to hospital.

Where the nearest relative has signed a 'section' form, the social worker has a responsibility to visit the home of the person admitted to hospital and to provide a report on the family circumstances.

A social worker's consent is also required under section 3 of the 1983 Act before compulsory treatment may be given. This 'section', of six months' duration, is usually passed on somebody already in hospital.

Today only *approved social workers* who have successfully undergone extra training are allowed to sign 'section' orders, but before the Mental Health Act 1983 any social worker could do this.

Many people suffer mental illness of a milder nature and do not need to be in hospital but still require community support. SSDs sometimes run day centres where individual counselling, group meetings, or other activities may take place. Social workers will generally aim to encourage a person's involvement in the society around him, since isolation often reinforces feelings of inadequacy or an inability to cope.

Fostering

Fostering is the bringing up of a child in local-authority care by substitute parents. It is one of the oldest services provided by local authorities and is sometimes referred to as 'boarding out'.

The *fostering officer* within the social-services department, normally a social worker of senior status, will have children who need substitute homes referred to her by other social workers and will seek appropriate foster placements for them among her vacancies. At the same time, she will try to recruit more people who are prepared to foster and will invite them to join in ongoing groups of existing or prospective foster parents. Groups are run to promote an understanding of the requirements of the work and to allow foster parents to share their experiences, express their views, and provide mutual support. The fostering officer will have to assess the suitability of applicants, and, in addition to individual interviews, the group sessions may assist her with this.

Local authorities pay foster parents an allowance to cover the cost of keeping the child, but they are not paid a salary. This stems from the thinking that people should not make a profit from looking after children. Nowadays, however, as the service is expanding to include provision for children of all ages and with a wide range of handicaps, allowances are being increased in relationship to the degree of difficulty and responsibility involved. In some areas of the country, with regard to 'hard-to-place' children, fostering is recognised as a full-time job and paid accordingly; in other areas, only the basic recommended allowances are paid.

Regular group meetings enable foster parents to be supportive to each other.

It may well be that foster parents will seek to adopt the child they have been fostering, and, under newly implemented legislation stemming from the Children Act 1975, they will be guaranteed a court hearing if they have had the child for five years. They may, of course, make application sooner. Not all foster parents want to adopt – they may wish to continue long-term involvement and still receive the fostering allowance, or they may apply to the court for custodianship, which is simpler and quicker to achieve than adoption and has some of its security benefits.

Fostering is a demanding job and requires a wide range of skills from the foster parents, who in turn need regular support. Visits from the child's social worker or even the fostering officer, together with group meetings of fellow foster parents, provide this support. Statutory boarding-out regulations require social workers to make regular visits and hold periodic *reviews* concerning the child. Foster parents will be invited to attend these reviews and to contribute to the local-authority plans for the child's future.

Since the 1970s, *specialist* fostering has developed in an *attempt* to provide for a wider range of children: older children, handicapped children, and adolescents with behaviour difficulties. The periods of foster care vary, too, from long-term care to short-term or emergency care following a family crisis.

Fostering should continue to expand, as it offers a more naturally supportive setting for children than that offered in residential care. (See later in this chapter for the different types of fostering services offered by SSDs.)

Adoption

This takes place when the court transfers the legal parental rights and responsibilities for a child from either the child's natural parent(s) or the local authority to the adoptive parents. Unlike when a child is fostered and the child remains in care, when a child is adopted the new parents assume all rights and responsibilities and local-authority involvement is ended.

Many SSDs operate as *adoption agencies* concerned with the placing of children and the recruitment of prospective adoptive parents. Where local authorities are not the sole agency, they may share this role with one of the many private voluntary adoption organisations which exist locally (the Catholic Child Rescue Society, for example) and run a joint service.

The nature of adoption work has changed over the years as fewer babies have become available for adoption. This trend reflects a growing social acceptance of single parenthood, developments in contraception, and to a lesser extent the availability of abortion in some cases. At the same time, the service has been extended to include children with special needs and older children. Mentally handicapped children were formerly considered 'inappropriate for adoption' – nowadays the right of any child to family life is increasingly being recognised.

Adoption work is complex because it is carried out within a legal framework. Once an adoption order has been made, the rights of the natural parents cease permanently; so, because of the irrevocability of adoption, the situation requires careful and sensitive handling. Giving up a child so that he will benefit from the care of another family takes strength, and the person(s) concerned need time and support from an experienced sympathetic social worker so that this step can be fully considered, understood, and valued.

Preparatory work is normally carried out by specialist family-placement social workers, some of whom will serve on the *adoption panel* made up of other social-work personnel from the local authority, specialists from other agencies (probation and voluntary organisations, for example), and recommended lay people (such as councillors). Meeting regularly, the panel makes recommendations on the appropriateness of adoption for particular children and the suitability of prospective adopters, to try to 'match' children to parents. Frequent meetings of the panel are essential, as undue delay can be harmful to the families and children whose circumstances are being considered. Natural parents can speed up the legal process and reduce their subsequent involvement by making an application to the court to 'free their child for adoption'.

The Children Act 1975 requires local authorities to appoint a panel of *guardians ad litem* (i.e. independent guardians in law) and *reporting officers*. This panel is made up from social workers, probation officers, and staff employed by relevant voluntary bodies. The principal duty of the reporting officer is to witness the natural parents' written consent to adoption, having first ensured that they do so freely, fully understanding what adoption involves. She will provide the court with a written report.

Normally a guardian *ad litem* is also appointed by the court only where the proposed adoption is contested (i.e. when the natural parents withhold their consent) or is particularly complicated. It is possible that the same person will be appointed reporting officer and guardian *ad litem* in the same case. The role of the guardian *ad litem* is to safeguard the interests of the child. She will visit the families concerned and carry out investigations before making a report to the court. Indeed, depending on his age, the views of the child may also have to be ascertained.

Much of the work of the local-authority adoption agency involves applications made by step-parents wanting to formally adopt the children they are already caring for. This applies in cases where one of a child's parents remarries (or marries for the first time) and the couple want to formalise their joint parental commitment. If such applications are granted, the natural parents surrender their natural parental rights in regard to the child and an adoption order grants both partners equal status as parents. Not all step-parents seek this legal status – some are satisfied with obtaining custodianship, which carries certain legal rights and is simpler to obtain.

Adoption is necessarily complex because of the essential legalities involved. However, the Children Act 1975, while increasing the statutory regulations, has sought to make this provision available to more children, particularly older children, who presumably might otherwise have had to spend their lives in residential care, without the benefit of life in a family setting.

Intermediate treatment

As a member of the children-and-family team, at least one social worker will specialise in intermediate treatment, or 'IT' as it is generally referred to. Her aim will be to help young people to obtain a better understanding of themselves and to enhance their self-respect.

Often children from deprived backgrounds, lacking proper parental support and without any educational achievement, become bored and frustrated and experience life in a negative way. These are the very children who are most likely to appear in court or to be received into care. The 'IT' worker, operating in the 'intermediate' area between the home and the courts, seeks to prevent this happening.

Most local-authority SSDs will have an IT centre where youngsters can go for group meetings or activities. 'Latch-key' provision in the form of rooms and meeting places may be available in the morning and early evening for those whose parents are out at work, and, indeed, the centre may offer 'drop-in' facilities throughout the day. During the group meetings, children are encouraged to discuss and share their feelings about matters which are important to them. Meetings are held on a regular basis with the aim of developing trust and friendship. Other activities, including Outward Bound courses organised from the centres, will try to strengthen a person's self-worth and sense of achievement.

Not all intermediate treatment is done in the locality of the child's home – residential IT centres exist for children who need a physical separation from their surroundings so that they can distance themselves from previous patterns of behaviour and learn new skills in a more therapeutic setting.

Not only social workers, but probation officers, education welfare officers, and youth and community workers are involved in intermediate treatment.

Reception into care
There are several ways in which a child can come into the care of the local authority, but these can basically be divided into two: children can be either (i) received into *voluntary care* or (ii) committed into care by the *court*.

Voluntary care　The local authority is a 'guardian of last resort', and children are admitted into care only when all possible alternatives have been explored and there remains no other course of action. Section 1 of the Child Care Act 1980 requires local authorities 'to make available such advice, guidance, and assistance as may promote the welfare of children by *diminishing the need to receive children into or keep them in care*', and so energy and resources are spent to prevent reception into care happening. However, it is sometimes necessary, 'in the interest of the child', for reception into care to take place.

The grounds for voluntary care are laid out under section 2 of the Child Care Act 1980. These conditions relate to children who are orphaned or have been abandoned, and to those whose parents are 'for the time being or permanently' prevented from properly caring for them. The most common reason for a child being admitted into voluntary care is the short-term illness of a parent. Most children who come into voluntary care return home within six months, the crisis having been resolved.

As the word 'voluntary' suggests, children coming into care under the Child Care Act 1980 are admitted with the approval of their parents, who sign a form consenting to care and who are financially assessed for contributions towards their child's maintenance. For the first six months, parents can at any time request the child's return home. After this period has elapsed, however, local authorities require 28 days' notice of parental intention to remove their child – this gives the SSD time to consider the consequences of such an action and to oppose the action legally if necessary.

Assumption of parental rights　Depending on the circumstances of the family, after a child has been in voluntary care for some time, the SSD may wish to apply for *parental rights* so that it may properly plan for a child's future. It may be that, during the time a child has been in care, he has shown a substantial improvement, both physically and emotionally, and the department may be reluctant to return a child home to a family whose circumstances may have deteriorated since the child's (original) removal.

There are a number of grounds on which the social services can apply for parental rights and take out what is known as a *section-3 resolution* (section 3 of the Child Care Act 1980). Some of these ways are relatively straightforward – for example, when a child has been abandoned (including when a parent has failed to make contact over 12 months). Others are more complicated and require the SSD to show that a return home would place a child in 'moral danger', or that his parents are 'unfit to care for or look after the child'. Whatever the grounds – and there are others – social services report to a committee of the local council who may then pass a resolution granting parental rights in respect of the child.

Sometimes parents welcome the local authority taking this responsibility, but, if they do not, they may take the matter to court and contest the decision.

Committal to care through the court   Children are committed into care through the court either because of something they have done themselves or because of something that someone else has done to them. The grounds for making a child the subject of a *care order* are laid out in section 1(2) of the Children and Young Persons Act 1969. This Act was passed to protect the child, and it states that a care order can be made only if without such an order 'a child would not receive the proper *care and control* thought to be necessary'.

Examples of the grounds for making the child the subject of a care order are that 'he is beyond the control of his parents or guardian' or that 'he has committed an offence'. In addition to local-authority social workers, the police and the National Society for the Prevention of Cruelty to Children (NSPCC) can initiate care proceedings. For example, an NSPCC officer may seek local-authority care for a child-abuse victim and bring him before the courts on the grounds that 'his proper development is being avoidably prevented or neglected' or that 'his health is being avoidably impaired or he is being ill-treated'. These grounds (section 1(2)a of the 1969 Act) are the most well used and, together with the section 1(2)f 'guilty-of-offence' condition, account for nearly three-quarters of the care orders made.

An alternative to the care order is the supervision order.

Supervision order   If the social services feel it would be more suitable, they may ask the court to grant a supervision order instead of a full care order. Such an order would place a duty on the social worker to 'advise, assist, and befriend' the young person (similar to the relationship a probation officer has with her client). The young person would then be able to remain at home and maintain his links with the community. A condition of the supervision order may be that the young person attends school regularly or takes part in an intermediate-treatment programme.

The supervision order may be converted into a full care order if necessary. Alternatively, if progress is made, the supervision order may be revoked before the maximum three-year period is over.

Place-of-safety order Any citizen who reasonably believes a child to be in danger (and that conditions exist which would lead to the child being made the subject of a care order) may apply to the court to have the child removed from his home to *a place of safety*.

It is normally a social worker who would make this application to the court. A 'place of safety' refers to any social-services community home, a hospital, or any suitable place 'where the occupier is willing to receive the child'.

If the courts are not in session, a social worker will have to go to the home of a magistrate and, under oath, describe the circumstances a child is in and state why removal is felt to be necessary. Once the magistrate is satisfied that urgent action is required, she will issue a warrant which the social worker may then use to remove the child. The social worker may not be able to gain entry into the child's home and, if this is so, she must then obtain the assistance of the police, as they are the only body with the power to force entry into someone's home.

When a child is detained in hospital for observation where child abuse is suspected, the hospital administrator may ask the social services to obtain a place-of-safety order to prevent the parents removing their child before a full investigation has been carried out. The child can then remain in the hospital.

A child can remain in a place of safety for up to 28 days, by which time the circumstances of the child and family would have been properly looked into. It may be that the child should then return home, but in more serious cases the local authority may wish to apply for an *interim care order* as a temporary measure before obtaining a full care order for the child at a later date when a hearing can be arranged and all the evidence be assembled.

There are a few other ways in which a child can come into the care of the local authority, but these are less commonly used. The Matrimonial and Family Proceedings Act 1984 provides grounds for the granting of care orders for children involved in divorce proceedings. Occasionally, children are made *wards of court* – this means that matters concerning them are decided by the High Court, even though the children may be accommodated by the local authority.

Access Before the Health, Social Services and Social Security Adjudications Act 1983, parents of children in the care of the local authority were denied access to their children if the local authority considered this to be in the child's best interests. Now parents have to be informed of any proposals and can be legally represented in court if they wish to contest decisions made by the social-services department about their child.

Home carers or family aids or home-care aids   In some areas, SSDs deploy home-care aids with families who have difficulty coping, in an attempt to reduce stress. For example, a young single mother with three closely aged small children and financial difficulties may be under a good deal of pressure which could result in a break-up of the family. As a preventive measure, a home-care aid could help the mother, either in her absence or while she is in the home, with routine care of the children – bathing, cooking, and cleaning etc. This may give the mother time and space to reorganise her routine and so help her to structure her daily living and to cope more readily.

Sometimes family carers step into the mother's or father's shoes in an emergency to look after children who may otherwise have to go into care. For example, if an unsupported parent needed to go into hospital, a 'live-in' family aid would enable the children to remain in their home surroundings and to continue to go to their local school.

Home-help service   This service is operated by all authorities, who may charge an assessed fee or nothing at all, depending on local policy.

Home helps are allocated to members of the community who, through age or physical infirmity, are unable to carry out certain tasks in their own homes. Some elderly people can manage simple cleaning tasks themselves, but bending to polish floors or stretching to take down curtains or clean windows may be beyond them. Others are more disabled and housebound – unable to get their own shopping or to collect their pension. These tasks would be undertaken by the home help.

According to individual need, the *home-help organiser* will allocate a certain number of hours help per week, so each home help will visit a number of different people during the week, some of them on more than one occasion.

Home helps provide a valuable service which goes beyond their caricatured 'Mrs Mop' image. Indeed, there are roughly twice as many home helps as there are local-authority field social workers. They provide a welcome social contact for an elderly person and often they stay over their allocated hours into their own time. Importantly, they can monitor an old person's ability to cope in the community and can recognise any signs of deterioration.

Night sitters   Some authorities have introduced a night-sitting service for elderly people at risk where sudden deterioration may occur and hospitalisation has been inappropriate or difficult to arrange. If it is a purely medical problem, then a doctor or, in an extreme emergency, an ambulance could be called. Otherwise, a home help will be sought from the standby rota to sit in with the elderly person until the morning when other services will be available. Night sitters can be arranged in advance in cases where relatives have spent a series of sleepless nights caring for someone awaiting hospital admission, or somebody terminally ill at home, so that they can have a break.

Wardens   Wardens are employed by SSDs to provide care for elderly and handicapped people living in *sheltered accommodation* – a series of independent living units. The warden's job is to call on the people living in the flats, usually twice a day, to offer help and ensure that they are not in difficulty. Very often the warden's home is linked to the flats by an alarm or intercom system, so that she can be summoned in case of any emergency. Wardens may use their experience to anticipate a deterioration in someone's condition and contact a doctor on their own initiative.

Physical adaptations to the home   The physically handicapped and elderly have obvious difficulties getting around, but adaptations to their homes can make this easier. Rails can be fitted to walls, particularly around stairs and in bathrooms, and special low-level baths can be fitted. Under the Chronically Sick and Disabled Persons Act 1970, local authorities are obliged to provide this form of help. In a limited number of cases, telephones can be supplied to house-bound people. Indeed, there is a whole range of uncomplicated fixtures which make life easier for those who are less ambulant – less able to move around freely – from a non-slip bath mat to the installation of a lift or hoist within someone's home.

'Meals-on-wheels'   SSDs deliver meals to housebound people unable to cook for themselves, ensuring that they have the benefit of regular, warm, nourishing food. A small charge is normally made, and in most cases the service is provided only on alternate days of the week. However, this service is often sufficient when supplemented by the support of neighbours and/or relatives.

Social work in medical settings
Some field social workers are based in hospitals and work directly with patients and their relatives. They may concentrate on helping particular age groups – young children or the elderly – or they may be more problem-orientated and be attached to psychiatric wards or alcohol-abuse treatment centres.

The tasks of a hospital-based social worker are varied and could include comforting patients who are anxious about treatment or a forthcoming operation. Some people may be worried about what is happening at home with regard to their relatives, or about how welfare benefits will be affected while they are in hospital. A social worker will look into these matters for them.

After a long stay in hospital, some people will experience difficulty fending for themselves in the community, and so the social worker needs to be sure that support will be available. The social worker may visit the home in order to establish the family circumstances and what kind of help can be relied upon. She may contact the area-based social services to see if

32

the patient is known to the SSD and to ask for any domiciliary services which may be appropriate (a home help or family aid, for example) to be arranged.

Patients relatives often need time spent with them to help them to come to terms with a loved one's sudden decline in health and the implications this may have for the rest of the family. Practically, a social worker could put relatives in touch with people in similar situations by referring them to relevant organisations (such as stroke clubs or the Multiple Sclerosis Society).

Social workers make a valuable contribution to the doctor's ward round by outlining the family circumstances and emphasising the social needs of the patient to medical staff.

Occasionally, social workers are attached to a GP's practice and see doctor's patients who have problems that are more of a social nature than strictly medical – such people often require the help of skilled counselling. Many people automatically go to a doctor when they have a problem, but, if the doctor lacks the necessary listening time and patients are prevented from fully expressing their difficulties, they may be put off permanently and refrain from seeking further professional assistance. The doctor may also refer particular patients to the social worker when she feels that the root cause of a continued illness is social stress.

Welfare-rights officers
As welfare benefits have become increasingly complex and difficult to calculate, some SSDs have added welfare-rights specialists to their personnel. It is difficult for a generic social worker to keep completely up-to-date with the frequent changes in the various allowances.

The main role of the welfare-rights officer is to examine someone's personal circumstances and inform him of the amount of benefits that are due. Not all social-security benefits are claimed by those entitled to them, and so some families undergo unnecessary hardship.

Social-security claimants have a right of appeal if they are refused a particular payment, but they may lack confidence to take the Department of Health and Social Security (DHSS) to a tribunal. The welfare-rights officer would be willing to act as someone's advocate, or to advise some-one who wanted to represent himself in these circumstances.

Debt counselling   It is not only people of limited financial resources who get into debt, but they are more likely to do so – particularly if they under-take hire-purchase or catalogue buying. The amount owing is likely to increase if professional money-lenders or loan companies, who often demand very high interest rates, are involved.

Being in debt can have a depressing effect on personal and family relationships, and support will be needed. Welfare-rights officers are usually skilled in debt counselling and can offer advice about money management and legal ways of repayment which are within a family's capacity.

The work of the emergency duty team

The area offices of most SSDs open between 8.30 a.m. and 5.30 p.m. Outside these normal hours, the standby team is on duty to deal with any emergencies which may arise. In larger urban areas more than one officer will be on standby duty at a time, whereas in some less populous area only one social worker may be involved, and this, among other considerations, limits the time spent with any one client. Some areas of the country have no separate standby service – instead, social workers work on a rota system following a normal day's work.

All kinds of emergencies occur outside office hours, and special arrangements have to be made. Designated residential establishments will have beds reserved for emergency admissions, and certain foster parents will be available to receive a child into care at short notice. Home helps will be contactable if their sitting services are required, and senior management will be available for telephone advice if necessary. Daytime field-workers may inform the standby team of family situations which they regard as being potentially difficult and outline the relevant circumstances in case the standby duty officer is forced to intervene during the night or over the weekend.

The existence of a standby team does not prevent the necessity of social workers working in the evening with their own cases, as the role of the standby duty officer is strictly concerned with emergency matters.

Problems that face the emergency social worker are usually precipitated by some kind of crisis, and it is part of her duty to resolve the situation as calmly as possible until the normal daytime services come into operation. If people contact the standby duty officer with routine requests which could wait until the following day, they will not be dealt with out of hours but will be referred to the daytime staff.

A standby social worker has to be adaptable in dealing with the range of problems she is presented with. The police may phone to say they have an elderly confused person found wandering in the road who is unable to tell them where he lives. The social worker may respond by checking with the establishments to see if any residents are missing, or visit the area office to see whether the name is known to social services and the address is obtainable from the files. If this procedure is likely to take some time, she may arrange for the gentleman to go to the local elderly persons' home and wait there. The social worker's enquiries may yield no information and the man may still have not recalled his address, so a bed would be made available for the night until he is eventually reported missing.

If acute family discord occurs at night when all members of the family are together, the social worker can be contacted to help settle the dispute. A wife may phone from a neighbour's house to seek refuge from her violent husband. Initially a place in a Women's Aid hostel will be arranged for a mother and children – a rendezvous and transport will have to be provisionally arranged as quickly as possible. However, if a visit by the social worker to the family home is likely to resolve the situation, then this will be made, but there are certain circumstances in which this course of action is plainly not appropriate.

If a child under 16 is held at the police station and the police are unable to obtain the child's parents, or the parents are unwilling to attend, the social worker's presence may be requested so that the child has the support of a 'responsible adult' before any questioning or fingerprinting procedure can legally be carried out. Similarly, the duty social worker has a responsibility to return children who have absconded from children's homes in the area. If the home is too far away, then a temporary placement at a local children's home will have to be arranged.

Since 1983, all standby duty officers have had to undergo extra training in order to become approved social workers able to administer the new regulations contained in the Mental Health Act 1983.

People who have difficulty coping often experience their worst fears when alone at night. They may seek help from the overnight duty officer. Her need to be available in case of other emergencies will limit her involvement, although reassurance over the telephone is often all that is required. The social worker is continually using her judgement to decide upon who should be visited. Sometimes, however, there is no choice.

A visit from a social worker, who will listen to the particular circumstances of the family and outline the support services available, will often resolve a crisis and render immediate action unnecessary. All contacts made with the emergency team are referred to the daytime staff the following day and followed up by the appropriate social workers.

People made homeless through unforeseen circumstances (a house fire or flood, for example) are the responsibility of the SSD 'out of hours', and the social worker may have to obtain places in a local-authority housing-department hostel if no other arrangements can be made. Married couples with children, elderly and handicapped people, pregnant women, all children under 18, and those under threat of violence in their own homes are all entitled to temporary accommodation. Capable single people or couples without children are not the responsibility of the local authority; however, the social worker would advise and direct them to hostels or hotels in the area if they present themselves as homeless.

The emergency duty team consists of experienced field-workers who need to be particularly flexible and resourceful, with friendly dispositions. Having to wake residential social workers up at two in the morning to request accommodation requires a little tact! The establishment and maintenance of good relations with other agencies, notably the police and the hospitals, is of course essential.

Day care

The local-authority SSDs provide *day centres* for families and various client groups. The broad emphasis of day care is to help people continue to live in their own homes, to which they return at the end of the day. Day care not only assists the individuals who attend the centres, but also provides respite for those involved in caring for them at home. Without day centres, many people would need full-time residential care.

Day care for the under-fives

Unit 2.

Day nurseries   Day nurseries usually provide facilities for children aged from six months (occasionally younger) to five years, although only under special circumstances are children admitted under 12 months. Places are normally allocated on a *priority basis*, with special consideration being given to children of single parents, children with language difficulties and special needs, deprived children, and those suspected or known to have been ill-treated. By providing a warm, caring, stimulating setting, the day nursery seeks to compensate for the limitations of the child's immediate environment.

The relatively inexpensive costs, the high standard of professional care, and the length of time they are open make day nurseries attractive to parents. However, the number of places available falls short of need, and – although provision varies throughout the country – waiting lists are common, particularly in inner-city areas.

Day nurseries provide a range of stimulating experiences for the under-fives.

Nursery centres   Nursery centres are a more recent development and are run jointly by the local-authority SSD and the local-authority education department. The aim is to combine the educational resources of nursery

36

classes with the caring aspect of the day nurseries. Staffed with social-service and education-department personnel, these establishments are equipped to prepare a child for school and to assist with children's language or speech difficulties. In some areas, nursery centres are gradually taking the place of day nurseries.

In addition to providing day centres for the under-fives, local-authority SSDs have to inspect and *register* the day nurseries, childminders, and play groups which exist in the *private* sector.

Childminders Childminders are people who care for pre-school children in their own home. They are not paid by the local authority and are free to charge their own fees (normally between 70p and £1 per hour). Depending on the size of the house and its facilities, childminders are limited in the number of children they may look after at any one time (normally three or four, including their own). They are obliged to be registered by local authorities, who need to be sure of the quality of care given and who ascertain that health and safety standards are met.

Childminders provide a flexible service and may be recommended to parents by the SSD. However, the services of a childminders are beyond the means of many families.

Under certain circumstances the SSD itself will pay the childminder to care for a child or children from a low-income family. Such children would normally qualify for a nursery place, but there may be a long waiting list. This form of *sponsored* childminding ensures the child some form of day care.

Playgroups Playgroups are not provided by the local authorities, but the SSD is obliged to approve and register them. Help may be given in the form of small grants, or the local authority may allow premises to be used for the group. Playgroups vary enormously in size, opening hours, and times of meeting – they provide a useful service where local-authority provision is missing. The under-fives specialist social worker will be aware of all the organisations in the area, including *parent-and-toddler groups* where mothers or fathers take their children on occasions in the week.

Family centres Family centres are a relatively recent concept in social work. As the name implies, they offer day care to both children and parents. The policy of each centre is different, but their primary function is to keep children out of care by trying to improve the quality of life within a family environment. The local-authority SSDs themselves may run the centres or, alternatively, they may be run by voluntary agencies (the Save the Children Fund, for example) and funded by the local authority.

Basically there are two types of family centre: structured and 'drop-in'.

Structured family centres Some family centres only take families referred to them by social workers or health visitors. Such families may have difficulty controlling young children or may be unaware of the play

In family centres, parents come together to share and enhance their skills in a group setting.

needs of their children. Whatever the problem, the whole family of the pre-school child are invited into the centre, where they are confronted with their difficulties and a joint pledge is made to work on these over a certain period of time.

For part of the time during the day, parents will be involved in group activities (for example, cookery, keep fit, and discussion groups) while their children play supervised and observed by care staff. Feelings of failure and inadequacy contribute to poor parenting, and it is hoped that from these group activities parents will gain mutual support and added understanding of the difficulties they all face as parents. At other times, parents and children participate in activities together in the presence of staff. It is hoped that skills learned at the centre will help families to manage better at home.

In order to discourage dependency, families normally attend for a fixed period of time only. Around fifteen families may be receiving support at the same time, although they will not all be engaged in the same activities of the centre nor will they always attend on the same occasions. During the school holidays, older children are encouraged to attend with the rest of the family.

Informal 'drop-in' centres   Other family centres offer 'drop-in' facilities which enable any parents in the community to come in and use the

38

resources of the centre. Parents may want to use the centre's cooker or washing machine and so have an opportunity to meet other parents in the area and avoid the isolation experienced by many mothers, particularly those who are single. Fathers, too, attend the centre, but are more likely than mothers to be out at work during the day. Nevertheless, they are encouraged to attend for part of the day.

Drop-in family centres may also run discussion groups or shared activities as they seek to help families in an informal and relaxed manner. Children are not normally left at family centres as they are in day nurseries, except on special occasions when the parent needs to be elsewhere (for a hospital or dental appointment, for example). Family centres are essentially concerned with the parent and the child and aim to improve their ability to cope with the stresses and strain involved in everyday life.

Adult day centres

The mentally handicapped   Local-education-authority special schools provide for the day-care needs of the mentally handicapped up to the age of 19. After this age, adult training centres (ATCs) offer both educational and workshop experience.

These centres – often large and old-fashioned – have been criticised because the contract work provided is undemanding, involving simple repetitive processes only, and the pay is very low. The value of keeping mentally handicapped people together in an institution, rather than encouraging them to find work in the community, is also questioned. However, the reality – particularly with high unemployment rates – is that the community does not seem eager to employ mentally handicapped people, and so, in a limited way, ATCs serve a useful function. For many who come from residential homes, the ATC meets their need to be in different surroundings and to be with other people. Others who come from their own homes also have this advantage, and their attendance provides respite for those at home.

The physically handicapped   Social centres exist for anybody who is registered as disabled and they provide a range of activities. Education classes are run in adult literacy, arts and crafts, and other subjects; and a committee is formed of the members to decide on future activities and outings. For any isolated or severely disabled person, these social centres provide a link with the outside world and a chance of regular social contact.

The mentally ill   Social withdrawal is a characteristic of mental illness, and day centres can help a mentally ill person become more involved in the community. Counselling or art-therapy sessions may help some people obtain more insight into their condition. Group meetings or assertiveness training may develop their confidence to deal with the outside world.

The elderly Most elderly persons' homes offer day care to elderly people living in the area who are not capable of looking after themselves fully. The provision of regular meals, social contact, and involvement in activities ensures that an elderly person is cared for in the day. Transportation is also arranged to and from the home. This resource, whether used daily or two or three times per week (depending on the demand for places), enables an elderly person to continue to live in the familiar surroundings of his own home. His ability to cope can be monitored by the staff of the home.

Day care in other centres is offered to residents of EPHs and gives them a chance to experience new surroundings and meet different people.

Residential services

Local-authority SSDs provide residential care for various people who are unable to be properly looked after in the community. Establishments differ in size, design, and character according to their purpose and the client group they serve. The primary function of all homes is the provision of day-to-day care of the residents.

Residential services for children
The great Victorian institutions housing hundreds of children are no longer with us, and the trend since the Children Act 1948 has been towards providing smaller homes. In recent years these homes have been forced to adapt to new demands and define their function more precisely.

Current child-care practice recognises that all children have a fundamental right to experience 'normal family living' and aims at limiting a child's residential experience. In the past it was common for some children to spend most of their childhood in residential care. Now, particularly for a child under ten years old, the aim is to restrict his residential experience to two years at the most – thereafter, the child should either be rehabilitated with his own family or be placed with a permanent substitute family.

Family group homes (FGHs) FGHs were developed in order to provide home surroundings which most closely represented normal family living. Places are made available for between eight to ten children of varying ages. The housemother is normally at home during the day, and her husband returns home from work to take up the role of housefather. Additional care staff may work on a rota basis to assist the houseparents, and the aim is to create a family atmosphere.

To accommodate such a large group of children, two council houses may be knocked into one to form a large home.

The advantage of the FGH is that children can be cared for locally, within their own community, and contact with their own parents is more easily maintained. FGHs were originally conceived as being suitable for long-term care, but they are now being used less for this purpose – partly because of the reduction in the numbers of children in care and partly because FGHs are too large to provide typical family experience.

Short-stay children's homes   Most children who come into care because of a family crisis (under section 2 of the Child Care Act 1980) return home within six months. For these children it would be disruptive to place them in an established family or community setting, so they are usually accommodated in short-stay children's homes. Here they will mix with up to twenty other children who also anticipate returning to their families soon.

Short-stay homes are often local, so they encourage the children to continue any community commitments they may have (youth clubs, Scouts, or Guides, for example) and they obviously permit children to carry on going to their usual schools.

Emergency units   All SSDs need emergency accommodation for children being received into care at any time of the day or night. Consequently, an emergency unit with a certain number of beds will be attached to one of the children's homes (logically it should be the short-stay home).

At one time it was considered necessary to isolate a child from other children when he first came into care, partly because of the risk of possible infection. He remained isolated for at least 24 hours, until the result of his medical examination became known. The production of his freedom-from-infection certificate (FFI), signed by the doctor, then enabled the child to integrate with the others in the home. This practice obviously added to the trauma of reception into care, and nowadays only a child known to have an infectious disease would be isolated. However, it is still necessary for children to be medically examined, and this is done as soon as possible following reception into care.

Coming into care is often distressing, but the tension can be reduced if children are received by experienced social workers in a setting properly prepared for them. Foster homes are increasingly being used for this purpose, particularly with regard to younger children.

Observation and assessment centres (OACs)   When a child is committed to care by the courts, it is up to the local authority to find the most appropriate accommodation for that child. Similarly, local authorities must decide on the most suitable home for children coming into care voluntarily. The most suitable home is not always apparent, so in some cases children may be sent for 'observation and assessment'.

Every authority has an OAC within its boundary, or shares this facility with a neighbouring authority. The function of the centre is to watch and study the behaviour of a child over a short period (usually six weeks). The child will take part in various activities, and education is provided on the premises. A team consisting of teachers, psychologists, social workers, and medical personnel will help to contribute to an all-round understanding of the child. Finally, a case conference (of all the professional people involved with the child) will be held in order to decide on the most appropriate placement – the child's own wishes having been ascertained.

Community or domiciliary assessment units   A recent development has been the introduction of the community or domiciliary assessment unit. Instead of the child being assessed in the centre, social workers from the unit will visit the home of a child about to come into care and will carry out an assessment. A number of visits will be made to the home by all members of the team before a recommendation is made. In this way a child may be placed in the most advantageous establishment – if it is necessary for him to come into care.

Some children may already be in care – placed for the time being with foster parents – when they are referred to the unit. The team may carry out an observation/assessment while the child remains in the foster home. Referrals come from schools and probation and education welfare departments, as well as from the field social worker, and the work done reflects the expanding role of residential workers.

Pre-adoption and pre-fostering homes   In most cases the social-work goal for children received into care is their rehabilitation into their own families. However, for some a return home is neither possible nor desirable, and once this becomes clear the aim for those children is to find a suitable permanent substitute family (i.e. one prepared to adopt or to foster long-term). Some children's homes have the function of preparing children for the change from residential care to a new family setting.

During the time a child spends in this preparatory children's home, he is allocated a member of staff who is known as his *keyworker*. This residential social worker's task is to form a special caring relationship with the child, to develop trust and confidence, and to enable the child to eventually make the transition to a new family. The keyworker will work closely with the field social worker and the family who propose to take the child. She will plan introductory meetings, visits, and short stays, and will be present for the final moment of transfer.

Community homes with education on the premises (CHEs)   Not all children who come into care are ready to be placed with a substitute family – it may be considered beneficial for them to live away from their home surroundings in a community setting for a period of time. CHEs came into existence following the Children and Young Persons Act 1969, replacing the more punitive approved schools which had existed before then. As well as providing formal education, CHEs offer a therapeutic setting aimed at developing the whole individual. Homes vary in the degree to which they are genuinely therapeutic, but most offer practical and social skills training, group work, and other activities. Links with the child's home are maintained with regular weekend/holiday leave.

Not all local authorities will have a CHE within their boundaries – some have to use the resources of a neighbouring authority.

In recent years the value of CHEs has been questioned – there has been concern about the poor standard of educational provision and the lack of social development for children. Local authorities are nowadays more inclined to place a child within the local community and to consider the use of IT programmes or specialist foster parents as an alternative.

Hostels and centres for independent living For older children about to be discharged from care, accommodation is provided which will help them prepare for living in the outside world. Hostel accommodation allows older teenagers a certain amount of independence (their own room and a front-door key, for example) while still providing basic communal care. In preparation for leaving care and finding accommodation for themselves, some children are placed for a few months in purpose-built flats. Under supervision, children will learn budgeting, cooking, and general house-hold skills which will equip them for the outside world.

Children who have been in care for a long time may be used to having things done for them, and the transition to living on their own can be extremely difficult. Without some assistance and preparation for their move, many children would be unable to cope with their new responsibility.

Homes for mentally handicapped children Although the policy of SSDs is to encourage children to remain out of care, some parents are either unwilling or unable to provide their handicapped child with the love and constant attention the child needs. It is therefore necessary for some children to live permanently in residential accommodation.

Residential establishments for mentally handicapped children are run by the local-authority SSD. During the day, the children attend a special school run by the education department before returning to their home in the evening.

Because of the severity of their condition, some children need constant care and attention and are able to do little for themselves. Others are more able but are limited in what they can do. High staff-to-children ratios ensure that children's individual needs are met.

Normally these homes are divided into smaller living units to accom-modate different age ranges and ability groups, each having access to a central play/social area. Sometimes similar homes exist for severely phy-sically disabled children.

Fostering services Since the 1970s, the use of foster parents by local-authority SSDs has increased. In 1977, for example, 34 000 children were boarded out in foster homes. In 1982 the number had increased to 38 700 (despite the fall in the numbers coming into care), accounting for nearly 42% of all children in care.

Foster homes have a number of advantages over residential estab-lishments – physically they more closely resemble a 'normal' family home; also, care is not affected by rotas or staff turnover; and, finally, they are usually less expensive to provide than many community homes.

At the same time, however, because of the intense complexity involved in foster placements, much preparatory work and support does need to be invested before placements are made.

Long-term fostering   This is the commonest type of fostering and simply involves a married couple (or occasionally a single parent) looking after a child or more than one child as they would their own, on behalf of the local authority. For this service the foster parents are paid an allowance which helps cover the added expenses of looking after the foster child or children. At a later stage the foster parents may seek to adopt the child, or they may be content to continue to foster.

Although technically they will have no legal rights over the child, if he is happily placed the local authority is unlikely to want to remove him from the foster parents. Recent legislation, stemming from the Children Act 1975, has made it easier for long-term foster parents to improve their legal security with regard to the child.

Short-term fostering   This situation exists where foster parents agree to care for a child until his home circumstances alter and his future care can be established. It may be that the child returns home after only a short period and the foster parents will stand by to receive another child in the future. For the sake of continuity, natural parents are often encouraged to visit their children in short-term foster homes.

Emergency fostering   In the mid-1970s, residential nurseries were common, and young children admitted into care in an emergency were placed in one of these centres. Today, most residential nurseries are closed and it is considered less traumatic for a small child to be placed in a foster home rather than a residential institution. Emergency foster parents have to be flexible and prepared to receive a young child at any time.

Specialist fostering   One of the reasons for the increase in the number of foster placements is the expansion of the service to include older children – teenagers, handicapped children, and those who were previously considered 'hard to place'.

Mentally handicapped children   Since the 1970s and the 1971 DHSS report *Better services for the mentally handicapped*, the aim has been to move more of the mentally handicapped out of residential homes and into the community. Some have been successfully placed with foster parents on a permanent basis.

Relief or respite fostering   This has developed to meet the needs of parents of handicapped children. Foster parents look after handicapped children for a day, a weekend, or a few days at periodic intervals in order to give the parents regular breaks.

Bridge fostering   This refers to the use of foster parents for children between placements. For example, an emotionally damaged child waiting for an adoption placement may be placed with bridge foster parents after one placement has been disrupted. Another use of bridge fostering would be before a child is ready to leave care – as a bridge to independence.

Treatment fostering   This provides for delinquent adolescents or youngsters whose behaviour makes them unsuitable for traditional fostering. The idea is that specialist foster parents, over a set period of time, seek to actively reduce the difficulties a youngster may have and help him return to his family or move on to independent living.

Some of these forms of specialist fostering are recognised as being demanding, thus they need greater expertise and professionalism. In some cases, local authorities acknowledge this by paying a higher allowance to foster parents.

Residential services for adults

Elderly persons' homes (EPHs)   Local-authority SSDs have a responsibility to provide full-time care for elderly people who are no longer able to be supported in the community. This duty derives from part III of the National Assistance Act 1948, and residential provision for the elderly is often referred to as 'part-III accommodation'.

Because of limited resources, not all elderly people who want to be cared for in an EPH can be accommodated, so places are allocated on a priority basis.

EPHs are established either in large Victorian homes or in more modern purpose-built accommodation. To a certain extent the type of building goes some way towards determining the way the home is run. Most modern purpose-built homes have been designed for *group living*, where it is possible for the more able residents to provide their own light meals and to retire to small lounges. The older establishments, with their centrally based kitchen facilities and large all-purpose lounges, are restricted in the degree of independence they can offer their residents.

After a period of rehabilitation in an EPH, it is possible that an elderly person may return to live in his own home. However, for most people admitted under part III, the move is a permanent one. It is therefore important that residents are encouraged to participate in the affairs of the home and to maintain their independence in as many ways as possible. Links with the community are maintained either by bringing people into the home (by holding garden fêtes or inviting school children or church groups to visit, for example) or by taking residents out (to day centres or on day trips).

45

Residential provisions for other people in need In the past, when residential establishments were first built, the policy was to place people with 'social problems' 'out of sight and out of mind'. Consequently, many psychiatric hospitals and other institutions for mentally handicapped and mentally ill people were built a 'comfortable' distance from major towns, where it was hoped that rural fresh air would help heal the mind.

Less was known about psychiatric illness and mental handicap at the beginning of the century – many people were quite readily admitted to residential care for merely displaying anti-social behaviour or behaviour which was not approved of or understood by those around them (mothers of illegitimate children and sexually promiscuous people, for example). It was not uncommon for people to spend their whole lives in institutions. Even today there are men and women who were admitted in their youth and have become so used to the way of living and so reliant on the care provided that they would be unable to cope for themselves in the outside world. This dependency on a residential regime is known as '*institutionalisation*'.

People still confuse mental illness and mental handicap, and this is partly because they were treated similarly in the past. Even the Mental Health Act 1959 (in force until 1983) covered both conditions (for example, mental subnormality was included along with mental illness) despite the fact that they are very different. Today more is known about both mental handicap and mental illness.

The mentally handicapped Mental handicap is permanent, but, with support and encouragement, the ability of a mentally handicapped person to function in society can be greatly improved.

Since the 1970s, the policy has been to encourage the integration of mentally handicapped people into the community, and many have been discharged from the huge subnormality hospitals. Some people have been transferred to smaller community-based residential homes where they are cared for and at the same time encouraged to involve themselves in the outside world. Regular use of local shops, public transport, and other amenities – with or without supervision – are practical ways of generating confidence in the residents.

Some of these residential homes have an *independence unit* which will consist of a flat for four persons where the more able residents can prepare for outside living, initially in a *group home*. In these group homes, situated in the community (on council estates or in private houses), four selected people will be able to manage their own day-to-day living. Regular supportive contact will be made by a social worker.

The mentally ill Group homes for the recovering mentally ill are becoming more common as the value of long stays in hospital is being questioned. Many forms of mental illness are thought to have been precipitated (in the first place) by the environment – stresses and tensions of family life, work demands, financial hardship, and personal interaction.

Separating people from the community is no longer considered to be the most satisfactory way of treating mental illness. Consequently, there is a shift of emphasis away from hospital-based psychiatric services towards a community-based system.

The advantage of group living to people who have experienced breakdowns is that many of the daily responsibilities can then be shared. *Joint-tenancy homes* enable people to live together in a supportive way based on collective decisions and agreements. *Core-and-cluster homes* are the ambitious projects of some local authorities – they involve a number of group homes being provided around a central resource from which social-work or medical support can be obtained.

The physically handicapped   Residential homes for the physically handi-capped are provided by most authorities for those who are unable to manage for themselves and have nobody to care for them. They are necessary only for the most severely disabled people, since many disabled people can function in their own homes, with support. An example of domiciliary support is where the SSD provides two home-care aids to live in and attend to the needs of a paralysed mother and her young child.

Other functions of residential establishments   Most homes – be they for the elderly, the mentally ill, the mentally handicapped, or the physically handicapped – provide *day care* for respective members of the community or residents from other homes. *Short-stay* periods (normally of one or two weeks) are arranged for those people in need of rehabili-tation, or simply to provide a break for those who care for them at home.

Sometimes a series of short stays is arranged a long way in advance (say four times over the next 12 months at three-monthly intervals) to ensure regular periods of care. This practice – known as *rotational care* – enables people to continue living in the community and provides respite for those who care for them.

With regard to the elderly, designated homes will be responsible for providing *emergency* beds in case the need arises to admit someone outside of office hours.

The patch system

So that their service is more accessible and visible to the community, some SSDs have developed the *patch system*. Here areas are divided up into a number of smaller neighbourhoods, depending on population size. Social workers operate from locally based offices and deal generically with all the work from their patch.

Some advantages of this system are as follows:

a) The neighbourhood system gives the worker an opportunity to become attached to a defined territory and to become more aware of its character and more committed to its well-being.

47

b) Greater accessibility in the area may lead to earlier identification of problems and prevent the need for crisis intervention at a later stage.

c) Patches are small enough for social workers to go about on foot, and this leads to more informal contact and enables the social worker to promote knowledge of the services of her department.

d) Local offices can be used to encourage community action and be a base for meetings of local people.

e) Where other local-authority services (for example, housing) operate from neighbourhood centres, there will be increased liaison between the agencies.

The main disadvantage of the patch system is that smaller offices will have fewer personnel upon whom to call, and there will be a lack of expertise at hand. This can be overcome to a certain extent if specialists work in all areas, either directly with clients or in an advisory capacity with social workers.

Conclusion

This chapter has outlined the services provided by the local-authority SSDs. Each authority runs its services differently and has its own priorities, although statutory obligations determine resource allocation to some extent. Legislation such as the Chronically Sick and Disabled Persons Act 1970 provides guide-lines for local authorities. Reports (the Barclay Report, for example) also influence policy, even if they do not result in statutory change.

Authorities are continually devising new ways of meeting clients' needs, and pilot and experimental schemes shape future developments in some work.

Not all the services are run exclusively by the SSDs – other statutory agencies and voluntary organisations provide support, as will be discussed in later chapters.

Over the past ten years it can be seen that the direction of social-service provision has moved away from residential care towards supporting people in the community. The use of family centres, home-care aids, and group homes for the mentally ill are all indications of this. The introduction of patch-based services by some authorities is a further commitment to this end.

It could be argued that changes in social work have been made with financial savings in mind, as, since the mid-1970s, SSDs have increasingly been forced to accept cuts in their services. The popularity of fostering may be explained thus: having a child in care placed with foster parents is likely to be less expensive than providing a place in a children's home. Alternatively, it could be pointed out that standards of social work have risen and that clients' individual needs are more closely considered. A good foster home is undoubtedly more appropriate for a child than his being allowed to drift into long-term residential care.

The Seebohm Report indicated that social workers should be 'genericists', working within family and community settings. Instead, although generically trained, social workers have tended to specialise in order to follow their own interests and be able to keep up with new developments. Patch-based social work may mean that social workers become more genuine all-rounders.

Appendix 1 – an example of the reception into care of four children following the admission to hospital of their parent

11.30   Phone call from Dr Bremner (a GP) to the social worker: Mrs Binny is displaying behaviour disorders and is neglecting herself and her four children. The GP has just returned from visiting Mrs Binny after being advised of her condition by a neighbour (Mrs Brook). He is of the opinion that Mrs Binny's mental state is deteriorating and that she now needs to be admitted to hospital.

Although she is refusing treatment, he is arranging for the consultant psychiatrist to see Mrs Binny in her own home this afternoon at 2.15. Could the social worker be present in order to carry out a 'section-2' compulsory admission to a psychiatric hospital if necessary?

The family is known to the social worker, who appreciates that Mrs Binny has had a psychiatric breakdown in the past and has been compulsorily admitted to hospital before. There is no support for the family, and if the mother needs to go into hospital again then the children will need to be received into care.

11.45   The social worker contacts the fostering officer and asks if provisional places can be obtained for children aged five, six, eight, and nine – to be available later that day.

12.00   The social worker telephones the GP back to arrange a time to meet so that he can collect the first medical recommendation form from Dr Bremner's surgery.

 1.30   The social worker visits the GP's surgery, collects the form, and discusses Mrs Binny's home circumstances with Dr Bremner.

 2.00   The social worker visits Mrs Binny and finds her very distressed and in a neglected condition. The surroundings of the home are unclean with used utensils, several days old, scattered around the living room. Dirty washing is heaped in the corner of the living room. She is complaining that voices inside her head are telling her what to do!

Mrs Binny does not seem to be aware that she is behaving abnormally, and, after abortive attempts at trying to communicate with her, the social worker feels, like the GP, that she needs to go into hospital. He informs Mrs Binny that another doctor will be visiting her.

 2.15   Dr Weir (a psychiatrist) arrives and speaks with Mrs Binny for some time. Although she is calmer now, Dr Weir feels that she needs to be admitted to hospital for a full assessment of her condition on the grounds that she is a danger to herself.

Dr Weir believes that a compulsory admission is in order and signs the medical recommendation form.

2.45 The social worker transports a subdued Mrs Binny to hospital, where he introduces her to the charge nurse on the emergency admissions ward. He hands over the three signed forms.

3.15 The social worker returns to his office. The fostering officer informs the social worker that she cannot get all the children together with one foster parent. Instead there are two places in each of two foster homes which are in fact next door to each other, so all the children will at least be near to one another.

3.30 Together with a social-work assistant (Paul), the social worker goes back to Mrs Binny's home to await the arrival of the children from school.

3.45 The social worker and Paul arrive at the home to find three of the children already at home and the next-door neighbour, Mrs Brook, in the house with them. Mrs Brook has anticipated that the children will be taken into care and has begun to collect their clothes.

4.00 The older boy arrives home, but not before Sally – the youngest child, who is very upset – has gone upstairs to the bathroom and locked herself in. The social worker has tried without any luck to persuade her to come out. The other children try this, but the door remains locked.

4.20 Mrs Brook goes upstairs and taps on the bathroom door. She tells Sally that her mother has returned and is downstairs. A few seconds later Sally unlocks the door and Mrs Brook brings her downstairs.

When she discovers that her mother has not come back, Sally begins screaming. Eventually she quietens down and is comforted by her older sister, Julie.

4.35 The social worker, Paul, and all four children go to the foster parents.

5.00 Arrival at the foster parents where the social worker takes the six- and eight-year-old boys.

At the same time, Paul takes the two girls to their temporary foster home next door and stays with them while they settle in.

6.00 The social worker and Paul return to the office.

Appendix 2 – an example of short-term social-work involvement by a social-services department (a deliberately oversimplified case-study)

Monday – 11.00 a.m.
Mrs Baker arrives at the social-services office and sees the duty social worker. She is concerned about her son Arthur (aged nine) who has recently begun to absent himself from school. Mrs Baker shows the duty officer a letter she has received from the school indicating Arthur's

absences over a two-month period. This is the first time that Arthur has ever stayed away from school, which he has always seemed to enjoy.

The duty social worker takes down some information about the family's history and present home circumstances. She tells Mrs Baker that another social worker will come and visit her and Arthur in their home during the week.

Tuesday morning
The case is allocated to a male social worker from the children-and-families team. (Not all offices have a special intake team for short-term work.)

Wednesday – 5.30 p.m.
The social worker calls on Mrs Baker at her home. The family live in a small terraced house. The social worker is shown into the main living room in which there are two comfortable chairs. Arthur is present, but withdrawn and a little apprehensive.

Arthur tells the social worker and his mother that he has stayed off school for a number of isolated days during the last 2½ months. He has spent the time wandering around the park or 'messing about on the wasteland'. None of his school friends has been with him.

He is unable to say why he stays away from school – he likes the subjects, particularly maths and geography, and has 'two close mates'.

At the suggestion of his mother, Arthur takes the social worker to show him his new bedroom – it is brightly furnished with new unit shelving, a small computer, and a small black-and-white television. Arthur says quite proudly that his mother decorated the room for him. The social worker goes downstairs to see Mrs Baker, while Arthur remains upstairs engaged at his computer.

Mrs Baker tells the social worker more of the family history: how Arthur's father left shortly after Arthur was born and how Mrs Baker has brought up Arthur single-handed. She met her present husband five months ago, having almost despaired at ever finding anyone with whom she had so much in common. They have been married for three months. Her husband works quite long hours as a sales representative and likes to relax when he comes home in the evening. He sometimes spends Sundays fishing at the local reservoir.

By the end of their discussion, the social worker concludes that Arthur's staying away from school could be a form of attention-seeking behaviour. He points out that, before his mother's recent marriage, Arthur and Mrs Baker spent a good deal of time together. Now that Mr Baker has moved into the home, Arthur may be feeling a little excluded – this is symbolised by the fact that there are only two comfortable chairs in the living room. He recognises that Arthur's material needs are adequately met – the child has, for example, a well equipped and cheerfully furnished bedroom – however, the social worker feels that, in her enthusiasm to establish her relationship with her new husband, Mrs Baker may have neglected Arthur's emotional needs.

Mrs Baker can see some truth in this appraisal and decides with the social worker that it might be useful if the family could do a few more things together. A third comfortable chair in the living room might encourage Arthur to spend more time with his mother and stepfather. Perhaps Mr Baker could take Arthur fishing one Sunday.

It is further decided that Arthur should not be criticised for his non-attendance at school – rather he should be encouraged to forget about the past few months and start going regularly.

Mrs Baker and the social worker feel that, if Arthur could be made to feel that he is still loved and wanted by his mother and could form a closer relationship with his new stepfather, he would begin to feel more secure. This might result in Arthur resuming his previous readiness to attend school.

Exercise 1 – emergency-duty social work

Below are a number of problems presented to an emergency-duty social worker working outside normal office hours. Imagine you are the social worker. How would you respond to the telephone calls and what kind of help would you offer? It is important to remember that the social worker would be basically concerned to find a practical short-term solution to each problem, which would later be referred for follow-up social-work support when the office next opens.

a) Sunday night – 12.05
The social worker receives a phone call from a Mr Jones who, together with his wife and two young children (aged three and five), is stranded just off the motorway but within the local-authority boundary, having run out of petrol. They have no money. They are 40 miles away from home and 30 miles from the hotel where they have spent the last week on holiday. Mr Jones is requesting overnight temporary accommodation and is presenting the family as homeless. If no help is offered, he threatens to inform the Sunday newspapers.

Note Under certain circumstances, local-authority housing departments have a duty to temporarily rehouse families presenting themselves as homeless in their area. Not many housing departments have overnight duty staff, so housing matters are dealt with by the social-work emergency-duty team and are referred the following day.

b) Saturday night – 12.30
Mr Taylor (44) is known to the social services. He is an unemployed single parent caring for his two sons in poor rented accommodation. He phones the overnight duty officer, saying 'The keys to my house are in the door.

The two children are upstairs in bed. I have had enough and am leaving. I am going to walk to the motorway and hitch south. I intend to go abroad.'

c) Saturday – 11.30 a.m.
A neighbour telephones to say that Mrs Heggarty fell during the night and was taken to hospital only to be discharged and returned home early in the morning. The neighbour feels that Mrs Heggarty is at risk and could fall again tonight. He says he has done 'all that a neighbour can, but I have my own family to be concerned about'. He would like the social worker to provide some help as, in the neighbour's opinion, Mrs Heggarty is deteriorating.

d) Bank holiday
Mr Walker telephones. He is angry about the lack of support there has been for his ageing and confused father. Mr Walker has spent three days of the bank holiday caring for his father, who is obstinate and difficult to manage. A request for a full-time place in an EPH has been refused in the past. Mr Walker is 'fed up with having to make a 50 mile journey every weekend and bank holiday to look after my father'. It has gone on too long, he says, and quite simply, 'I am transferring the responsibility of my father to you.' With this statement he puts the telephone down.

e) Weekday – 7.00 p.m.
Mrs Simpson is distressed as she speaks to the social worker over the telephone. Her husband has just been physically violent towards her and her son (14). He has left the home but threatens to return to 'finish the job' later. He has now presumably gone back to the pub. Mrs Simpson is using her neighbour's phone, but she is frightened that her husband will return home any minute. She has two other children, aged seven and nine.

f) Weekday – 8.00 p.m.
Nigel Jones phones to say he would like a social worker to accompany him to the local psychiatric hospital. He is not prepared to go by himself. Further, he says he has a piece of glass held against his wrist and that if someone doesn't come soon he will inflict an injury on himself. He says he will give the social worker 20 minutes to arrive.

g) Weekday – 11.30 p.m.
Mr Grundy is a 56-year-old disabled man with an artifical leg. He phones from a public call box in the town centre to say he is unable to get back home, four miles away, because he cannot afford the fare. He sounds as if he has been drinking. There is no late-night bus service, and he would like to be transported home by the social worker.

Exercise 2 – Day-care allocation for the under-fives

You are the social worker with responsibility for allocating day-care places for the under-fives. You have one vacancy in a day nursery, one vacancy in a family centre, and two places in a nursery centre. It would be possible to place two children with registered childminders, although their fees are £1.20 per hour. The social-services department would be prepared to help a family meet these fees for one child in the case of hardship. How would you allocate the available places among the families below? What advice would you give to the families you are not able to offer a place?

a) *Mr and Mrs Stewart* are two doctors in their late twenties. Mrs Stewart would like to return to general practice now that their daughter Norma has reached 12 months of age. She would be able to hold surgeries on alternate evenings to her husband.

b) *Mrs Fasoon* (31) has recently separated from her husband and has custody of the two children, Ali (seven) and Suriya (two-and-a-half). She has an opportunity of working at her cousin's factory and would welcome this for financial reasons and for the social contact a job would bring. She has no friends or relatives near to where she lives. Mrs Fasoon would like a day-nursery place for her daughter.

c) *Mr and Mrs McDermott* are in their late twenties and have three children – Rita (six), Asa (five), and Aileen (three). The family live in rented accommodation of poor quality and, since Mr McDermott was made redundant, have accumulated debt problems. The two school-age children both wet the bed, and neighbours have complained to the housing department about shouting they hear coming from the house late in the evening. Mr and Mrs McDermott would like Aileen to be offered a place in a day nursery, so that the parents can spend time 'free from the children'.

d) *Mrs Davies* (37) is married with two children – Thomas (seven) and Roseleen (three-and-a-half). Her husband works full-time in a well paid job, and Mrs Davies has spent the last few years looking after the home and the children. Mrs Davies has a history of psychiatric illness and, according to her husband, is beginning to display signs of disturbed behaviour. He feels she may need to go into hospital again. Mrs Davies requests a day-nursery place for Roseleen.

e) *Miss Nelson* (27) would like to return to full-time education in order to pursue her interest in a career caring for people. She has two children, one of whom is at primary school. She requests a day-nursery place for her two-year-old daughter, Julie. Miss Nelson is a single parent with no relatives or good friends living nearby.

f) *Mr and Mrs Wong* work long hours running a family business and have four children, two of whom – Amy (four) and Fran (three) – are under school age. They would like Amy and Fran to be placed in a day nursery. English is not spoken in the home, and the parents would like their children to mix in an English-speaking environment. Previously the children were cared for by their grandmother, who has just died.

g) *Mr Casson* (30) is a travelling salesman who spends some nights away from home. He is a single parent and until now his daughter Bernie (aged two-and-a-half) has been looked after mostly by Mr Casson's mother. His mother had a stroke recently and can no longer care for the child. Mr Casson requests a day-nursery place for Bernie. His brother's family, who live nearby, will look after Bernie when Mr Casson works away from home overnight.

h) *Miss Griffiths* is 19 with a young son Daniel (aged two). She lives alone and has become quite depressed recently. The health visitor who calls to see her and the child feels that, although the baby is loved, it is very understimulated. Miss Griffiths has never worked but would like to take up the offer of a job as a lunchtime barmaid at a local pub, in order to have the chance to meet more people.

i) *Mr and Mrs Taylor* are a young couple in their twenties. Their only child Alan (aged three) is physically handicapped. Alan has to wear a caliper on his deformed right leg. His parents would like him to mix more with other children and are requesting a nursery place.

Exercise 3 – role-play – a case conference

The following account describes the issues involved concerning Paul, a 15-year-old boy who is attending a community home with education on the premises. At the case conference, Paul's new social worker will recommend that Paul be allowed to return home. Your group will be allocated the various roles of the personnel involved and will have to re-enact the case conference.

Roles

1. Paul's new social worker
2. Head of the home (and chairman of the meeting)
3. Motor-mechanic teacher
4. History teacher
5. Houseparent
6. Other member of staff (role can be invented)
7. Paul's mother
8. Paul's stepfather

Situation

Paul Yates is 15 years old and has been in care since the age of nine. When he was 13, having previously been returned 'home on trial' to his parents, he appeared in court charged with taking and driving away cars. He was also due to appear for non-attendance at school. Since his court appearance, he has been at a community home with education on the premises (CHE) ten miles outside the city centre. In the last few months his behaviour has deteriorated and he has been disruptive in class. Paul admits that he has been a bit unco-operative but feels that he has been picked on by one member of staff in particular – his history teacher.

Family background

Paul's mother and father are divorced. His mother remarried a friend of her ex-husband, and all three – mother, father, and stepfather – have a close relationship. Mr Yates and Paul's natural father were themselves in care as children and later experienced Borstal and prison. All three adults are contemptuous of social services. As far as Paul is concerned, they argue that he has already spent 18 months in a community home and has already 'done his time' (equating the time Paul has spent at the community home with a prison sentence). They point out that Paul made good progress during his first 12 months and that his social worker promised that he could return home after the next case conference, three months later. This case conference passed and Paul was not discharged. Since then his behaviour has deteriorated. The parents, who visit Paul every Sunday, feel that Paul is 'not a bad lad' and should be given a chance to return home, where his parents will give him support. They feel that the social worker, Miss Tarrow, let him down by not obtaining his discharge as she previously promised.

Attitudes

1. Paul's new social worker

Paul's new social worker (replacing Miss Tarrow, who is going on a course) has seen Paul twice at the community home and finds him quite a likeable boy, despite his surly exterior. Paul is bitter about remaining at the community home and, like his parents, feels that he has 'done his time'. The social worker feels that Paul's being in a community home is not helping him to develop: rather it is reinforcing his resentment of authority.

In one month's time the establishment will be holding case conferences on all the children. At this meeting you would like to recommend that Paul is discharged and returned home, for the following reasons:

a) You feel that Paul has been let down by his previous social worker and that his current behaviour is a reflection of his disappointment.
b) You feel that Paul will not gain significantly from remaining in the community home.
c) You want to work purposefully and practically with Paul over the next few years – you want to give him an opportunity of accepting responsibility and receiving trust and to be able to show maturity.

You discuss this proposal with Miss Tarrow, who is not very hopeful of this being a successful move. Although she had at one stage considered Paul's return home, she felt that it would be too much of a risk and so changed her mind. She feels that the whole family are not really to be trusted in what they say.

In order to gauge the possibilities, you discuss the situation with Paul, without promising anything definite. Paul sincerely promises that, if he were allowed to return home, he would stay out of trouble. Further, he would agree to attend school regularly until he is allowed to leave, even though he is sure he will not like school. He would welcome the opportunity to show that he can be trusted.

At the secondary school Paul previously attended, provisional arrangements are made with the head-of-year, who agrees to grant Paul a school place. He is willing to give Paul another chance, but – knowing Paul from the past – realistically indicates that he is doubtful about Paul's ability to comply with the arrangement.

You discuss the case with your principal officer and outline your intentions. He is prepared to back you in your decision to request Paul's discharge. (Note: Legally the local authority can withdraw any child from any home at any time – but to do so without involving the community home would be to act in bad faith and jeopardise future relations.)

2. Head of the home (and chairman of the meeting)
You are the head of the community home, which you run on rather strict disciplinary grounds. Reports from staff suggest that, although Paul made good progress in the first 12 months, his attitude and behaviour has deteriorated recently. You would like Paul to remain in the school at least until his sixteenth birthday, in six months' time, by which time he may have learned to be more responsible and co-operative. You are not anticipating a request for Paul's return home but would object to such request because of the effect it would have on the other children at the home, if granted.

3. Motor-mechanic teacher
You have a good relationship with Paul, who works well and enthusiastically in your group. Paul confides in you occasionally and often talks about his mother, whom he would like to go back to live with. He gets on well with his father and stepfather and agrees that it is a 'funny situation' with them being so close. Paul responds to individual attention and informal instruction.

4. History teacher
You feel Paul that needs to be 'taken down a peg or two'. He is not interested in your lesson and does not respond willingly to instruction. Rather he encourages others to be disruptive. You feel that he needs to understand that he cannot get away with antisocial behaviour.

5. Houseparent
You like Paul but have noticed his recent unco-operative attitude. Paul normally willingly does his share of work in the unit. He was recently involved in a fight with another boy on the unit and had been spoiling for a fight for some days. You feel he should remain in the school and learn to accept disappointments and things which do not go his way.

Task
Take time to identify with your particular role and act out the case conference (about 30 minutes).

The case will begin with the social worker presenting the case for Paul's return home. All members of the group will then make contributions to the discussion. Ten minutes from the end of the meeting, Paul's parents will be invited in to the conference to be given a chance to have their say and to learn of the main arguments so far put forward.

Following the role-play
Spend some time reflecting on the experience. Consider how the parents waiting outside the room must have been feeling, how Paul was feeling, and whether these parties should have been included from the outset of the case conference.

Exercise 4 – residential-care allocation for the elderly

Each of the following people has been recommended by a social worker to the admissions panel of the elderly persons' homes. Unfortunately there are only two places available. Which two people do you feel need to be admitted?

a) *Mrs Musgrove*, aged 83, lives alone in first-floor council flat. Two years ago she suffered black-outs and is now quite confused, although physically fit. She fell and broke an arm during a recent black-out and has been cared for by her elderly brother and sister, who are both in bad health. Her short-term memory is poor, and she feels that her neighbours are stealing things from her. She hides objects, forgets where she has put them, and then blames neighbours. (In fact she has no contact with neighbours.) Recently she has wandered into the neighbourhood and has been unable to find her way home.

   She is visited by a home-care aid, has day care for seven days a week, a home help, and 'meals-on-wheels' three days a week. The elderly relatives do not feel capable of providing any more support and would like Mrs Musgrove's request for a full-time EPH place to be granted.

b) *Mrs James*, aged 85, lives in a ground-floor flat. She suffers severe arthritis and is visually impaired. Since breaking a leg in a fall, she has lost confidence to do anything for herself.

   Mrs James is frightened, and her anxiety increases when local teenagers congregate outside her flat. It has been broken into once.

   Last year her only grandson (20) volunteered to sleep on the settee in her home each night and to make her a cup of tea and her breakfast in the morning. His mother would visit during the day and do the shopping.

   Recently Mrs James' grandson obtained a job, and he now feels that he needs a proper night's sleep in preparation for the next day and no longer stays with his grandmother. Mrs James' daughter visits less often, as she is experiencing marital difficulties and has been to see the doctor about her anxiety. As a consequence, Mrs James is reverting to previous behaviour – staying in bed all day, unable to do anything for herself, and becoming depressed.

Mrs James does not receive any domiciliary services, but her daughter would like her to be admitted to an EPH full-time.

c) *Miss Grant*, aged 64, retired from a responsible job four years ago and lives on her own in rented property where she has been all her life. When she left work she weighed 9 stone. She now weighs over 20 stone.

The loss of her main role in life on retirement reinforced Miss Grants' loneliness and isolation and she became depressed. She began to eat excessively, to the point where she became ill and went into a coma. She went to hospital and her weight reduced a little. On being discharged she became known to the social services. Soon she began overeating again, no longer used her upstairs bedroom, and lived in one downstairs room. She had managed to become totally housebound and in need of help. She was on the telephone and often phoned neighbours to request help at any hour of the day.

Domiciliary support services have been brought into the home, but it is now felt that her physical size renders Miss Grant beyond domiciliary care. She is impossible to move by one person.

The social worker recommends that Miss Grant be given a full-time place in an EPH where her weight can be slowly reduced and eventually she can be rehabilitated to her own home.

d) *Mr Manning*, aged 91, lives in a ground-floor warden-controlled flat. An ex-alcoholic, he has three children whom he left when the youngest was four and the oldest was ten. They remember him as a violent man. He continued his job but left the family in poverty. Until her death, the children's mother was nursed by the second daughter, who is now 60.

Mr Manning is slightly brain-damaged from alcohol abuse and is lonely and confused. His eyesight is deteriorating. He wants to be looked after. One daughter still visits him occasionally out of a sense of duty. She blames him for her mother's early death and refuses to provide him with the emotional support he craves.

e) *Mr and Mrs Millerman* are aged 79 and 81 respectively. Mr Millerman has always presented a tough image and beaten his wife and daughter. Since he lost the sight of his right eye last year, he has become depressed, neglecting himself and expecting his wife to do everything for him.

Mr Millerman has exhibited characteristics of mental illness, insisting that the lights be turned off because he is frightened of switches. He also insists that his wife stay in the house all day.

The daughter visits, but is contemptuous of her father and speaks only to her mother. Mrs Millerman has recently had a stroke which has led to her being confused.

The social worker has noticed a gradual deterioration of Mrs Millerman's condition and observed her with black eyes and bumps on her head. Mrs Millerman claims that these are the results of falling, but the daughter contests this.

The social worker is concerned for Mrs Millerman's physical safety and feels that she would like to get away from her husband.

f) *Mr Latham* is aged 79. His wife is fit, active, and very proud of their recently modernised home. Mr Latham was formally a strong man and a 'bit of a womaniser'. Both their children have drifted off and have not been heard of for many years.

Mr Latham has suffered two strokes and lost the use of his left side. He is unsteady on his feet and needs constant care and attention. His wife feels resentful of his behaviour. He uses the commode in front of visitors and urinates when he feels like it. She thinks he is deliberately attention-seeking. Further, his sexual urge seems to have increased and he is making excessive demands on her. He masturbates publicly.

The social worker would like Mr Latham to be considered for a full-time place, as this is the wish of both Mr Latham and his wife, who is finding the strain increasingly difficult.

Questions for essays or discussion

1. Receptionists in social-services departments are normally the first people seen by people seeking help. What kind of skills do you think a receptionist needs in order to deal with clients who might be angry or distressed?

2. What do you understand by the term 'preventive social work'. Discuss which practices which can be included under this heading.

3. You are a nursery officer (nursery nurse), working in a day nursery, attending a staff meeting. The officer-in-charge would like to encourage more parental involvement in the day nursery. What suggestions would you make?

4. From a client's point of view, list the advantages of social services being provided from neighbourhood offices. Can you think of any drawbacks to the client under the 'patch' system?

5. Many elderly people are supported in the community by relatives and neighbours. Some neighbours offer no help. What kind of assistance could reasonably be expected from the neighbours of a frail 75-year-old man receiving day care on six days a week? He is unable to cook for himself but can manage to wash, dress, and get himself to bed. His only daughter lives 150 miles away and visits once a month.

6. Members of ethnic minorities in the UK have been slow to come forward to offer their services as potential foster parents. Why do you think this is so?

As a consequence of this, most social-services departments are actively involved in recruiting more foster parents from all ethnic minorities. Write down your views on whether you feel it is important for a black child to be brought up by black foster parents.

Further reading

1. *Social workers - their role and tasks*, the report of a National Institute for Social Work working party set up in October 1980 under the chairmanship of Peter M. Barclay ('The Barclay Report'). (Bedford Square Press, 1982). An up-to-date review of the work carried out by social workers: an analysis of social problems, social policy, and developments within social work.
2. *The newest profession*, Eileen Younghusband (*Community care*/IPC Business Press, 1981). A short competent history of the development of social work.
3. *Images of ourselves - women with disabilities talking*, edited by Jo Campling (Routledge & Kegan Paul, 1981). A number of women give their personal accounts of the experience of physical disability, their various struggles, and the attitude of society.
4. *Fostering in the eighties*, Jane Rowe (British Agencies for Adoption and Fostering, 1983). An up-to-date account of the varying developments within fostering.
5. *Welcome to St Gabriel's family centre*, Chris Warren and Joy Adamson (Church of England Children's Society, 1983). A description of the work of one particular family centre, written by two ex-workers from the family centre.
6. *The client speaks - working-class impressions of casework*, John Eric Mayer and Noel Timms (Routledge & Kegan Paul, 1970). A view of social work from the client's perspective.

3 The Probation Service

Introduction

The Probation Service is one of our society's responses to crime, along with the police and prison services and various smaller agencies. The Probation Service provides a social-work service to the courts in the UK – except in Scotland, where it does not exist as an independent agency and its functions are performed by the *social-work department* (the Scottish equivalent of the social-services department). The work of the Probation Service applies to both the criminal and the civil courts of England, Wales, and Northern Ireland.

Most of its work relates to the criminal courts, and in working with offenders it has as its central task the providing of alternatives to imprisonment. In the financial year 1981–2, the Home Office calculated that the average weekly cost of keeping someone in prison was £195, whereas the average weekly cost of someone on probation was £10. Apart from being much cheaper, though, it is also thought more constructive to keep a convicted person in the community, rather than in custody.

The Probation Service is a locally, as opposed to nationally, organised service, and there are 56 area Services in all. In 1986, there are approximately 6000 probation officers, with about 5000 ancillary and support staff most of whom are professionally unqualified. The total cost of the Service in the financial year 1983–4 was approximately £150 million.

Although each probation area is locally organised, the Service receives official guide-lines as to its policy from the Home Office, a part of central government.

The work of the Probation Service is rather complicated, both professionally and as regards its financing. Probation officers are social workers, and those who become probation officers now must possess the Certificate of Qualification in Social Work (CQSW) awarded by the Central Council for Education and Training in Social Work (CCETSW). As well as being social workers, however, they are also 'officers of the court', and they provide much assistance to the courts. This means that not only the Home Office but also benches of local magistrates (or Justices of the Peace) have a certain amount of authority over them and the work they perform.

The financing of the Probation Service is shared – 20% of the total cost is at present met by local authorities and the remaining 80% by the Home Office, from central-government funding.

This chapter will provide a brief history of the Probation Service, an account of the organisation and structure of the Service, and details of the work performed by probation officers both for the criminal courts and for the civil courts as well as other, more specialised, duties. A final section will look at current innovations and possible future developments.

History

The history of the probation service can conveniently be divided into three periods:

i) nineteenth-century origins,
ii) the period of establishment, 1907–70,
iii) from 1970 to the present day.

Nineteenth-century origins

As with social work generally in the UK, the origins of the Probation Service are to be found in the work of the charitable philanthropists and voluntary pioneers of the late nineteenth century.

During the second half of that century, drunkenness and alcohol abuse were social problems which caused particular concern, especially in the cities and large towns. The abuse of alcohol was often brought about or worsened by social deprivations like unemployment, poverty, and appalling housing conditions. People were frequently brought before the criminal courts for drunkenness and other related offences, and a large proportion of these people would be sent to prison.

In 1876 a Hertfordshire printer called Frederick Rainer wrote to the Church of England Temperance Society (which still exists today, incorporated into the Church of England Council for Social Aid) expressing his concern about such people. He felt that, once a person had been convicted and imprisoned by the court, there seemed no hope for her – on release from prison, it was likely that further offences would be committed which would soon result in a further term of imprisonment. Rainer could see no end to this sad process, which is called '*recidivism*', unless something were done for the offender. He even sent five shillings to help the society start some kind of practical work with these people.

Rainer was only one of many concerned people, and in August 1876 the Temperance Society appointed the first, unpaid, *police-court missionary*, in London. Many more appointments followed, and by 1900 what had become known as the *police-court mission* employed 143 missionaries. It is interesting to note that only 19 of these were women.

What did the missionaries actually do? They made enquiries into the background of people who appeared before the courts and, if the courts so agreed, they accepted responsibility for their care and supervision. Sometimes they even helped financially, by providing money as a security so that a person could be bailed and not kept in custody. Much of the work performed by missionaries with offenders involved matrimonial conciliation and assisting with difficult children.

The police-court missionaries rapidly earned respect and credibility for their work from the courts. While they were doing so, there were other interesting developments abroad, which came to have a bearing on the history of the Probation Service.

Developments abroad   In Boston, Massachusetts, USA, in 1878, a Probation Act had introduced the appointment of what were called 'probation officers' there. Members of the newly formed Howard Association (a penal-reform group in Britain) went to the USA to learn about the new ideas in Boston, and they returned enthusiastic about what they had seen. Along with others, some of whom actually worked in the British criminal courts, they acted as a powerful pressure group in trying to bring about changes similar to those in Boston.

In 1887 they met with partial success, and the Probation of First Offenders Act of that year introduced a system of releasing a first offender from a possible sentence of imprisonment, provided that she committed no further crimes. It was similar to what we now call a 'conditional discharge' – a person receives no punishment from the court as long as she stays free from further criminal activity.

Although this Act did not authorise supervision of the offender, it was a first move in this direction. The credibility which was being built up by the police-court missionaries meant that in 1907 an Act of Parliament was passed which *did* permit local authorities to appoint probation officers whose job it would be to supervise offenders.

The period of establishment, 1907–70
Between 1907 and 1970 the Probation Service became officially established as the agency providing a social-work service to the courts.

The Act of 1907 mentioned above was the Probation of Offenders Act. It contained the basic principles of probation as we know it today. A local authority could appoint probation officers to 'advise, assist, and befriend' those people convicted by the courts. Unfortunately, however, it was only 'permissive' legislation – it did not force local authorities to appoint probation officers. Such 'mandatory' legislation was not introduced until the Criminal Justice Act 1925, which meant that local authorities *had* to appoint probation officers (although many areas were still slow in actually doing so). Nevertheless, these two Acts of Parliament did mean the establishment of the Probation Service as a statutory (that is, an official State-provided and State-funded) service.

From 1925 onwards, the Probation Service expanded and became an increasingly professional service. In fact, the Probation Service pioneered training for social workers. In 1936, the Home Office introduced maintenance grants for students intending to become probation officers. To administer and control this scheme, the Home Office established the Probation Advisory and Training Board. At the same time, it began to inspect the services provided.

Probation officers formed a professional association as early as 1912. This was the National Association of Probation Officers (NAPO). One of the first debates to take place in the Association is still very much alive today – that of the court-officer (or controlling-agent) role versus the social-worker (as caring agent) role. For many, this debate was (and is) irresolvable, as they believed that even caring contained within it elements of controlling.

Following the Second World War, the Criminal Justice Act 1948 repealed the original Probation of Offenders Act 1907. The 1948 Act established the organisation of the Probation Service as we know it today (to be discussed later in this chapter). One of the changes which the 1948 Act brought about was that it was no longer required to insert the actual supervising probation officer's name into the probation order made by the court.

In 1962, the Government set up the Morrison Committee to examine the work of the Probation Service. As a result of the Committee's report, the role of the Probation Service became very much expanded. From being a social-work service to the courts, it became a social-work service to the whole penal system. Most importantly, it became responsible for 'after-care' of those adult offenders being released from prison. This expansion of role even meant a change of name, and in 1965 the Probation Service became the Probation and After-Care Service.

The Morrison Committee's report contained a definition of the Service: 'the submission of an offender, while at liberty, to a specified period of supervision by a social caseworker who is an officer of the court'. 'Social caseworker' is a fairly accurate description of the probation officer, even today. Basically it means a social worker who is doing 'one-to-one' work with an individual.

The many changes which have taken place in recent years as a result of parliamentary legislation form too large and complex a subject to discuss in any detail. However, one interesting change which took place as a result of the Criminal Justice Act 1967 was that the law no longer required that only a female probation officer should supervise girls and women.

The Children and Young Persons Act 1969 was a very important piece of legislation. One of the changes it introduced was that a probation order for juveniles (in law, those under 17 years old) was to be called a 'supervision order'. It is interesting that the 1969 Act used the same phrase 'advise, assist, and befriend' as had originally appeared in the Probation of Offenders Act 1907 when referring to the supervisor's role.

Since the 1969 Act, either probation officers or local-authority social workers can supervise juveniles under the terms of a supervision order. Arrangements differ from area to area, and it is therefore not possible to give precise details about this. The 1969 Act also introduced 'intermediate treatment' for juveniles.

The Seebohm Committee's report of 1968 recommended one unified department for social services. In England and Wales the Probation and After-Care Service was to continue and to remain independent, but as from November 1969 it ceased to exist in Scotland and became part of the social-work department.

From 1970 to the present day

Since 1970, the number of probation officers has continued to rise, and there are now approximately 6000. As well as this increase, the number of ancillary (largely unqualified) staff has also grown dramatically.

There is no doubt that, alongside the expansion in numbers of proba-tion officers, the work and the responsibilities of the Probation Service have grown tremendously. In fact many people involved with the Service feel that the growth in the workload of the Service has stretched resources to the limit, if not surpassed it.

Changes in the 1970s included the supervision, on their release from prison, of increased numbers of people who had committed more serious offences. This was known as the system of *parole*, which was originally introduced in 1968. The introduction of parole meant that prisoners were released early but, although being supervised in the community, were tech-nically still serving their sentences of imprisonment. Not complying with the requirements of their parole 'licence' could mean immediate return to prison.

The Probation Service has always had as a paramount aim the provision of alternatives to imprisonment. The Powers of Criminal Courts Act 1973 introduced *community service* for offenders aged 17 or over. This meant that they could perform unpaid work of service to the community, as a sentence of the court. It was originally intended to be an alternative to im-prisonment, and it is still largely used as such. It meant that – as with parole supervision – probation officers were increasingly supervising people who had committed more serious offences.

Another important area of work is the providing of information about individuals' personal circumstances and offending behaviour to the criminal and civil courts, as well as to custodial institutions. These report-writing responsibilities of the Probation Service have steadily increased over the past few years. The preparation of reports is time-consuming, involving as it does consulting with individuals and other agencies, as well as checking probation records.

The Criminal Justice Act 1982 has affected the work of the Probation Service in important ways. It introduced a return to the situation before 1965. As from 24 May 1983, the words 'and After-Care' ceased to be a part of the official name of the Service, which is again plainly called the 'Probation Service'.

The 1982 Act also introduced new requirements which could be made as part of supervision and probation orders. These requirements can limit the activities of offenders more than previously, as well as involving them in other activities aimed at diverting them from offending.

A very recent and significant development regarding the Probation Service was the publication in April 1984 by the Home Office of a *'Statement of national objectives and priorities'* for the Service. This was the first time in the history of the Probation Service that any such state-ment had been issued by the central authority. The statement is a brief document which sets out the present work of the Probation Service and

66

possible developments for the future. It has come under criticism from the National Association of Probation Officers for 'its failure to provide a positive programme for the future development of the Probation Service'. Two other substantial criticisms from NAPO are the low priority the statement gives to after-care work with offenders released from custody and the low priority it gives to the civil work of the Service.

The organisation and structure of the Probation Service

The powers and duties of the Probation Service are set down in the laws of this country. They are to be found in particular in the Powers of the Criminal Courts Act 1973 (as amended by the Criminal Law Act 1977) and the Criminal Justice Act 1982. In addition to this legislation, the 'Probation Rules' (which are 'statutory instruments') also contain official directives for the work of the Probation Service.

The Probation Service is organised both nationally and locally.

National organisation

As far as central government is concerned, the Home Secretary is the government minister responsible to Parliament for the Probation Service. Under the Home Secretary's authority is the Probation Department of the Home Office. The head of this department is an assistant under-secretary of state. This department has two divisions, and is part of the Civil Service. It has a certain degree of control over the Probation Service, and it exercises this control or guidance by way of memorandums sent to the local probation areas.

Also based at the Home Office is the Probation Inspectorate, which has power to inspect local probation areas and make recommendations. It also has a certain amount of responsibility for the recruitment and training of probation officers.

Local organisation

The Probation Service is largely a locally organised service. There are 56 different probation areas. Some areas coincide with county boundaries, while others are simply a part of a large city.

Each probation area is responsible to a *probation committee*. This committee is made up of local magistrates, judges, and others who are not justices but co-opted lay persons. This committee meets regularly to discuss probation matters, and will be involved in appointing new staff as well as disciplinary matters.

Probation areas are further divided into smaller areas which are known as *petty-sessional divisions* (PSDs). A PSD is an area covered by one local magistrates' court. A group of magistrates in these areas forms a local *probation liaison committee*. This meets at least three times a year and tends to be fairly closely in touch with the work of the local probation office. Local probation officers are present at these meetings, and take part in them. A wide range of matters can be discussed, ranging from the case of a particular individual on probation to more general topics and current issues of interest or concern to either the magistrates or the probation officers. Each probation officer is accountable to this committee.

Structure of a local probation area

The chief probation officer (CPO)   The chief probation officer (at present only 9% of them are women) is responsible for the work of the probation area he is appointed to. The CPO has to liaise with the Home Office and the area probation committee and – through assistant chief probation officers – has to oversee and organise the work of the Probation Service in the area.

The assistant chief probation officer (ACPO)   Each probation area will have two or more ACPOs. They will usually be more closely involved than the CPO in the work carried out by the teams of probation officers in the local offices. Their duties can be either general or specific – for example, some with specific duties are responsible for the training of officers; others for hostel provision. Those with general duties will link local teams, ensure that area policies are implemented, and assist the CPO in the formation of area policy.

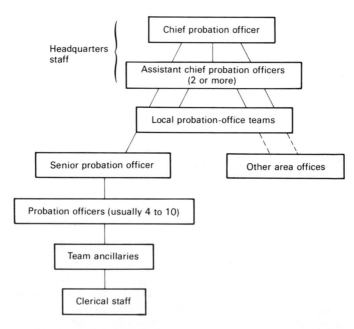

Structure of a local probation area

68

Generally, the CPO and ACPOs are based in the county or area headquarters, which will often be central, while all other staff will be locally based. It is unusual for headquarters staff to supervise offenders.

The senior probation officer (SPO) The main task of the SPO is to supervise the work of the team of probation officers for which he is responsible. This means a general overview of the team's work as well as the personal supervision of each individual officer. Another important role is to act as a link between headquarters and the team, and to ensure that correct policy is carried out by officers. The SPO is also the main channel of communication between the team and the local probation liaison committee.

Much of the SPO's time will be spent in meetings with other agencies in the local community, and often in being the 'public face' of the local probation officers.

Many SPOs carry a case-load of clients whom they supervise in addition to their other duties. The number of cases will vary with each individual.

The SPO is also responsible for the work of the team ancillaries (usually unqualified staff) plus the secretarial staff.

The probation officer The probation officer (often known as the 'main-grade' probation officer) is responsible for his own case-load (the total number of people under his supervision). In addition to this, a probation officer may carry responsibility for a specialised office resource – such as a local landlady scheme, or a drug-abuse phone-in line, or groupwork with offenders.

Details of the work of the probation officer are to be found in the following parts of this chapter.

The probation ancillary The employment of probation ancillaries varies considerably from area to area. Some employ none, whereas others employ a large number.

Usually the ancillaries are professionally unqualified – in fact they are often people who intend at some time in the future to qualify and work as probation officers.

The work performed by ancillaries can vary a great deal, and often depends on the needs of a particular probation office. Sometimes they provide general support or back-up for probation officers. Others will spend a great deal of time in court, taking details of cases and providing reports. An ancillary might run an accommodation scheme or a special project of some kind. In a few offices the ancillary is given the rather privileged opportunity to start new innovations in the local community and to involve the probation office more in its activities.

Voluntary associates Almost all probation officers involve in their work a group of individuals known as voluntary associates (VAs). These volunteers are very important to the work of the probation office, partly because they reflect the early beginnings of the Probation Service. Volunteers from the community – interested and concerned people, often with great compassion and human understanding – have made valuable contributions to the work of the Probation Service throughout its existence. Something a volunteer will be able to offer, as compared with a probation officer, is much more time, and often longer may be spent with just one individual offender.

It is usually felt to be important that the volunteers attached to a particular probation office should have some kind of group identity, and so meetings and common activities are arranged, either by a probation officer or by one of the volunteers themselves. Some kind of training – say in counselling skills – may even be offered to the volunteers. Many volunteers have been involved with the Probation Service for a considerable number of years, and they make an extremely valuable contribution.

The tasks carried out by voluntary associates vary a great deal. They can be similar to the tasks of the probation ancillary, as mentioned above. They are more likely, however, to involve one-to-one work with particular clients, sometimes intense and in-depth. In contrast, tasks may be simple practical ones – for example, driving a mother and child to see a husband in prison, or helping an individual to transport furniture to her newly found home.

Voluntary associates do not receive payment for their work but can, if 'accredited' by the Probation Service, receive expenses for petrol or fares for example.

The recruitment of new volunteers to the Probation Service can – as every 'volunteer organiser' knows – be a difficult, time-consuming, and arduous task! However, the Probation Service generally exerts a great deal of effort and encouragement to recruit them. Many volunteers have full-time jobs in a field of work which bears no resemblance to the caring professions, but their contributions are very much valued and appreciated. The very fact that many of them have ordinary jobs often makes them more acceptable to clients.

Work for the criminal courts

The probation officer's work involving the criminal courts can be subdivided as follows:

a) the provision of reports for various courts and custodial institutions (such as detention centres and prisons), giving information on individuals' personal circumstances and offences;
b) the supervision of offenders in the community;
c) the care of offenders in custody;
d) the after-care of offenders on release from custody;
e) other general duties.

Each area will now be dealt with in detail.

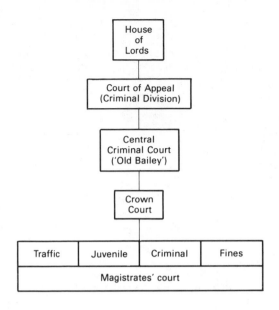

```
                    ┌─────────────┐
                    │    House    │
                    │     of      │
                    │    Lords    │
                    └──────┬──────┘
                ┌──────────┴───────────┐
                │  Court of Appeal     │
                │ (Criminal Division)  │
                └──────────┬───────────┘
                    ┌──────┴──────┐
                    │   Central   │
                    │  Criminal   │
                    │   Court     │
                    │ ('Old Bailey')│
                    └──────┬──────┘
                      ┌────┴────┐
                      │  Crown  │
                      │  Court  │
                      └────┬────┘
    ┌─────────┬──────────┬─┴────────┬─────────┐
    │ Traffic │ Juvenile │ Criminal │  Fines  │
    ├─────────┴──────────┴──────────┴─────────┤
    │            Magistrates' court           │
    └─────────────────────────────────────────┘
```

Basic structure of the criminal courts in England and Wales

The provision of reports for various courts

This area of the Service's work has grown dramatically over the past 20 years.

For the courts, information is provided on individual offenders in what are called '*social enquiry reports*' ('SERs' for short). They will contain details of the offender's history, family and domestic situation, education, and personal relationships. They are usually compiled and presented to court only after a person has pleaded guilty, or has been found guilty, of an offence. This is because, in theory, in British law a person is thought innocent until proved guilty, and it would be unfair to inquire into her situation and intimate life details if she has committed no crime. This also means that an SER can include details of the offender's attitude to the offence, and this will be important for the court to know when it is sentencing. The report will normally conclude with a recommendation from the probation officer, based on a considered judgement as to how the offender might most effectively be diverted from further offending and possibly suggesting one of a range of sentences intended to achieve this.

Once completed, the SER is the property of the court, but the offender (or, in the case of a juvenile, the parents) has a right either to read the report or at least to know the contents of it.

When the court is ready to sentence an offender, copies of the SER will be handed by the probation officer in court to the magistrate or judge, and

71

In court, probation officers are frequently questioned on the reports they submit.

also to the clerk of the court, who is responsible for the running of the court's business. After the report has been read, the magistrate or judge will frequently ask the probation officer about details of the report before deciding on a sentence.

The preparation of SERs is a very time-consuming task, and some estimates reckon that on average a probation officer spends one-third of his time preparing them. A single report may take up to five hours to prepare and write. In order to complete the report, the offender will normally be interviewed more than once, possibly in company with members of her family. The probation officer may also need to contact other agencies or professionals – for example the police, the offender's doctor (who would usually want to gain the consent of his patient before divulging any personal details), social workers, etc. – to collect or verify information. In the case of a juvenile still attending school, contact will normally be made with the school and a report will be obtained on the young person's progress there.

An SER is like a 'shop window' for the Probation Service, in that it is a part of a probation officer's work which is held up to scrutiny by those outside the Service. There is a certain degree of confusion about the purpose of reports. Probation officers will tend to think of them as documents of a social-work nature, whereas magistrates and judges view them

72

more as an aid to sentencing. The truth is that they are both at the same time. Many thousands of SERs are prepared by the Probation Service every year, and the time saved by the courts as a result is considerable.

You will find an example of an SER in exercise 1 at the end of this chapter.

Reports for custodial institutions (detention centres, youth-custody centres, prisons)

The Probation Service also prepares reports for custodial institutions. An institution requests these, and their purpose is to provide information about the home situation and release plans of offenders serving sentences. These reports will involve the 'home' probation officer in visiting the home and family of the offender, or may involve the probation officer in attempting to secure accommodation for the release of an offender who is homeless. These reports tend to be shorter than SERs and less time-consuming in their preparation.

You will find an example of this kind of report in exercise 2 at the end of this chapter.

The range of sentences open to the criminal courts in England and Wales

Absolute discharge   No punishment is involved, but a criminal conviction is recorded.

Conditional discharge   No punishment is involved as long as the person does not commit any further crime for a period of up to three years.

Fine   The Crown Court can impose unlimited fines, but there are various limits in the magistrates' court. If people fail to pay fines, they can later be sent to prison.

Supervision and probation orders   Minimum length six months, maximum three years.

Community-service order   Allows people to perform unpaid work in the community, usually as an alternative to being sent to prison.

Attendance centres   For young people under 21. Orders vary from 12 to 24 hours. Offenders attend on a Saturday morning or afternoon and take part in sporting activities and education (for example, home crafts, physical exercise, or personal hygiene). Often an alternative to custody for football hooligans.

Detention centre   A custodial sentence for males aged 14 to 20. Minimum three weeks, maximum four months. Intended to impose a 'short sharp shock'.

Youth-custody centre   For males aged 15 to 20, females aged 16 to 20. A custodial sentence which lasts anything from four months upwards.

Prison   For all those aged 21 or over. No minimum or maximum length of sentence.

Suspended sentence   A prison sentence can be suspended (or put off) for up to two years. If the offender commits no further crime during that period, she does not go to prison. However, if she does offend again, it is very likely that she will go to prison, but this may depend on how serious the crime.

Partially suspended sentence   Applies only to those over 21. Depending on the length of custodial sentence a minimum of one-quarter and a maximum of three-quarters of the sentence can be suspended (i.e. served in the community).

Deferred sentence   Introduced as recently as the mid-1970s, this means that sentencing is simply 'deferred' (or put off) for up to six months. At the end of the period the court decides on, the offender returns to court to be sentenced. It is hoped that in this period of 'deferment' she will have made some progress in her personal situation.

The Rehabilitation of Offenders Act 1974   This Act – which applies to England, Wales, and Scotland – was intended to relieve the burden of past criminal conviction on people who had committed crimes.

If an offender remains free of further convictions for a specified period of time (what the Act calls the '*rehabilitation period*'), she becomes, in the terms of the Act, a '*rehabilitated person*', and the conviction becomes '*spent*'.

This is very important when a person is applying for a job, because it means that she may not have to declare criminal convictions, depending on the sentence she received at court.

Some rehabilitation periods are fixed:

Sentence	Rehabilitation period
Imprisonment between 6 months and 2½ years	10 years
Less than 6 months' imprisonment	7 years
Fine or community-service order	5 years
Absolute discharge	6 months

If the person was *under 17* (i.e. a juvenile) when convicted, then all of these periods are cut by half.

Some sentences carry variable rehabilitation periods.

Sentence	Rehabilitation period
Probation order or conditional discharge	1 year or until the order expires (whichever is longer)
Supervision order	1 year or until the order expires (whichever is longer)

For people sentenced to more than 2½ years in prison, their conviction is *never spent*. Under the Act, *suspended prison sentences* are counted as if they are prison sentences.

As regards a job, the Act means that an employer *cannot refuse to employ someone* (nor *dismiss someone*) because of a *spent conviction*. However, it is very important to state that some jobs and professions are excluded from the Act. They include:

a) the police force,
b) the prison service,
c) the Probation Service,
d) traffic wardens,
e) teachers in schools or colleges of further education,
f) the social services,
g) the National Health Service (doctors, nurses, dentists, etc.),
h) the youth service,
i) veterinary surgeons.

Someone applying for work in these fields *has to record even spent convictions* on her application form. If she did not disclose spent convictions when asked, then, if appointed, she could be dismissed at any time.

The supervision of offenders in the community

Probation order   This applies to an offender over 17 years, who will appear in an adult or magistrates' court. In law, a probation order is not technically a sentence of the court: it is rather an *alternative* to a sentence. The length of a probation order can vary from six months to three years and will depend on various factors, one of which may be the seriousness of the offence. An order can only be made if the offender *consents* to being placed on probation.

A probation order contains three legal requirements:

 i) that the probationer keeps in touch with the probation officer,
 ii) that the probationer notifies the probation officer of a change of address and employment,
iii) that the probationer should lead an 'honest and industrious life'.

Some probation areas consider that, in the present economic climate, with high unemployment, the requirement to live an 'industrious' life is redundant and are making moves to have it deleted.

In addition to these standard requirements, other requirements can be inserted into a probation order. These might be, for example, that a probationer lives at a specific address (this may be a hostel) or undergoes psychiatric treatment, or that she participates in specific activities arranged by the Probation Service.

If a probationer fails in any of these requirements, she is said to be 'in breach' of the probation order and can be returned to court and sentenced again for the original offence.

The probation officer has a lot of freedom as to how someone is supervised on probation. Meetings can be arranged as necessary, and there are no legal constraints about this. Sometimes meetings will be in the probation office, at other times in the offender's home. The home will often provide a more natural setting, where the atmosphere can be more relaxed.

In many cases, the committing of an offence might signify a crisis in an individual's life. When the probation officer meets with her, he may discover massive fuel bills, hire-purchase payments owing, or other worrying or confusing problems. Fuel may have been cut off, the individual might be threatened with eviction from her home, and so on. Often the probation officer has to work very quickly in helping the person to face up to and deal with problems, and this can mean that, by the time a person's case comes to court for sentence, the crucial or decisive work may already have been done.

Supervision order   A 'supervision order' is the term given to a probation order (usually made by a juvenile court) on a young person under 17. One difference from an adult probation order is that the court does not have to gain the consent of the juvenile to the making of the order. (Local-authority social workers supervise these orders as well as probation officers, particularly if the young person is under 14.)

A supervision order contains similar general requirements to those in a probation order, and again similar additional ones can be made.

In addition to this, what is called an *intermediate-treatment* (IT) order can be made. This is a growing area of work, introduced by the Children and Young Persons Act 1969. In the early years of IT, progress in many areas of the country was very slow and spasmodic – in some areas IT provision hardly existed at all. However, this situation has now changed. The Criminal Justice Act 1982 laid a duty on local authorities to provide intermediate treatment. As a result, much activity is going on, and probation officers are getting more involved.

The phrase 'intermediate treatment' was originally intended to mean provision for juveniles which bridged the gap between an ordinary supervision order in the community and a custodial sentence – in a detention centre, for example. It was 'intermediate' and was intended to increase the chances of diverting a young person from custody, and indeed from further offending.

IT involves a wide range of activities. It most commonly means juveniles meeting as a group and then taking part in some kind of common activity. Sport can figure, or 'outdoor pursuits', or a probation officer may lead a group where the focus is more directly on members' problems

Intermediate treatment can develop self-confidence.

rather than physical activity. In many areas motorcycle groups are organised, or cars repaired. These activities have been thought particularly useful for young people involved in crime concerning motor vehicles (such as theft of vehicles or driving while disqualified) as they tap an interest they have.

The Government has recently made available greatly increased finance for IT schemes. For the three years from 1983, the Department of Health and Social Security (DHSS) was allocated a total of £15 million to spend on this provision.

Community-service order (CSO) An offender aged 16 or over can be made subject to a community-service order. The individual concerned has to agree to it being made. The order means that over a period of one year, the person must perform unpaid work in the community as directed by the Probation Service, which runs the scheme. The times to be worked are from 40 to 120 hours for a 16 year old, and from 40 to 240 hours for anyone over 17.

The kind of work performed varies a great deal. Examples are redecorating an elderly persons' home, gardening for a children's home, or cleaning footpaths or waste ground. Work must not be performed for any profit-making concern.

If the person fails to work satisfactorily, she is 'in breach' and can be returned to court to be sentenced again.

As originally intended when introduced by legislation in 1973, community service was a strict alternative to imprisonment, and most probation areas still apply this principle. One pleasing aspect is that many people who perform community service are subsequently offered permanent employment by the organisations they have worked with.

The care of offenders in custody
Anybody receiving a custodial sentence will be sent to one of three types of establishment:

 i) detention centres,
 ii) youth-custody centres (formerly known as 'Borstals'),
iii) prisons.

  i) *Detention centres*   These are provided for males only, aged 14 to 20 years. When introduced, after the Second World War, they were intended to act as a *'short sharp shock'* in diverting the young person from further offending. The minimum sentence is three weeks, the maximum four months.
 ii) *Youth-custody centres*   Until May 1983, these were known as 'Borstals'. It is unclear yet as to whether the change of title signifies a more profound change of regime. They exist for both males (aged 15 to 20) and females (aged 17 to 20). Whereas the old Borstal-training sentence was for an indeterminate period between six months and two years, a young person sentenced to youth custody can spend anything from four months and upwards in such an institution depending on the sentence of the court. If under 17, however, there is a maximum sentence of 12 months.
iii) *Prisons*   Any offender over the age of 21 can be sent to prison, and there is no minimum or maximum length of sentence. There are different types of prison, and the atmosphere and regime can vary a great deal. Many of our prisons are old (often Victorian) buildings, simply not built to cater for the numbers they contain today. Some of the more modern prisons are able to offer a reasonably constructive regime, and a very small number actually offer industrial work to their inmates.

There are different categories of prison as regards security, ranging from 'open prisons' (for those regarded as no security risk) to top-security gaols. One prison – Grendon Underwood in Buckinghamshire – is known as a 'psychiatric prison' and offers various therapeutic programmes for many of its disturbed inmates.

No matter what type of institution an offender is sent to, the 'home' probation officer retains some responsibility for her welfare throughout the sentence, and after release.

This involves the probation officer in visiting his client, communicating by letter, and keeping in touch with the client's family as well as possible. Often a court appearance results in a husband, wife, or family breaking

Probation officers provide a necessary link between the prisoner and the outside world.

off all contact with an offender, and a probation officer may feel it right to work towards a reconciliation. As a custodial sentence means a difficult time for all involved – and when you consider that most convicted prisoners can receive only one short visit every month from members of their families – it can put an impossible strain on relationships. The probation officer has to work within the difficult limitations of this situation.

Welfare officers in prison probation departments In addition to the 'home' probation officers, there are probation officers working full-time in all prisons and in most detention centres and youth-custody centres. They may be known as 'welfare officers' rather than probation officers, and in larger establishments they work in small teams known as a 'welfare department'. Being on site, in close proximity to those serving custodial sentences, they can react fairly swiftly when a problem arises and can, if necessary, contact the home probation officer, who can in turn contact the prisoner's home. Often there is no need to make contact with the home probation officer, and welfare officers simply contact the prisoner's home directly.

The after-care of offenders on release from custody
All males released from *detention centres* are subject to supervision which lasts for three months. This means that they are officially required to

report to a probation officer on release, and that for the next three months they are supervised very much as if they were on probation.

All males and females released from *youth-custody centres* are also officially subject to supervision. This runs for a minimum of three months, but is frequently longer and depends on the length of sentence the individual had received.

For men and women released from *prison* there is no official (or statutory) requirement to be under the supervision of a probation officer, unless they are in one of two categories:

i) If they are released on *parole* (i.e. if they are granted early release), they are subject to the official supervision of a probation officer until the date when they would normally have been released. Technically they are still serving their prison sentence, but are doing so in the community.

ii) Offenders who have received a *life sentence* of imprisonment but are released from prison are then subject to a *'life licence'* for the rest of their life. As you are probably aware, this applies to quite a number of people in the country as a whole, because most people receiving life sentences are in fact released before their death. Individuals on a 'life licence' are under the statutory supervision of a probation officer.

Voluntary after-care Apart from those categories of statutory after-care mentioned, anybody released from prison can request 'voluntary after-care'. This means that, while she is still serving her prison sentence, she can contact the probation service in the area in which she intends to live, and ask for assistance. Alternatively, she can request help after her release. The problem she is asking for help with does not have to be of any particular kind. If a probation officer felt able to assist, then he would attempt to do so; if not, he would probably refer the person elsewhere.

Purpose of after-care The main purpose of after-care is to help the individual readjust as effectively as possible to life in the community. Receiving a custodial sentence is a major disruption in a person's life, and it nearly always also means a disruption for relatives and friends. Frequently, family or friendship ties are broken or damaged when a person enters custody, and it is the probation officer's main consideration to assist in this difficult situation.

Apart from this, other after-care tasks are often of a practical nature. Many are made homeless when sent to prison, or they lose furniture and other property. Some require help with education or training courses on release, or even assistance in job-finding. The probation officer can, and frequently does, help with these kinds of problem.

One of the most difficult challenges to the probation officer is the case of the 'recidivist' – a person who commits new offences at fairly regular intervals and who is therefore quickly returned to court. This situation can go on for years – perhaps, for a very few people, for an entire lifetime – and it is important that, faced with this situation, the probation officer does not 'give up' on the individual. He should continue to show warmth and acceptance and not give the impression that he expects the offender to fail again. People we call 'recidivists' need to believe in themselves in order to break the vicious circle of offending and court appearance.

Other general duties

Record-keeping The probation officer is required to keep written records of all people who form part of his case-load. These should contain a record of every meeting with an individual. Apart from this, the probation officer is expected to provide thorough summaries of the progress of each case, perhaps three or four times a year. Every case file, as well as containing these details, will also hold any reports a probation officer has prepared for the court, and copies of all letters written or received in regard to the case.

Office duty Most probation offices have an 'open-door' policy. This means that a probation officer will be on duty during normal office hours (usually 9 a.m. to 5.30 p.m.) to assist anybody who walks in off the street. Most offices have a 'rota', which means that each probation officer in the team takes a turn at office duty. Each day on duty will be quite different – some hectic, some quiet. Some days will throw up problems which the probation officer can feel able to assist with, and on other days problems will seem quite intractable. Many difficulties presented cannot be suitably dealt with by a probation officer, and the person seeking help will be referred elsewhere, say to the local social-services department or citizens advice bureau.

Unlike the social-services department, the Probation Service does not provide 'out-of-hours' or emergency services to the community. If a serious problem does occur outside office hours, the social-services department could deal with it, and contact would later be made by the two agencies.

Court duty While a criminal court is sitting, it will be able to call for the assistance of a probation officer. Most probation offices will have a court duty rota, and each probation officer will take a share in being available to the court. Duties in court will include passing SERs to the magistrates or judge and answering questions on defendants or on social-welfare resources in the local community. The probation officer is also accessible to any member of the public in court who may be distressed, or may simply have a question to ask. The probation officer will also check on defendants who are in custody before appearing in court, and will make visits to the cells to see them.

Other tasks   It is not possible to mention all the tasks a probation officer is likely to have to fulfil, but they may well include the following.

The probation officer has to attend many different kinds of meeting. These will include staff meetings of his own team; case committees (or meetings with local magistrates); and meetings with other agencies in the area, such as the social-services department or the local education office.

The Probation Service arranges professional staff conferences and in-service training activities, and the probation officer will take part in these.

In addition, many probation officers – often in their own time – devote a great deal of energy to setting up new projects or resources for the local community. This will be discussed later in this chapter (see under 'specialised work').

Work for the civil courts

Divorce-court welfare work
When a marriage is dissolved (usually in the *county court*) and there are children by the marriage, the judge dealing with the proceedings has to be certain that the arrangements made for the welfare of the children are the best possible in the circumstances. When the judge is uncertain about the arrangements – especially where younger children are involved – he can call upon the Probation Service for assistance.

Working in another role, as a *'divorce-court welfare officer'*, a probation officer can be asked to make enquiries about the welfare of the

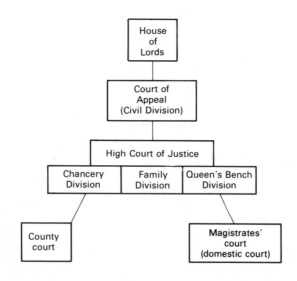

Basic structure of the civil courts in England and Wales

children and to then report back information to the court at a later stage, in order to assist it. These enquiries might be simple and be done in a few weeks time, or they might be complicated and take many months to complete. Usually, the case will not be listed again and be proceeded with until the divorce-court welfare officer's report has been 'filed' in the court's office.

The divorce-court welfare officer is concerned not so much with financial arrangements or simple practical matters, but with the following:

i) *Care and control of the child or children* This normally refers to where the child will actually live after the divorce has been made absolute. One parent will be awarded the care and control of the child and will have the child living with him or her on a day-to-day basis.

ii) *Custody of the child or children* In law, having the custody of a child means having certain rights to make important decisions about the child's life, such as where she is educated, whether or not she enters a particular religious faith or denomination, or whether to move to live permanently abroad. It is obviously very important to a parent to have these rights. It is now more common for a judge to award 'joint custody' to parents. This means that, no matter which parent the child lives with (i.e. which parent has 'care and control'), both parents have an equal right to make and be consulted about these important decisions.

iii) *Access* As the child will live with only one parent after the divorce, the othc. parent will request (and will nearly always be granted) 'access' to the child. This means seeing and meeting with the child, and it can take place in the home of either parent or in any 'neutral' location. Particular arrangements will depend on each case and, generally speaking, judges would rather parents amicably made their own arrangements. The court only intervenes when problems are experienced.

The overriding concern of the divorce-court welfare officer is always the *welfare of the child*. Everything else takes second place.

Matrimonial supervision order If the judge in a divorce hearing foresees either short-term or long-term problems occurring in regard to children, he can make this order. It places the child or children under the official supervision of a divorce-court welfare officer until the age of 18. Applications for the order to be discharged before then can be made by either parent or by the divorce-court welfare officer, but this decision lies finally with the court. (Social-services-department social workers can also supervise such orders.)

Compared to the probation officer's work for the criminal courts, divorce-court welfare work does not take up a great deal of time. In most

83

areas, each probation officer will perform divorce-court welfare work, but a few probation areas have set up 'civil-work units' to specialise in civil work, thus releasing probation officers for other tasks. A probation officer might work in a civil-work unit for some time and then return to mainstream work.

Conciliation

Many people involved in divorce proceedings and the welfare of children are very critical of what they call the *'adversarial approach'* to family breakdown. Divorce proceedings have traditionally been carried out as if they were a contest or fight between the two parties – a struggle to get the better deal. It is felt that this is a sad and inappropriate misdirection of human resources, and in the past few years there has been the growth of an alternative to it – the *conciliation scheme*.

Conciliation has elements of preventive work in it and basically attempts to help husbands and wives to make decisions themselves regarding the welfare of their children, rather than take the matter to court.

The Probation Service, as well as voluntary agencies (such as *marriage-guidance councils*), is very much involved in encouraging such schemes, and this means that in the next few years the whole organisation of divorce-court welfare work may radically change.

Adoption

Under legislation which has only recently come into force (despite it being part of the Children Act 1975), probation officers can be involved in *adoption proceedings*. The probation officer can have two different roles: *guardian ad litem* (or *guardian 'in law'*) and *reporting officer*.

If adoption proceedings are in *dispute* (perhaps because one of the 'natural parents' does not consent to the adoption), then a probation officer can be appointed as 'guardian *ad litem*'. This means that the officer will be independent of the agency which *placed* the child for adoption (for example, the social-services department or a private adoption agency), and it will be his job to represent the child through the court proceedings and to safeguard the child's interests.

When there is *no dispute*, a probation officer can be appointed as a 'reporting officer'. This will involve reporting to the court on the situation, welfare, and best interests of the child.

The Children Act 1975 set up new *'panels'* of social workers, probation officers, and certain independent carers. From these panels, reporting officers and guardians *ad litem* are appointed by the courts to oversee the interests of children in adoption proceedings.

Most adoptions are dealt with by the *county court*, but some are heard by the *juvenile court*.

Specialised work

Other than the general duties already mentioned, there are probation officers who work in different and more specialised ways.

Hostels

Having run hostels for young offenders for some fifty years, the Probation Service introduced hostels for older, adult offenders in the early 1970s. They cater for both males and females, many of whom will have committed quite serious offences and could well receive a custodial sentence. However, the court can, as an alternative to custody, make a probation order and include in it a requirement that the offender resides in a hostel for up to a year.

Going to live in a hostel can be traumatic change in a person's life, and it will often be her first taste of life away from her own home or home area.

If offenders leave the hostel for a long period without permission, or if their behaviour is unacceptable, they can be returned to court and be re-sentenced. The organisation and regimes of hostels vary a great deal, but they are generally supportive while encouraging those living in them to examine their life-style and how they might constructively change it.

The *warden* in charge of a hostel is a qualified probation officer, and there will also be a liaison probation officer from the team covering the area in which the hostel is situated.

Day centres

There are an increasing number of day centres run by the Probation Service. They are of two types:

i) *'Drop-in' day centres* have quite a free policy on admission. Normally, people using the centres will be offenders or will have had some connection with the Probation Service in the past. Especially in the large cities, many of those using day centres will be homeless or rootless, and there will often be a high proportion of people who abuse alcohol. There will be a range of activities in a day centre. People can simply sit and chat to friends or to staff. There will usually be card or other games offered, but there will also be the opportunity for counselling by a probation officer. Some day centres extend their activities to organising a football team or short holidays.

ii) A few day centres have a more official use, and people will use the facilities only when referred by the court, as a condition of a probation order. Activities may be similar to those at 'drop-in' day centres, but there will be more emphasis on a therapeutic programme, group work, and other social-work interventions. Originally this type of centre was known as a 'day training centre', but this name has now been dropped. Some of the staff working in this type of day centre will be qualified probation officers, and again there will be liaison officers from a local probation team.

Community-service schemes

Senior staff who organise community-service schemes will normally be qualified probation officers. This is full-time work, and the probation officers involved will not have the usual case-load and other duties mentioned earlier in this chapter.

Staff who actually supervise offenders on community service are known as 'sessional supervisors' and are usually professionally unqualified. However, many of them have technical or trade skills which they use in this work.

Those running community-service schemes will have to seek out possible work opportunities and keep in contact with those work placements already in existence. Much tact is required when the behaviour of those people on the community-service schemes upsets the people they are working for!

Community service allows offenders to be more positively involved in their local community.

Other specialised work

There have been occasional experiments with '*detached*' probation work. This means that a probation officer is not based, as usual, in an office team. Instead, he works from his own home or some other 'neutral' base, and the focus of the work is very much to meet young people on their own territory. The approach will be informal, and will often involve young people who may be using drugs, or glue-sniffing, and who are generally rootless or drifting.

There is no doubt that working in this way can be very satisfying, but it is extremely draining, because the officer has to rely on his own initiative and stamina and does not have the support of a team or office staff. As a result, it is doubtful whether anyone can work for very long as a 'detached' officer.

Many probation officers spend much of their time (often their *free* time) setting up new *projects* or *resources in the community*. These can range from *homelessness* projects, to *drama groups*, to *'phone-in' counselling services* for drug users or their parents. Others pursue new forms of *group work* and also *life- or social-skills training*. All these activities are valuable, and can be described as *'preventive work'* – helping the client to build up personal resources and capabilities which will make resorting to criminal activity less likely.

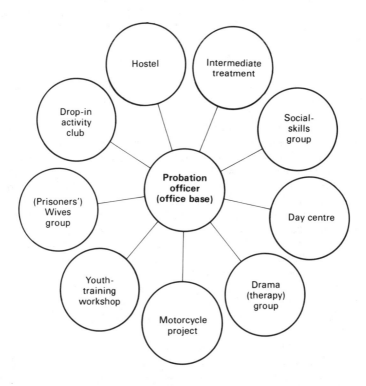

In recent years, some believe that the probation officer has increasingly become a *manager of resources*. Here are just some of the possible resources in the local community that the probation officer may be able to draw on.

Current innovations and possible future developments

The Probation Service has traditionally been viewed as a *social casework* agency, and this is still largely true today. It means that most probation officers, most of the time, work on a one-to-one basis with individual offenders.

Groupwork

However, over the past fifteen years, more and more *groupwork* has been taking place, and many in the Service are very enthusiastic about innovations in this way of working. Taking part in a group often feels very challenging to an offender, but it seems that the experience is more intense than taking part in one-to-one work. Being in a group can help to break down any inhibitions the client may have.

Drop-in or activity clubs

These are being organised more and more frequently. They are places with an informal atmosphere where offenders can come and play games or chat with friends or probation officers or the volunteers who often run them. Sometimes the office waiting room (which can be a very bleak and forbidding place) is used for these activities in the evenings.

Differential working

Some probation areas and offices are experimenting with '*differential working*'. This means that – rather than all the officers in a team having general case-loads – the total office case-load is categorised in various ways. The team may *differentiate* between different groups of offenders – for example, those released from custodial institutions, or those requiring long-term work due to difficult and complex problems. Smaller teams of officers will be set up within the large team to take on different types of work. For example, there may be an '*intake*' team (as with the social-services department), which will assess all new cases coming to the notice of the office; then there may be a '*long-term team*', or a team which deals only with *civil* work, or with *report writing,* or with offenders receiving *after-care.* Differential working can offer clients more help with '*life- and social-skills training*', which is designed to help them cope better and build up their own resources.

It is felt that this approach can use officers' time more efficiently and release some members of the team to specialise for a time. There is a great likelihood of this way of working becoming more common.

Victim support schemes

The past ten years have seen more interest shown in the *needs of the victims* of all types of crime. Although the Probation Service exists primarily to provide support for the offender, a large number of officers and senior staff have been enthusiastic about victim support schemes – many have contributed a great deal of hard work to their setting-up. In doing this, they work alongside interested and caring members of the community, and this co-operation is felt to be valuable by both sides.

The scheme means that a victim will be visited as soon as possible after the crime was committed. Help will be offered – largely counselling and emotional support – but no pressure is put on the victim to accept this assistance. The growth in the numbers of these schemes is an encouraging sign of a more aware and sensitive community.

Reparation

A new development under discussion in the Probation Service, which is related to the aims of the victim support schemes, is the concept of *reparation*. In itself, this is of course a very old idea, but the Service is exploring the possibility of the offender providing a more direct and specific service to the victim. The community-service schemes, started in the mid-1970s, have an element of this, but they do not usually provide help directly to an individual who has suffered as a result of crime. A reparation scheme could include financial compensation from the offender to the victim. In September 1985, four experimental schemes were launched – in Carlisle, Coventry, Leeds, and Wolverhampton.

A multi-racial society

In recent years, the Probation Service has become more aware of the problems and tensions which can occur in a multi-racial society. Many areas have taken practical steps to improve their work with ethnic minorities. Some have appointed specialist workers, themselves often drawn from minority groups, to speed up progress. These workers – frequently ancillaries – can increase the knowledge of probation officers about the culture, religion, and life-style of minority ethnic groups. They can also organise specific activities designed to cater for these groups and involve them more in the local community.

Conclusion

Despite the importance of its work, the Probation Service tends to be a rather 'invisible' agency in our society. If asked, most members of the public would probably have very little idea of what probation officers actually do. To a certain extent this is understandable and good – the very nature of probation work requires a great deal of confidentiality, and this means that the probation officer tends to be unobtrusive.

On the other hand, the attitude of 'leave crime to the professionals' (the courts, police, probation, and prison services) is not healthy or positive. Crime is generated by, and in, society. It is a social factor, and people who commit crime either remain living in society or return to it after a period in custody. Therefore it is the responsibility of the whole community to co-operate in dealing with crime and in devising ways to prevent it, or at least to alleviate its damaging effects.

Despite the aim of the Probation Service to provide *alternatives to custody*, the prison population continues to rise steadily. An increased building programme will be able to cater for 49 000 people in all forms of custody in England and Wales within the next few years.

Some would say that this highlights the need for the Probation Service to put more effort into *preventive work* which would stop crime happening in the first place. In answer to this, many would reply that resources are already stretched, without adding to already considerable duties. The intervention of a probation officer does contribute to diverting an offender from further criminal activity, but this is on a small scale compared to the total crime which occurs in our society.

A probation officer enjoys a great deal of freedom to work as he chooses. There is also a considerable amount of *autonomy* – he can make important decisions about people in his care without a great deal of reference to senior staff. So, although the Probation Service could be called a '*bureaucracy*', it might be described as a 'shallow' bureaucracy.

The main-grade probation officer can fairly quickly make direct contact with the chief probation officer at headquarters. CPOs and ACPOs will visit office teams on a reasonably regular basis.

This freedom and autonomy can be the source of great *job satisfaction*, which is important in social work today, as pressures on professionals increase and social and economic conditions worsen.

Today the Probation Service is at a crucial stage in its development. There exist pressures and influences for change which could radically change the way in which it carries out its duties.

Those in the Service, and those of a more liberal political view, want to see it expand as a caring social-work service providing help for damaged members of our society, as well as an element of control.

Those who support a '*law-and-order*' perspective would like to see it change from being a key social-work agency to being what in the USA has become a '*community correctional agency*'. It would provide monitoring and surveillance of offenders, control, and punishment.

One experiment run by the Probation Service recently is known as '*tracking*'. Largely an import from the USA, it involves juveniles reporting one or more times a day to a 'tracker' – a part-time worker, often a former policewoman or teacher. It is a way of 'keeping tabs' on young offenders.

'Tracking' is a radical departure from the traditional social-work role. It does nothing to give young offenders a greater insight into their behaviour. It does nothing to encourage more constructive ways of dealing with temptations or difficulties they experience. It is far more likely to lead young people into 'playing the system' rather than to consciously and willingly choose to change the way in which they behave.

The next few years will provide the answer to the question 'In which direction will the Probation Service move?' In 2000, will it be a *social-work service* or a *surveillance service*?

Appendix 1 – office duty – a possible morning's work

9.30   Two homeless men who had earlier been waiting for the office to open, enquiring about cash help and possible accommodation. Phoned the local Cyrenian shelter and made arrangements for them to go there.

10.20   Mother in with 15-year-old son. Worried about his court appearance in ten days' time. Explained juvenile-court procedure and generally tried to calm and reassure her. Told her a duty probation officer would meet her and speak with her at the court, on the day.

11.00   Another probation officer's client arrives, very distraught because the expected Girocheque from the DHSS had not arrived this morning. Telephoned the DHSS and managed to arrange a special interview for this afternoon, with the possibility of an emergency payment being made.

11.35   Young woman from London (50 miles away) arrived. She is on probation there, and has moved to live here without notifying her officer. She was concerned about this. Telephoned her officer in her presence, and they spoke together. She will come to see me on a weekly basis, and if she looks like settling we shall arrange for the order to be transferred to this office.

11.50   Telephone call from social-services department, enquiring as to whether we have had any contact with a Mr and Mrs Barton, as Mrs Barton has applied to be a childminder. Checked our records and phoned back to say we did not know them.

12.30   Police phoned to notify us that they had an Andrew Johnson, a juvenile, in custody, having been arrested for shoplifting. They could not find either parent at home. As we know Andrew from the past, I telephoned his father at work, and we arranged to go and see Andrew while the police interviewed him, at 1 p.m. Phoned police and notified them.

Appendix 2 – persons supervised by the probation service

The table on page 92 shows the persons supervised by the Probation Service in England and Wales by type of supervision, from 1978 to 1983.

Appendix 3 – a typical week in the working life of a probation officer

The diagram on page 93 shows a typical week in the working life of a probation officer.

Note In many weeks, a probation officer will work longer hours than shown in the diagram. The official working week is about 39 hours. When crises occur concerning clients, the week's plan will be discarded as the officer responds to the immediate situation.

Persons supervised by the Probation Service in England and Wales, by type of supervision (totals and percentage changes)

Type of supervision	1978	1979	1980	1981	1982	1983*
Probation	40 970	40 650 (−1%)	46 150 (+14%)	50 870 (+10%)	51 830 (+2%)	51 760 (−)
Community service	10 970	12 410 (+13%)	16 220 (+31%)	18 970 (+17%)	19 990 (+5%)	20 840 (+7%)
Supervision (C & YP Act)	17 080	16 290 (−5%)	17 590 (+8%)	17 410 (−1%)	16 110 (−7%)	15 330 (−10%)
Total statutory after-care	31 460	29 700 (−6%)	31 820 (+7%)	34 360 (+8%)	34 180 (−1%)	22 980 (−34%)
Voluntary after-care	22 570	24 690 (+9%)	24 860 (+1%)	25 000 (+1%)	25 220 (+1%)	26 300 (+4%)
Total, all forms of supervision	124 310	124 390 (−)	136 920 (+10%)	146 880 (+7%)	148 170 (+1%)	140 420 (−6%)

* *Note* All annual figures as at 31 December, except 1983 (this figure as at 30 June). As from 1 July 1983, some members of the National Association of Probation Officers failed to submit statistics giving details of their work-loads. As these are used in providing national statistics, figures after 1 July 1983, would not be accurate. (Source: *Probation statistics, England and Wales,* published annually by the Home Office.)

Time	Monday	Tuesday	Wednesday	Thursday	Friday
9 10 11 12 1	Magistrates' court duty	Paperwork Staff meeting with full team and SPO Visit client in police cells	Present report in local juvenile court Two clients seen in office	Office duty: report and record writing at office (+ 2 clients called in on off-chance)	Attend fines court with two clients Several interviews in office
	Lunch				
2 3 4 5 5.30	Five clients seen in office	Visit to local detention centre to see two clients	Attend case conference (with social-services department) to discuss a mutual client	Talk to 6th form in local comprehensive about work of Probation Service Three clients seen in office	Visit to local school to discuss a client with head and year teacher Home visits to four clients
	Tea				
6 7 8 9 10		Home visits to three clients	Report writing at office	Attend meeting at local Council for Voluntary Service as a committee member	

A typical week in the working life of a probation officer

Exercise 1 – a social enquiry report

Fordshire Probation Service
Probation officer's social enquiry report

To:	Newtown Magistrates Court
Concerning:	John Harold Hastings
Address:	6 Parkgate Villas, Newtown
Date of birth:	18.12.50
Age:	34
Date of hearing:	21 June 1985
Offence:	Burglary of food warehouse

1. Mr Hastings lives with his wife and three children in a three-bedroomed rented council house. The children are two boys, aged 5 and 7, and a girl aged 4. It is Mr Hastings' second marriage. He has two children by his first marriage, but he does not have any contact with them, due to the extreme antagonism of his previous wife. I have visited Mr Hastings' present home, and the quality of care and cleanliness is poor. Mrs Hastings (aged

28) has not been in good health for several months, and she appears to find it difficult to manage the home and to look after the children.

2. The defendant left school at 16, with poor academic qualifications. He fairly quickly found work as a guard on the railway, and he remained in this employment for the next six years. He was dismissed following an incident just before Christmas, where he and some workmates got drunk during a lunch-time and were unable to perform their duties satisfactorily.

3. He then drifted for a considerable time and, apart from drinking heavily on regular occasions, he also began to abuse 'soft' drugs. In March 1974 he was found in possession of cannabis at a party which the police raided. For this offence he was fined, but only a month later a similar conviction resulted in his being placed on probation for two years.

4. The probation officer who supervised him at this time felt that he made good progress, and there was no evidence that he continued to use illegal drugs. He committed no offences while on probation, and towards the end of the order he met and started to 'go steady' with a girl who later became his wife. They married just before the birth of their first child, and their situation looked promising.

5. Unfortunately, Mr Hastings tells me that, after just six months of marriage, the relationship between him and his wife began to break down, and he now describes them as simply not being 'compatible.' Despite many months of unhappiness, and sometimes violent arguments, a second child was born in 1977. Soon after the birth, his wife left the matrimonial home and went to the Women's Aid refuge in the town. Mr Hastings says that he resorted to drinking heavily, to try to ease the depression and guilt experienced as a result of his wife's departure. The next few months he describes as 'the worst of his life', and it was only the meeting of his present wife – at that time a barmaid in one of the several public houses he used to frequent – which lifted him from his depression.

6. He made a great effort, managed to curtail his drinking so that, he says, he was never drunk, and after a few weeks he and his present wife began to live together. He has even managed to find short-term jobs for varying periods of time, but is at present unemployed. His last job was as a gardener with the town's parks and gardens department. This ended just three weeks ago, when he says his foreman discovered he had to come to court to face a burglary charge.

7. The actual circumstances of the offence, according to the defendant, are that he had met an old school friend very late one night in the local 'Fandango' club. Mr Hastings was not drunk, but he had had a disagreement with his wife earlier in the evening and had gone out to try to 'cheer himself up'. His friend had recently been dismissed from his job at the food warehouse which they later burgled. Apparently his friend was very much the worst for drink and had suggested that they go to the warehouse and break in. Mr Hastings foolishly agreed to go along, partly because he is currently struggling financially. In fact the family have outstanding fuel bills totalling £384 and hire-purchase agreements which add up to another £270.

8. I believe that Mr Hastings is a rather weak-willed man who has allowed other people to influence him to detrimental effect. I also believe that in the past he has suffered from depression and that, faced with difficulties, he has tended to 'give up' rather than make an effort. Over the past four weeks, I have interviewed him both at home with his family and on his own at my office. I am certain that he is attempting to be more positive about himself, and he has the tremendous support of his wife, who is showing great resourcefulness, despite her bad health. In the light of this, I feel that the best disposal open to the court today is . . .

R.W.

Questions

a) If you were the magistrates reading this report, how would you sentence Mr Hastings? (You can use the guide to sentencing on pages 73–4 to help you. Read the section through completely before trying to decide.)
b) Give reasons for your decision.
c) Do you consider Mr Hastings has a bad *criminal record* (that is, his previous convictions for criminal offences)?
d) If you were a magistrate, to what extent would you be influenced by previous convictions?
e) Do you feel that Mr Hastings needs *control* or *care* or a mixture of both? Give full reasons for your opinion. Imagine you are Mr Hastings. How do you think you would feel about your present situation and your future?

Exercise 2 – a home-circumstances report for a custodial institution

The subject of the report is eligible for release on *parole* in three months' time.

To: The Governor
                    HM Prison
                    Springtown
Re: Keith Hendry 55013 'C Wing'
Home address: 21 Bute Crescent, Newtown
Age: 24

1. Mr Hendry received a three-year prison sentence for causing *grievous bodily harm* to a youth aged 18. In December 1984 he was transferred to Springtown, having served four months of his sentence elsewhere. I understand that staff at the prison feel that he has settled in and made good progress, and he is given various responsible jobs on the wing.
2. He had married only six months before he was sentenced, and a baby girl (Ruth Bernadette) was born just two weeks before he entered custody. He has received regular letters and visits from his wife, whom I have visited at the matrimonial home, and I believe their relationship is a sound

one. He has also had regular visits from members of his own family.

3. Successful at school, he gained two A-levels and had found work in London as a computer programmer. He commuted from Newton to London each day, a journey of two hours each way. I feel that it is because he was one of six young men involved in a fight at a local disco that the Crown Court decided on a fairly severe penalty.

4. I also know that the youth whom Mr Hendry struck in the fight has moved with his parents to live in the West Country, so there is no possibility of problems involving reprisals on his release.

5. I do not believe that his remaining in prison any longer will serve any useful purpose. He very much regrets what he has done, and being deprived of the company of his wife and daughter, as well as the loss of his well-paid job, has been a punishment in itself. I therefore have no hesitation in recommending that Mr Hendry be granted parole.

R.W.

Questions

a) If you were a member of the local *parole review committee*, would you have any hesitation in recommending to the parole board Mr Hendry's release? Give reasons for your decision.

b) As a professional carer or social worker, would you agree with the probation officer's conclusion? Why/Why not?

c) Should society punish people for crime as well as think about their welfare? Why/Why not?

d) Do you feel that violence towards other people is more serious than other crimes (theft, burglary, and fraud, for example)? Give reasons for your opinion.

Exercise 3 – priorities

You are a probation officer and have just returned to work on a Monday morning after three weeks' summer holiday. You are greeted by your secretary, who informs you that there have been several crises involving your case-load while you have been away and that, as a result, there are urgent things you need to do! The specific problems you are faced with are as follows:

i) Ten days ago an 18 year old who has abused drugs for over two years telephoned the office to say he intended to take an overdose in order to 'do himself in'. Although a colleague has visited his home three times since, he could see into the flat and there appeared to be nobody there. Repeated knocking at the door met with no response.

ii) Mr and Mrs Allen came to the office four days ago in a very agitated state. Their daughter Jane (aged 15) had, by her unruly behaviour and her staying out late at night, driven them to despair. They were also angry with her and were threatening to exclude her from home if her probation officer did not intervene quickly on his return. Mr Allen is disabled, and he and his wife are at home all day.

iii) Just ten minutes before you arrived at your office this morning, the police telephoned to say they had picked up Jenny Underwood (on probation for shoplifting) on the hard shoulder of the motorway, during the early hours. They had soon discovered that she had been physically beaten and sexually assaulted and was near collapse. She had been rushed to the local hospital, and a doctor there had asked that her probation officer be consulted and that he should come immediately.

iv) In the waiting room on your arrival at the office is Fred Skerman. On seeing you enter, Fred hurries to tell you that he requires £2 immediately for the train fare to a place three stations down the line. As usual Fred is penniless, and, if he does not catch the train in 12 minutes, he will miss the opportunity of travelling to Brighton for some labouring work – his first chance of paid employment in 2½ years.

Questions

a) Which of these four problems would you deal with first? Why?
b) Order the remaining problems and describe how you would deal with them, giving reasons for your decisions.
c) If you were a probation officer, what would you regard as a real emergency? Why?

Exercise 4 – role-play – a probation-office staff meeting

Setting
A local probation office – the weekly staff meeting which usually lasts about three hours every Tuesday morning. All who should be are present.

Roles

1. Stuart – senior probation officer
2. Sue
3. David
4. Herma
5. John ⟩ probation officers
6. Karen
7. Jan
8. Charlie
9. Carol
10. Geoff – team ancillary

The meeting
Most of the 'business' of the meeting has been dealt with – for example, allocating new work and discussing the agenda for the probation-liaison-

committee meeting later in the week. The team is now turning to a thorny problem which it has to resolve.

Discussion background

Bob (aged 45) and Andy (aged 52) are two homeless men who both have a 'drink problem'. Both have appeared in court on several occasions and they are well known to all the local probation officers. They spend nearly all their time together. At night they sleep wherever they can – in a derelict building or any makeshift shelter. During the day (when they have money) they drink together, usually sherry or cider. They sit around the town centre, trying to attract the attention of passers-by – even begging for money from them on occasion. Only rarely do people become upset by their behaviour when approached by them – they are usually inoffensive.

It is February and the weather is very cold. As a result, Bob and Andy are spending more and more time during the day sitting in the probation-office waiting room. Sometimes they chat together; at other times they may take a 'nap', having lost sleep during a rough night outside. However, recently they have upset one or two people who were waiting to see probation officers – their language has been very bad, they have occasionally demanded money or cigarettes, and some people have found their lack of personal hygiene offensive.

The team's attitudes

Karen and *Charlie* feel very strongly that, as team policy, Bob and Andy should be excluded from the office, except when they have a specific need to see a probation officer.

David and *Jan*, who have responsibility for seeing Bob and Andy respectively when they come into the office, adamantly disagree.

Geoff also disagrees. As the team ancillary, he has special responsibility for a local single-homeless project.

Stuart, as the office senior, is mindful of the public accountability of the office and tends to feel that Bob and Andy should be excluded if they are upsetting other people.

Herma and *Carol* are keen that the office should be a 'community resource' and feel that the team should therefore pursue an 'open-door' policy.

John and *Sue* do not feel very strongly about the issue either way, but they are both good at raising useful points which move the debate along.

Task

Allocate the ten roles and set the discussion in progress. You have 30 minutes and *must* resolve the problem today.

Following the role-play

As a group, you might like to consider how you reached a decision. If you were unable to decide, you could examine why. You might also like to think about how you felt in your role, and how you dealt with these feelings. Sharing in the group in this way will probably mean that you are looking at issues about *teamwork* and at general questions about how teams or groups come to make decisions. Study the *process* of reaching a decision.

Exercise 5 – case-study

Read carefully the following case-study, taken from a probation officer's case-load. Answer the questions which follow it. In this case study you are *Colin's* probation officer.

Colin's history

Colin is a single man, aged 28. He has an older married sister whom he only sees occasionally. His parents live locally.

While still at school, aged only 15, he became involved with a group of people who were taking illegal drugs. He and two others at the school began to experiment with various kinds of drugs. At 16, Colin tried a 'hard' drug – heroin – for the first time and a few months later was dependent on it. He became involved in criminal activity – stealing cars and driving them to London in order to buy drugs on the 'black market'. When 18 years old, he was sentenced to one year's youth custody – his first custodial sentence.

In the ten years since then, his situation has steadily worsened. After a few casual or short-term jobs, he has not worked at all for the past seven years. He has now had four custodial sentences and a large total of criminal convictions which include theft, burglary, and possession of illegal drugs.

His steady downward drift over the past few years has sadly exhausted the large amount of goodwill shown him by his ageing parents. They have been very supportive, having forgiven him for a great deal of unkindness and thoughtlessness. There have been brief times when Colin has resisted resorting to drugs but, when under pressure or facing a new or difficult challenge, he has eventually given way. He has become more and more isolated. He has no real friends, and his few acquaintances are all involved in the buying and selling of illegal drugs.

The present situation

On Wednesday of last week, Colin was released from a two-year prison sentence, received for burglaries at two local chemist shops. He is taking up your offer of voluntary after-care.

While he was in prison, his parents told him in a letter that they regrettably wanted no further contact with him – they felt exhausted and needed to conserve their own energies by being alone for a while. So, he could not return to live with them as previously. Through the local landlady scheme run by the Probation Service, you found lodgings for Colin with a very understanding middle-aged couple. They are aware of his history and the potential problems.

Colin has had no drugs since starting his last prison sentence. He suffered from sickness, sweating, and stomach cramp as he underwent 'cold turkey' (i.e. a complete and sudden withdrawal from drugs, without any assistance or medication whatsoever) at the start of the sentence. He feels confident that he will not resort to using drugs now he is released. You are not so sure, being especially worried that so many idle hours and his lack of social contacts will make him vulnerable. He has no girl-friend.

Due to this vulnerability, you intend to see him very regularly – two or even three times a week for the first few weeks.

Questions
As Colin's probation officer,

a) How would you set about introducing him to other people in the community, with whom he might become friendly, in order to discourage his contact with the local 'drug scene'?
b) You want to try to reconcile Colin with his parents but realise this will not be easy and will require sensitive handling in order to be successful. How would you set about doing this?
c) How might you encourage Colin to remain drug-free?
d) If in time you suspected that Colin was again using 'hard' drugs, what signs would you look for which might confirm your suspicions?

Questions for essays or discussion

1. Do you think that supervising *offenders* (as a probation officer) is more difficult than working with *non-offenders* (as a social worker)? Give reasons for your answer.
2. *Recidivism* is a difficult and discouraging problem for a probation officer to deal with. Why do you think some offenders go on committing crimes repeatedly, even after being punished – sometimes with a prison sentence?
3. Do you think that judges and magistrates have a good understanding of the environment, life-style, and problems faced by offenders? Give reasons for your answer.
4. The 'short sharp shock' regime in some detention centres has recently been extended to *all* such centres. Is this an effective way of encouraging people to refrain from crime in the future, or do they require help rather than punishment? Fully explain your answer.
5. Four experimental *reparation* schemes have started, in which offenders will make direct amends to the victim or victims of the crimes they have committed. Some people fear that the thought of later meeting the offender will discourage people from reporting crimes. Do you think that offenders should make direct reparation to the victims of their crimes or not? Give reasons for your answer.
6. *Tracking* is a recent import into our penal system from the USA. If you were a juvenile subject to tracking, would you accept it as being of

benefit, or would you resent it as an unwarranted interference? Fully explain why you feel the way you do.

Further reading

1. *Probation and after-care – its development in England and Wales*, Dorothy Bochel (Scottish Academic Press, 1976). A very detailed history of the Probation Service.
2. *Probation – a changing service*, David Haxby (Constable, 1978). A review of the work of the Probation Service, with proposals for changes in its role.
3. *Act natural – a new sensibility for the professional carer*, Bruce Hugman (Bedford Square Press, 1977). An excellent account of a 'detached' probation project in Sheffield.
4. *Probation officers' manual*, F.V. Jarvis (Butterworth, 3rd edition 1980). The standard reference work, comprehensive in its coverage.
5. *The Probation and After-care Service*, Joan King (Butterworth, 3rd edition 1969). Edited on behalf of the National Association of Probation Officers – a good general survey of the work of the Service.
6. *Probation work – critical theory and socialist practice*, Hilary Walker and Bill Beaumont (Blackwell, 1981). A radical critique of the Probation Service.
7. *Working with offenders*, edited by Hilary Walker and Bill Beaumont (BASW/Macmillan, 1985). A lively up-to-date discussion of a range of practical issues in the Probation Service.

4   Other statutory services

In addition to the local-authority social-services departments and the Probation Service, there are other agencies which provide services within the caring network. Some of these services are run by voluntary organisations and others are provided by *statutory agencies*. This chapter will focus on the services provided by the statutory agencies and will include the work of those in the health service, local-authority education departments, and local-authority housing departments. The work carried out by State-funded community projects and the role of community workers will also be outlined, and a brief look will be taken at community police work and the Department of Health and Social Security.

Statutory organisations are those bodies which have been set up following specific legislation and are obliged by law to provide and maintain services to the community. More simply, the word 'statutory' refers to services which are run by the *State* via local authorities or by regional offices of central government.

The health service

The health service is concerned with the nation's physical well-being and (in the case of psychiatric disorder) its mental health. Care is provided in various medical institutions: the general practitioner's surgery, health centres, clinics, hospitals, hospices, and nursing homes. However, the major part of health-service personnel's work is carried out in a hospital setting.

The health service is administered by 14 regional health authorities which in turn are divided into 192 district health authorities, the boundaries of which often coincide with those of the local authorities, although there is sometimes an overlap. There are also 90 family-practitioner committees.

Living in the 1980's is becoming increasingly stressful for many members of society, particularly if they belong to families affected by poor housing, unemployment, low income, or single parenthood. The general lack of community involvement and the absence of the supportive extended family often means that people are isolated in their distress. Consequently a large number of people who contact the health service – usually through their own doctor – do so with problems of a psychological/social nature. It may be that they would be better advised to seek help elsewhere, but it is possible that they go to their GP partly because they are unaware of the existence of other helping agencies.

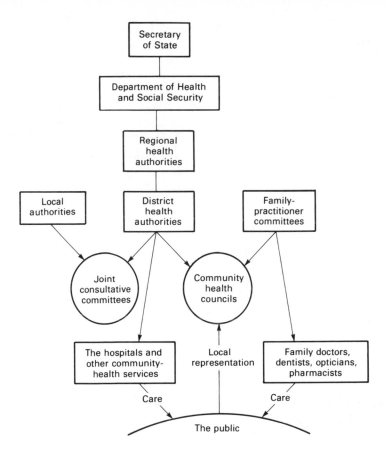

Structure of the National Health Service in England

Primary and secondary health care

'Primary health care' refers to the work that is carried out in the community by medical personnel. It is now more common for health-service workers to be based in health centres, and increasingly they are working together in teams.

A primary-health-care team involves co-operation between general practitioners, health visitors, district nurses, practice nurses, and recep-tionists. Meetings are arranged with the purpose of co-ordinating their schedules and observations for the benefit of the people whom they mutually serve. (In cases where a social worker is attached to a GP's practice, she will also be included in the team.) Observations made by, say, the district nurse may be useful to the GP, health visitor, and social worker alike. Each person's role is clearly prescribed, but each person will benefit from an appreciation of the involvement of other professional carers.

	Hospitals	Community – e.g. clinics, health centres and GP's surgeries	Individuals' homes
Medical doctors	●		
Psychiatrists	●	●	●
Psychologists	●	●	●
General nurses	●		
General practitioners		●	●
Psychiatric nurses	●	●	●
Mental-handicap nurses		●	●
Health visitors		●	●
District nurses		●	●
Practice nurses		●	
Social workers	●	●	●
Occupational therapists	●	●	
Physiotherapists	●	●	
Speech therapists	●	●	

'Secondary health care' refers to work carried out in hospital settings, and sometimes the term 'tertiary' is used to describe the health care provided in long-stay institutions.

The general practitioner (GP) or family doctor
The GP's traditional 'knowledgeable' role within our culture and the prevailing belief that there are 'pills for all ills' encourages many people to initially seek help from their local GP. Since most people are already registered as patients, they will find their local doctor easily accessible, and some may have developed a trusting relationship through previous contact.

On the other hand, some patients may be reluctant to reveal an inability to cope to a doctor whom they have known for sometime – they may choose to go elsewhere, or even not look for help with something they interpret as personal failure. Yet it is important that people suffering psychological stress are helped at an early stage, before an escalation of the problem occurs. Other people may feel that they need to present a legitimate symptom (a cold or headache, for example) before concerning the doctor with an underlying anxiety.

The interrelationship between psychological and physical illness is now more widely recognised. Some physical illnesses are known to bring on associated psychological disorders, and similarly there is evidence that stress and anxiety can induce *secondary* physical illness. The word '*psychosomatic*' is frequently used but often abused in describing this relationship. It refers to an illness which has definite physiological symptoms, but psychological factors also can be associated with the development, maintenance, and treatment of the illness. For example, a person suffering from an ulcer may not have experienced any psychological stress – the illness will be independent of the person's life-style. For other ulcer sufferers, stress factors will be seen to contribute to their physical condition and a reduction in their anxiety level will result in improved physical health and a more rapid recovery.

The main task of the GP is to detect signs of serious illness, and the focus of her diagnosis will be on this aspect. Doctors are restricted by time – it is common for GPs to see their patients at intervals of less than five minutes. Longer sessions with individual patients will mean an increased delay for those in the waiting room. It is therefore often impractical and inappropriate for the GP to undertake a counselling role.

Not all GPs have been trained in psychiatry or have gained counselling skills, but since 1983 all doctors wanting to become GPs must undergo vocational training involving two years in a hospital setting and a further year spent attached to a general practice; thus it is possible for an interested GP to develop skills in this area. Nowadays it is less common for GPs to work single-handed – most are based in group practices, often in health centres. This arrangement enables doctors to share their areas of expertise.

A patient suffering from the effects of anxiety may be prescribed tranquillisers by the doctor in the hope that the resultant reduction of physical discomfort may enable that person to deal with the causes of the problem. This treatment, plus the knowledge that there is nothing physically wrong, may be sufficient to encourage some people to combat their difficulties themselves. However, not all psychological states respond well to drugs – a course of counselling may be necessary in addition to, or instead of, medication.

An important role of the GP is to refer patients to more relevant agencies – some people suffering from psychological/social problems may be directed to voluntary counselling agencies, the Probation Service, or the Marriage Guidance Council. Sometimes a GP will refer a patient to the social-services department, either to the local office or, where possible, to the social worker attached to the group practice, particularly where practical information or resources (day-nursery places, for example) are required. Because of their training, social workers are more likely to be 'non-directive' in their counselling compared to GPs, who may tend towards being 'authoritarian', given their preoccupation with speedy diagnosis.

GPs can also refer patients to a psychologist when anxiety states and emotional difficulties are seriously affecting someone's everyday life. However, there are certain severe mental disorders that are more than just more serious forms of unpleasant emotional states – they are regarded as mental illness. Where the illness is of a psychiatric nature (such as schizophrenia), the GP will refer the patient to a psychiatrist. All general practitioners are required to work within the 'section' procedure of the

Mental Health Act Act 1983 with those people who are suffering mentally to the extent that they are a danger either to themselves or to other people.

The practice nurse
A practice nurse is sometimes employed in a GP's surgery or group practice to carry out routine practical treatment. This allows the doctor to spend more time with other patients.

The clinical psychologist
The health district's clinical-psychology service is aimed at meeting the needs of all members of the community. Today *clinical psychologists* can be found in every setting of the health service and, rather like local-authority field social workers, they can carry generic or specialised case-loads.

In 1976 the Trethowan Report recommended a ratio of one clinical psychologist to every 25 000 of the population. However, the implementation of the recommendations of this report has varied from district to district. Some districts have no psychology service of their own, whereas others have developed large departments and have demonstrated the need for more than the recommended number of clinical psychologists.

Clinical psychologists are not doctors – they are trained to rely, in the main, on the application of scientific principles in the assessment and treatment of individuals. When they are engaged in 'psychotherapeutic' approaches to working, clinical psychologists sometimes refer to 'theories of behaviour', but by their very nature these cannot be described as purely scientific in the strictest sense of the word.

Clinical psychologists will see as out-patients people who are suffering from phobias (irrational fears), obsessions, anxieties, and other mental or physical conditions if these affect the sufferer's normal functioning and if the condition itself is amenable to psychological treatment. Referrals will usually come from general practitioners, but psychologists will respond to approaches from individuals themselves or other agencies, being careful always to inform the person's GP.

We all suffer anxiety in certain situations and experience mood changes and bouts of depression, but for some people these states of mind are severe and continuous and this seriously affects their ability to cope with their everyday lives. The psychologist works towards helping people gain more control over their emotional states.

A person who suffers from a phobia feels an exaggerated fear, or terror, of an object or situation which is quite out of proportion (and sometimes quite opposite) to the feelings experienced by the average person when confronted by a similar object or situation. Fear of spiders (arachnaphobia) and an exaggerated fear of venturing from known places of security and safety (agoraphobia) are examples of phobias. Psychologists might treat these anxiety states through the behaviour-therapy technique of *systematic desensitisation*. This involves the application of relaxation skills aimed at controlling anxiety.

106

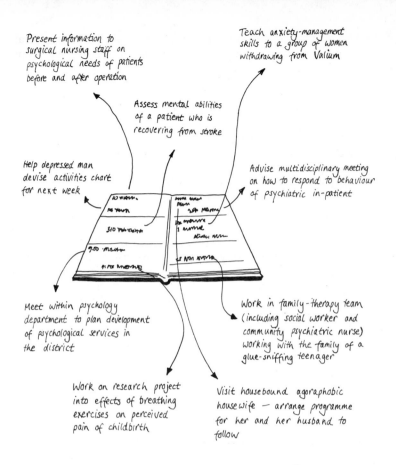

Present information to surgical nursing staff on psychological needs of patients before and after operation

Teach anxiety-management skills to a group of women withdrawing from Valium

Assess mental abilities of a patient who is recovering from stroke

Help depressed man devise activities chart for next week

Advise multidisciplinary meeting on how to respond to behaviour of psychiatric in-patient

Meet within psychology department to plan development of psychological services in the district

Work in family-therapy team (including social worker and community psychiatric nurse) working with the family of a glue-sniffing teenager

Work on research project into effects of breathing exercises on perceived pain of childbirth

Visit housebound agoraphobic housewife — arrange programme for her and her husband to follow

Tasks normally carried out by a psychologist specialising in adult mental health

As well as seeing out-patients, clinical psychologists will also see patients who are already in hospital and those who attend for day care. They will be concerned with the psychological aspects of medical conditions, both physical and mental. A clinical psychologist will assist individuals who may be suffering from severe mental disorders, to help them come to terms with any associated anxiety or depression. Similarly, they will help people experiencing physical illness to deal with related emotions.

In long-stay hospitals, psychologists will work more organisationally, preparing the environment to suit patients' needs. For example they may be involved in designing large clearly readable signs for elderly confused patients and/or suggesting work programmes aimed at maximising the potential of mentally handicapped people. Where rehabilitation into the community is the goal, psychologists undertake the assignment and development of social-skills training.

Treatment is only part of psychologists' functions – sometimes they are involved in psychological testing (of the effects of brain damage, for example), or they may undertake or advise others on research. These last two aspects of clinical psychologists' work involve skills which are very different from those required by others in the caring professions.

The psychiatrist

The psychiatrist is a medically qualified doctor who has completed, or is undergoing, further specialist training in psychiatry. She is normally based either in a general hospital with psychiatric facilities or in a psychiatric hospital (a 'mental hospital'). For some of the time she may also work in a general-practitioner health centre, a psychiatric day hospital, in prisons or other security units, or in special hospitals (such as Broadmoor). The psychiatrist also liaises with group homes and day centres within the community.

Referrals may come from a GP; the patients themselves, either directly or via the casualty department; other medical practitioners in hospital; psychologists; or social workers.

Psychiatrists may work individually or as part of a multi-disciplinary team where their work is shared and may overlap with that of other professionals involved.

Problems dealt with by the psychiatrist   The main problems dealt with by the psychiatrist are as follows:

a) *Major psychiatric illness* – including schizophrenia, manic–depressive illness, and dementia.
b) *Less serious illnesses* – anxiety, phobias, depression, obsessional illness, and psychological problems of surgery or physical or mental handicap.
c) *Alcohol and drug addiction.*
d) *Self-injury/overdose.*

Functions of the psychiatrist   Initially the psychiatrist is concerned to assess patients referred and make a *diagnosis* of the mental disorder, if present. She will then go on to make a *treatment plan*. This may involve the patient being admitted to hospital as an in-patient, a day patient, or an out-patient – depending on the severity of the illness. The psychiatrist will consider the possible involvement of other professionals, including the psychologist or social worker, and the use of any appropriate community resources. The use of drugs or other physical treatment will be decided upon, and the psychiatrist will make long-term plans based on diagnosis, response to treatment, and likely prognosis as well as the availability of follow-up support within the community.

Method of assessment   On seeing the patient for the first time, the psychiatrist will take a detailed history of the problem as the patient sees it and will note previous illnesses or psychiatric problems. She will then gather information about the patient's family and personal history, before making an assessment of the patient's current mental state. Once the diagnosis is made, a proposed plan of action will be outlined and discussed with the patient and others involved – including members of the family. Some people have no insight into the mental illness they are suffering and may not recognise the seriousness of their condition. Where the psychiatrist feels that such a person is a danger either to himself or others, she is empowered to compulsorily admit and detain him in hospital under sections 3 and 4 of the Mental Health Act 1983, as outlined in chapter 2.

A typical week in hospital-based practice   A typical week for a psychiatrist working in a hospital might include the following tasks.

a) *Assessing patients referred from casualty departments* – those who have taken overdoses or have tried to injure/kill themselves, and those who seem 'psychiatric' to the casualty doctor, such as an old person who has 'fallen' at home and is suspected of being demented or depressed.

b) *Seeing newly referred patients at clinics* – interviewing and considering appropriate further action, including investigations of alcohol consumption or physical disease which may cause mental problems, such as thyroid disease.

c) *Meetings with patients on the ward or in a day-care setting* and discussions with staff about such patients' progress.

d) *Out-patient classes for regular attenders* – these are mostly people who have been in-patients at some time and have recovered or those who have always been treated as out-patients. With the increased emphasis on community care, more people are being seen as out-patients throughout their illness, rather than being admitted to hospital, as removal of someone from his home environment can be counterproductive.

e) *People at home* – visits to a person's home are carried out by psychiatrists. This practice is particularly relevant for the elderly, who are best assessed in familiar surroundings – this is known as a 'domiciliary' psychiatric assessment.

f) *Teaching and administrative work* – this involves consultation with other staff and attendance at case conferences with staff or with particular patients and other workers.

In all circumstances, the psychiatrist is responsible for the *medical* aspects of treatment, including physical well-being and the action of drugs and their side-effects. She also has some legal responsibility for the care of the patient and for ensuring, for example, the safety of a patient with a mental disorder or that of others who may be in contact with the patient.

Mental disorders and illness which psychiatrists may be involved with It is not within the scope of this book to explain the details of the different forms of mental illness, but, for the purpose of familiarity, the main classifications are outlined below and some explanation is given concerning the meaning of some of the terms used.

a) *Mental handicap* Mental handicap results from brain damage, often from birth, but it is not a mental illness – although mentally handicapped people may also suffer mental illness.
b) *Psychoses* These mainly include schizophrenia and manic–depressive illness (mania and depression) – see below for explanation.
c) *Neuroses* These include anxiety states such as hypochondria and 'phobias', anxiety/depression, and 'depressive neurosis'; 'obsessional disorders'; and 'hysterical neurosis'.
   People with neuroses have some insight into their problem, which is very often an exaggerated form of their normal behaviour.
d) *Personality disorders* This term refers to problems of personality and character development.
e) *Drugs* This category includes alcoholism and drug dependency involving both *illicit* drugs (such as heroin) and *prescribed* drugs (such as tranquillisers).
f) *Organic states,* including confusional states such as 'delerium' and dementia.

Psychosis corresponds to the general image of 'madness' – 'insanity', with a breakdown in understanding of the difference between real and imaginary events.

Mania is a state of over-excitement, with unrealistic optimism, grand plans (but poor execution) and increased energy, and reduced sleep and food consumption. People with mania often have episodes of depression at some time – hence 'manic–depressive' psychosis. Manic–depressive illness is a disorder of mood which tends to recur, a number of episodes being separated by periods of well-being.

Schizophrenia is a term for a group of various conditions in which the thinking process may be disorganised, alterations of mood and perception may occur, and unrealistic ideas (such as that all someone's thoughts are being recorded and played back to others) or hallucinations may be experienced as definite realities. There may be changes in the personality and behaviour, even when the other experiences are not present. Some people recover fully from an episode of schizophrenia; others need long-term treatment and have some disabilities in between the episodes of obvious illness.

About 1% of the population (of any race, country, or sex) can expect to suffer from schizophrenia at some time in their lives, and rather fewer from manic–depressive illness. There is a tendency for both disorders to have an hereditary element.

Most people with 'depression' do not have manic–depressive psychosis but have a depressed mood, often associated with adverse factors in their lives. This may be known as *reactive* depression.

Psychosis generally requires psychiatric treatment with drugs or occasionally more controversial treatments including electric convulsive therapy (ECT – 'shock treatment') or even surgery. On the other hand, most other psychiatric disorders may be usefully treated by psychological treatments including psychotherapy and other 'talking therapies', and physical treatments may or may not play a part.

The health visitor (HV)

The health visitor is essentially concerned with the promotion of health and the prevention of ill health within the community. She will visit people in their own homes, mainly expectant and nursing mothers and families of children under-five. Her task is principally educational – she will advise on child care, child needs, and child development.

The health visitor has a statutory obligation to visit all new-born babies. She normally takes over from the midwife 10 days after the birth of a child and continues to visit the home of the child until he reaches school age (when responsibility for the child is transferred to the schools health service).

Referrals from the midwife form the bulk of a health visitor's case-load, but she is not always exclusively involved in the care of the under-fives. She may be required to identify the needs of the elderly or handicapped people within the community and to visit them in their own homes to offer medical and dietary advice to those in need and those who care for them.

A call by the health visitor is often welcome.

The HV may be based geographically, covering a specific area, or she may be attached to a GP's practice, in which case her clients will mainly consist of those on the doctor's list. She is, however, an independent professional with the responsibility of deciding whom, and how often, she needs to visit, and she is free to accept referrals from outside the health service (from social services or voluntary organisations, for example).

The size and nature of the health visitor's case-load will to some extent determine her priorities with regard to frequency and duration of visits (similar to field social workers). She will need, for example, to closely monitor suspected child-abuse situations. Because of her early involvement with families and her training, she is in a good position to detect early signs of non-accidental injury and she may undertake preventive work before the situation becomes more serious.

Not all of her work is done in clients' homes – part of her promotional health role is to hold group sessions at health centres (mothers' groups, anti-smoking groups, and anti-stress groups, for example) or to provide health talks to schools, with which she may be in regular liaison. She also visits handicapped and elderly people in residential establishments as well as children in local day nurseries and nursery schools. Some health visitors specialise in working with minority ethnic groups within the area.

An essential part of a health visitor's task is to ensure that a child's progress is normal – physically, emotionally, and socially – and to offer help and support to the family. She is not required to provide counselling for non-health issues, but she must be able to respond sensitively to distress.

Because of her general helpful advisory role, the HV may soon gain the confidence of the parents whom she visits and they may express to her their concern about any social or emotional difficulties they are experiencing. The health visitor may be able to offer advice, but at the same time she needs to be aware of the role of other caring agencies and resources within the community so that she can refer when she feels this to be appropriate.

Although a health visitor has no legal right of entry into someone's home, most people welcome her practical advice and the opportunity of having their anxieties about child care resolved. In some cases, a visit from the HV reduces the isolation some parents feel when they are at home all day with no adult company.

The district nurse
The district nurse may head a team of nurses, including auxiliaries and enrolled nurses, and is responsible for carrying out nursing care within the community. She will visit sick people of all ages in their own homes, most of whom will be elderly or chronically sick. Because of changing life-styles within society, it is now less common for married children to live close to their parents so many elderly people live alone, or with their spouses, without immediate family support. This often means that a caring role is forced on someone who is himself or herself limited by personal frailty. The district nurse is an important social contact who is able to monitor a

person's ability to cope within the community.

The GP and the hospital refer cases to the district nurse where home nursing is necessary. She visits to apply dressings, give injections, generally attend to medical needs, and to encourage the development of independence and rehabilitation. When attending to the terminally ill, she needs special skill in helping the patient's relatives come to terms with the prospect of the imminent death of the family member. She will enrol the help of other agencies in some cases – for example, she may request respite care in a social services' home where a partner, or the family, is feeling the strain of providing continuous care.

The community psychiatric nurse

Community psychiatric nurses are principally concerned with enabling people who are suffering mental illness to remain in the community and stay out of hospital. They follow up patients discharged from hospital and visit them in their own homes, where they may administer injections or check that prescribed drugs are being taken. They will look for signs of deterioration and will be able to observe behaviour changes and any signs that medication is not being taken regularly.

Psychiatric nurses need to be aware of community resources, local voluntary mental-health organisations, group meetings, and services offered by other statutory bodies. Liaison will be made with disablement resettlement officers (DROs) with the aim of helping people find work if possible or a place in a sheltered workshop. The debilitating effect of being out of work and the related social isolation can adversely effect someone's chances of recovering from mental illness.

People who have spent periods of time in psychiatric hospitals may lack confidence socially and may also need encouragement to combat the social stigma or prejudice that society sometimes attaches to those who are known to have suffered mentally. Here the community psychiatric nurse may work as an advocate, attending a job interview with a client to ensure that his personal qualities are understood by a prospective employer. With the current employment situation, not everyone can hope to find work, but it is harder for those who are vulnerable in some way.

Community nurses may also receive referrals from GPs who have seen patients in their surgeries and require a fuller psychiatric assessment to be carried out in a person's home. In some areas community nurses are used to support people who would otherwise be on medication, encouraging social involvement and an ability to cope without drugs.

Liaison between the hospital and half-way houses and other hostels for assisting the recovery of the mentally ill will also be done by community psychiatric nurses, who may also visit people in the hospital wards for a period before they are discharged.

Paramedical personnel

There are various 'paramedical' workers belonging to the health service, most of whom, like doctors and nurses, work in hospitals. An exploration of their role is contained in the following outline of a community based co-ordinated service.

Teams specialising in services to the mentally handicapped

In some areas, where the density of population allows, it is possible for a comprehensive service to be offered to particular client groups. For example, teams have been created specialising in the services to the mentally handicapped, drawing resources from both the district health authority and the social-services department. A typical team includes a psychiatrist, a clinical psychologist, a speech therapist, a community (mental-handicap) nurse, an occupational therapist, a physiotherapist, and one or two social workers. The team is based together in one room (perhaps in an adult training centre or any other convenient community building), which makes liaison and mutual understanding of each other's roles simpler.

The idea of providing a team approach to mental handicap has existed for some time – since the mid 1970s – with the release of finance from the regional health authorities (hospitals) to the district areas (the community). The money was transferred primarily to support *resettlement* – i.e. to assist those people who were being discharged after long periods in hospitals to live in hostels or group homes within the community.

Although there is bound to be some overlap of responsibility, each team member has a prescribed role, outlined below.

The psychiatrist The psychiatrist is concerned to help mentally handicapped people who may also have mental-illness difficulties (depression, for example). As well as seeing people in group homes, the psychiatrist will specialise in seeing all mentally handicapped people within the community. As a member of the team, she will be available in a consultative capacity to the other members and usually attends on a sessional basis.

The clinical psychologist In order to help mentally handicapped people adjust to the new demands of community living, the psychologist may create personal programmes for each individual. These will be based, after thorough scientific assessment, on realistic targets and will involve rewarding advancement of social competence. Known as 'behaviour-modification treatment programmes', they aim to increase a person's ability to integrate socially. Living day by day closely with others in a group situation after years spent in institutional care, where many routine living tasks were carried out by the caring staff, requires some adjustment. The psychologists' individual personal programmes will seek to assist with this change.

The speech therapist The speech therapist will aim to increase a mentally handicapped person's ability to communicate. In cases of severe

Treatment methods which may be used by practitioners within the health service

Job title	Physical treatment: drugs, surgery, etc.	Psychotherapy: individual, group, or family therapy	Behaviour therapy	Social-skills training
Psychiatrist	●	●	●	●
Psychologist		●	●	●
Psychotherapist		●		
Social worker		●		
Nurse (e.g. community psychiatric nurse)	●	●	●	●
Occupational therapist			●	
General practitioner	●			

handicap, she may concentrate on teaching an understanding of basic sign language and developing the Makaton system (an extension of the basic sign language, including gestures) for both the handicapped person and those who will be helpers (either family or other group-home members). Some of this work may already have been started in the hospital setting.

The community nurse (mental handicap)   In addition to providing basic nursing services, the community nurse will be involved in implementing the individual programme plans designed by the psychologist. She will try to increase an individual's control over bodily functions, including toileting and personal hygiene.

The occupational therapist (OT)   She will be principally concerned to increase a person's general ability to function. Part of her role will be to assess someone's present difficulties, and she may also carry out programmes designed by the team's clinical psychologist. She may engage the mentally handicapped person in simple exercises concerning the recognition of money, the use of the cooker, and other basic living skills that the client needs to acquire in order to achieve independence.

The physiotherapist   Like the other team members, she will have a special interest in working with mentally handicapped people and her role will be to encourage clients to maximise their physical potential. Long periods in institutional care with related inactivity, boredom, and overconcern with the importance of food may result in some mentally handicapped persons developing weight problems. The physiotherapist may design exercises to combat this. Where mental handicap coincides with physical handicap, she will concentrate on specific exercises aimed at strengthening certain limbs.

The social worker(s)   The social worker's task is to see that the clients' needs are being met and to consider ways of improving their quality of life. Practically, the social worker may advise on welfare benefits and resources within the community (meetings and social groups, for example). She may seek to involve the members of small group homes in choosing the colour schemes and furnishings of their new homes, or make suggestions for holidays and provide the brochures and other information which may help a client choose where to go and then follow this up by making the practical arrangements. She will also help with personal matters such as clothing and budgeting and will accompany clients on shopping expeditions. Essentially the social worker will be concerned with the relationships of those who share the home and will be ready to listen to complaints or any problems they may have.

Team social workers will not only be concerned with those who are living in group homes – they may also visit mentally handicapped people who are living at home with their parents. They will also go to see relatives of people in hospital who may be concerned about their future and the future of their handicapped relation. (For example, an elderly parent may need emotional support and reassurance about a mentally handicapped son who is likely to spend the rest of his life in an institution.)

In areas where these specialised teams have been created, the work of the team has concentrated on mentally handicapped adults – in particular, those being transferred from hospital to be cared for in the community. Services for mentally handicapped children and other adults continue to be provided by social services in the usual way. The advantages gained by special teams who work from the same base are that contact between the different agencies is more easily made, both internally on a daily basis and formally at meetings; an understanding of each other's roles is made easier; and good relationships and improved communication make for an efficient service. Because the workers come from different organisations, they are normally supervised by seniors from their own disciplines.

The education department

Local-authority education departments ('local education authorities' – LEAs) have a statutory duty to provide education for all children between the ages of five and 16. In addition to this, where children are considered to have *special needs* the range of facilities is extended to accommodate children from the age of two, and occasionally earlier, and educational provision is made beyond the school-leaving age, usually up to 19.

A child's educational needs are related to his learning ability and to social, emotional, and physical factors. The education department provides caring services in recognition of this.

Standards of educational provision vary enormously throughout the country, and some authorities are involved in experimental schemes of work, developing an 'alternative curriculum' or establishing a social-work service within schools.

The under-fives

Education departments are not legally required to provide education services for ordinary children under five, but many do. In 1983, 42% of the UK population aged three and four attended nursery or primary schools, about 47% of these attending on a part-time basis.

Unit 2

Nursery schools and classes Some nursery schools exist in accommodation separate from infant schools and are devoted solely to children between the ages of three and five. More commonly, educational provision is offered in reception and nursery classes which are part of a primary school. They provide the same functions and are staffed by teachers who are responsible for planning the day's activities. In their work, teachers will be assisted by qualified nursery nurses who will help to create a stimulating, secure, caring environment aimed at meeting children's emotional, social, and intellectual needs.

For those children whose home situation lacks stimulation and parental encouragement, an educational nursery setting is designed to help them develop skills and to 'catch up' with more fortunate children. However, places in nursery schools and classes are not allocated according to social need – they tend to be determined by availability. For example, in 1984 Newham education authority provided full-time or part-time places for 3564 children under five, whereas another London borough – Bexley – provided only 595. In the same year, Nottinghamshire Country Council offered a total of 9544 places, compared with 84 places provided by Somerset County Council.

Private nursery schools exist, but the fees required obviously exclude children from low-income families.

Nursery schools and classes help prepare children for ordinary school and soften the trauma of transition from home to school.

Many nursery schools will encourage the involvement of parents by inviting them to participate in the classroom or to be involved in school social activities. Attention will be paid to the needs of those children from non-English-speaking families – books, stories, pictures, food, and the celebration of their festivals will reflect the diversity of the multicultural society in which we live. Children will also be encouraged to take part in a wide range of activities – to engage in fantasy play and to develop practical skills that avoid restrictions of rigid sex-role stereotyping. Boys will be encouraged to express their caring nature – for example, they will be allowed to nurse dolls, to play in the home corner, and to join in cookery sessions. Similarly, girls will be encouraged to develop practical skills and to express their physical nature – for example, to play with cars, bricks, and so on. Even by the age of five, children will have picked up what is expected of them by the adults in their lives, and a nursery class gives them an opportunity to challenge their ideas of expected social behaviour. A boy who refuses to wash up during fantasy play because 'my dad never does the washing up' can be encouraged to question this and develop a broader recognition of what other mothers and fathers do in the home.

Nursery centres As already mentioned in chapter 2, nursery centres are a recent development, run jointly by the social services and the education department, aiming to combine education and social care in the same setting.

Primary schools

A primary school may provide a young child with his first experience of a large social setting. It may also be the first time he has been outside the familiarity of his home environment. The transition from home to school is best made gradually – it is therefore considered desirable for parents to share their young children's initial primary-school attendances. Children

118

who can build on playgroup or previous nursery experience are at an advantage compared to those who are separating from home and family for the first time and who may suffer distress at this.

Although the major role of teachers is an educational one, because they see children for so long and so often they are in an ideal position to observe disturbed behaviour and to recognise deprivation and distress. They may feel the need to refer children to education welfare officers, educational psychologists, or the social services. Owing to their proximity, especially at times when children change for PE lessons, they may also identify signs of non-accidental injury and report this to the agencies concerned.

Most children settle and enjoy their initial school experience, and, although absenteeism is known to occur, it is not usually a significant problem early in a child's school life.

Secondary schools
Secondary schools are essentially concerned to meet the educational needs of pupils within the school, and teachers are responsible for pupils who are in their charge. However, a child's formal education has to be seen within a social and emotional context. A child whose family life is stressful and disturbing may present behaviour difficulties at school which may be seen to affect educational progress. At the same time, it is possible for children to be suffering a disadvantaged home life but for their social problems to go undetected because their behaviour is not outstandingly different from that of other pupils. The curriculum of many schools often presents difficulty to such children, especially where the school concentrates on academic excellence.

The teacher Most secondary schools make provision for counselling and pastoral care, giving teachers time to be available to children to help with all matters, including academic issues.

Class tutors These will normally be responsible for between 15 to 30 children and – rather like the form teacher of the past – will be concerned with regulations, reasons for absence, discipline, and notes of trips and school events. The teacher may see a child on an individual basis at the beginning or end of the school day as part of a structured personal and social education programme. Children who present serious difficulties or those children who require disciplinary action can be referred to the year tutor.

Year tutors As head-of-year, the year tutor will have a reduced teaching load to allow her to carry out a pastoral-care role. She will be involved in the usual straightforward disciplinary action for standard misbehaviour and also in the more serious matters which may involve outside agencies. She will need to be aware of the functions of other organisations and will liaise regularly with outside personnel including the education welfare officer, whom she may see weekly.

Occasionally year tutors will make home visits to see parents (when the parents are genuinely unable to visit the school), but their involvement can only be limited. In some cases they will, when appropriate, refer to other organisations (such as social services). It may be that some pupils feel more comfortable disclosing their problems to another member of the teaching staff, and where this is the case the information will be relayed to the year tutor, as it is important that she is aware of the difficulties that children in her year may have. Serious disciplinary cases will be referred to the deputy head (pastoral) and may even go beyond, to the head of the school or to the board of governors.

Unit 2

Special needs

Since the Education Act 1944, local authorities have had an obligation to provide education for children who are handicapped in some way. Following the Warnock Report in 1978, the Education Act 1981 extended the designation of '*special needs*' to a wider range of children and stressed that, where possible, education should be provided within an ordinary school setting.

Classification In the past, children with 'special needs' were rather narrowly defined and included the more obviously physically disabled – the 'blind' and partially sighted, hearing-impaired, epileptic, and physically handicapped children. Crude labels describing children as 'educationally subnormal' (ESN) or 'maladjusted' are no longer used. Special-needs categories are now more wide-ranging and include those children with learning difficulties. Learning difficulties are currently classified as mild, moderate, severe, and specific. These may be associated with physical and sensory difficulties, speech and language difficulties, or emotional and behaviour difficulties.

As a consequence of the Education Act 1981 (section 5), all children who are considered to have special needs have the right to be made the subject of professional assessment and have a statement drawn up outlining their needs. Once this statement is made, it is maintained and reviewed throughout the child's life. The early detection of a child's needs is crucial, so the obvious priority for education departments at the moment is to consider those children under the age of five. However, there are some children who have experienced schooling without their special needs being catered for, so education departments are also concerned with current 13 to 16 year olds.

A statement of special needs can be made at any stage in a child's life at the instigation of parents, the education department, or any outside body. A child's own feelings have to be taken into account, and parental involvement is considered essential at all stages of the child's education. An appeal procedure is available for parents wishing to challenge educational decisions made on their child.

It is estimated that one in five children will need some form of special education during their school lives.

Within an ordinary secondary school there will probably be a teacher responsible for special education. In most cases she will be the *named person* statutorily concerned with the maintenance of the child's special-needs statement and for liaison with the parent and the child and other agencies.

The educational psychologist   An educational psychologist may play a principal role in the assessment of a child's special needs. As a non-teaching member of the education department, the educational psychologist can be seen as neutral, so the child may more freely indicate his needs and express whether or not they are being met by the school. The psychologist is also equipped to scientifically test a child's educational ability and to consider the most appropriate form of provision. There will be other agencies involved in assessing a child's needs – for example, a full medical report is required – however, usually it is the educational psychologist's responsibility to co-ordinate the assessment.

Integration   The Education Act 1981 stressed that, where possible, children's special needs should be provided within *mainstream education*. This recognised the mutual benefit and increased understanding that handicapped and ordinary children would gain from interaction within an ordinary school setting. It is not, of course, possible to accommodate all special needs within mainstream education, so alternative provision has to be made available.

Types of provision   The following types of provision are made for children with special needs:

Within the ordinary school   After a child has been 'statemented', attempts will be made to provide for his needs within the school. For example, if a child is unable to climb stairs because he suffers from asthma but is required to attend school in a high-rise building, he may have his timetable altered so that he can attend lessons at ground level. Similarly a child with impaired hearing may be able to attend an ordinary school with the aid of a special radio microphone (transmitting only to him) which he passes on to successive teachers. Some schools will act as a resource for particular handicaps and may have a lift installed in order to meet the needs of wheelchair-bound children.

It must be stressed that physical handicap is not viewed as a drawback to learning ability.

Special classes within ordinary schools   Some children's needs will be better catered for in smaller, more intimate groups. In some areas, the 'disruption in schools service' (DISS) will provide extra staffing within the school for a small number of children who have been disruptive in class. These children – who may not have any special learning difficulties – will undertake group work aimed at developing personal growth, adjustment, and preparation for life outside school. For most of the time, pupils will be involved in 'experiential learning' – i.e. learning by doing – which is likely to be non-examinable. The overall aim will be to increase a child's independence and self-belief, and this may involve special classes, a specially designed curriculum, or some withdrawal from mainstream lessons.

Special day schools   A decision to send a child to a special day school will be based on professional evidence and parental agreement. For children whose needs cannot be accommodated within mainstream education, special schools provide skilled support, often within purpose-built establishments. Schools for sight-impaired children and severely mentally handicapped children are examples of specialist provision. Experienced staff who work within low pupil/teacher ratios are concerned to maximise a child's independence.

There will always be a need for special schools, but, with many present pupils now being transferred to ordinary schools where possible, the number of these establishments is likely to fall. Where a special school shares the same site as a secondary school, special-needs children will interact with ordinary children and the stigma sometimes attached to those attending special schools will be reduced. For severely physically disabled children who attend special schools, it is recommended that efforts are made to enable them to spend their last year at school in an ordinary setting and so ease their transition to the outside world.

Residential schools (therapeutic communities)   For some children it is necessary to spend some time away from the environment which has contributed to their learning difficulties – for example, children who have developed very serious behaviour difficulties and who come from unsupportive homes. Special therapeutic establishments will be concerned in developing the whole individual within a community setting. Other children – for example, those with severe mental or physical handicap, those who are emotionally disturbed, and those who have done badly at school and are in need of smaller groups – will also need residential provision where there is less pressure.

For children who, for various reasons, are unable to live at home but are able to attend ordinary school, the local authority may provide local residential establishments for both short- and long-term use. Those children who have been persistently absent from school may also spend some time in a residential establishment, their return home being conditional on an improved school-attendance record. These children need not necessarily be in the care of the local authority, as social-services departments are reluctant to receive a child into care purely on educational grounds.

Home-tuition service   The home-tuition service is available to children who, because of their circumstances, are unable to attend school.

Pregnant schoolgirls and children immobilised by broken bones or suffering serious illness may receive lessons by a peripatetic tutor in their own homes or hospital until they can return to school. Children considered to be 'school phobics' (having a serious psychological aversion to attending school) may receive education in this way over a short period.

'Section-11' teachers The Local Government Act 1966 introduced special aid for areas with a large proportion of Commonwealth immigrants. Nowadays, some of the money is used to finance specialist teaching. 'Section-11' teachers, funded by the Home Office, are allocated to schools in order to provide additional help to children who come from non-English-speaking homes. They either may be involved in teaching English as a second language or may help with 'mother-tongue' learning.

The school psychological child-guidance service

Before the Social Services Act 1971, this provision was part of the school health service, but following the 1974 reorganisation of the National Health Service, the school psychological and child-guidance service became administered by the education department. It is a multi-disciplinary service – social workers are employed by the SSD but seconded full-time to the education department; similarly, child psychiatrists will be paid by the district health authority to work within the educational setting.

A typical team might include a senior social worker, three or four social workers (usually experienced and level 3), five educational psychologists, and three specialist teachers (tutors). Child psychiatrists may attend on a sessional basis and be available for consultation by the team. An open referral system is in operation whereby anybody can refer, including the parent or the individual child involved. In practice, most referrals come from the school via educational psychologists, education welfare officers, head teachers, or year tutors and from social services and general practitioners.

Regular meetings ensure collaboration between team members, and at allocation meetings the team decides on which worker is to become involved with the child and his family. This decision will be made after investigation into the nature and location of the problem. If the behaviour difficulties are considered to be closely related to a child's home life, it is likely that a social worker will be involved initially.

Social workers may see the whole family and engage them in 'family-therapy' sessions; alternatively, they may work individually with the child using simple behaviour-modification techniques. For example, a child with an enuresis problem will be encouraged to develop control over his bed-wetting by the use of a 'star-chart' or something similar. In using this approach, the social worker will draw up a chart with the days of the month outlined. This chart will be displayed in the child's own home and he is then able to record (with a star or tick) each dry night and thus observe progress. The involvement and co-operation of parents is

123

important to the success of this exercise – for example, the child's progress may be positively reinforced if the child is given praise or more tangible rewards. Sometimes a child's bed-wetting can be seen as a symptom of family stress, and it may be more appropriate for the social worker to work with the whole family and help them deal with their difficulties and so reduce the anxiety felt by the child. In other cases, social workers might work with groups of parents, children, and other professionals.

Educational psychologists are also involved in therapeutic measures, but they are primarily concerned in the assessment of a child's learning difficulties. Each educational psychologist is allocated to a certain number of secondary schools and their feeder primary schools. Because of their regular contact with schools, educational psychologists are the main source of referrals. They are themselves involved in special-needs assessments and in recommending residential schooling where appropriate. Parents have to give their permission for an educational psychologist to be involved with their children, and this consent can be dispensed with only in very exceptional cases where it is felt that without intervention a child would be deprived of his educational needs.

Teachers who are part of the child-guidance-service team may see children at the child-guidance centre or in the school. They may involve children in regular group activities in either setting. In addition to normal educational instruction, they may also be responsible for the continued observation and assessment of behaviour. Children who respond to such close and individual attention may eventually advance sufficiently to be able to continue their education in an ordinary school.

The schools' psychological and child-guidance service is a specialised agency primarily concerned with children's problems that are manifested within an education context. Various methods of intervention are used, including goal-setting, task-focusing, and contract-based work (see chapter 7). Because of the intensive nature of their involvement, child-guidance workers have restricted case-loads. Parents are encouraged to be involved and are informed of the agencies' proposals concerning their work with the child. In many areas of the country there are waiting lists for children who need to be helped in this way.

The alternative curriculum
It is now recognised that the established curriculum of many schools has failed in the past to meet the needs of all children, particularly those who for various reasons have not been able to cope with academic demands. About 60% of school-leavers have no formal qualifications and are ill-prepared for the outside world. The inappropriateness of the curriculum has been identified as contributing to children's disaffection with school and resultant non-attendance. As part of the European Economic Community Lower Achievers Project, some education authorities have now responded with the provision of an *alternative curriculum* for those aged 14 to 16.

Common features of the alternative education offered to children in their last two years of compulsory schooling include small groups with high staff/pupil ratios and an emphasis on co-operation rather than competition. Work is marked on a continual-assessment basis emphasising progress achieved, rather than by competitive external examinations which grade success and, for some pupils, tend to generate failure.

More time is spent with individuals in project work, and contracts are designed to motivate apprehensive inhibited youngsters by providing the experience of success. The essence of a contract is that it is drawn up by both parties: the teacher and the pupil. They agree on the aims, objectives, and content of a work programme and have a mutual responsibility to adhere to that programme. Out-of-school activities include community projects and Outward Bound sessions as well as a variety of work-experience and leisure activities. In addition, links are made with further-education colleges. Within the alternative curriculum, young people are encouraged to achieve familiarity and competence in areas of technology, design, numeracy, literacy, and communication skills. In some cases children are offered residential experience – the aim being that they should learn about their own needs in the context of the needs of others in a group situation.

To facilitate these changes in the curriculum, education authorities are acquiring the use of other community resources and are opening up schools to various members of the community who may be able to make a contribution towards a child's education.

Sometimes it is policy to offer this alternative, more practical, curriculum only to 'non-examinable' children. Where this is the case, such a policy may have the consequence of 'stigmatising' the children involved. Furthermore, it denies access to a stimulating and purposeful range of educational experience to those children who are exclusively engaged in academic learning.

The careers service

Youth-advisory services existed in many forms before 1973, but in that year the Employment and Training Act placed a mandatory duty upon all local education authorities to provide a careers service, defined as 'an employment service for persons attending or leaving educational institutions other than universities although university students may use the service'. The service was also to be open to those people who had ceased full-time education.

Careers officers are involved in a two-way process of trying to assess and match the needs of both young people and employers. Their work involves seeing pupils in schools, beginning when they are making signifi-cant subject changes at the end of the third year and also concentrating on helping those about to leave school. Pupils may be seen on an individual basis, so that the careers officer can take note of, and assess, their ambi-tions and inclinations and comment on the practicality of their choices.

125

Alternatively, interested pupils may be seen on a group basis. At the same time, in order to keep up-to-date, careers officers will visit industry, the professions, and other services and will advise about the employment of young people and also canvas for vacancies in the current job market.

The work of the careers service is a continuous process and is available to young people once they have left school – its liaison with further-education establishments and familiarity with Youth Training Schemes (YTS) and other Government training measures for the unemployed are of course essential. Careers officers may be involved in starting young people on YTS and be responsible for monitoring them while they are undergoing selected courses. In addition, the careers service produces literature, holds conventions, gives talks, and generally contributes to the dissemination of information relating to employment opportunities.

Most careers workers see a wide range of young people with differing abilities and ambitions. Others feel the need to specialise, in order to be up to date and to be able to provide an expert concentrated service. Some local authorities have teams specialising in helping handicapped young people and those who are unemployed.

Team working with handicapped young people Employment opportunities are problematic for many young school-leavers, but finding employment is even more of a problem for young people who are handicapped in some way. Employers of more than 20 people are legally obliged to make available at least 3% of the workforce vacancies to registered disabled people. In many cases a person's disability in no way interferes with job performance and he may go about a job in the normal way. He may, however, need support and intervention to counteract any prejudice that employers may have.

Mentally handicapped young people have a harder task in finding work, but they can be assisted in their search and also be advised about various training opportunities that exist in some further-education colleges or adult-rehabilitation centres. Although capable of employment at different levels, mentally handicapped youngsters are dependent, initially, on a sympathetic and understanding employer.

Team working with unemployed young people Careers officers working with unemployed young people will be concerned with those who have been unable to find permanent work since leaving school or since following a Youth Training Scheme course. Many of these youngsters will be keen to seek help from careers officers, and others will respond after some encouragement from them. However, some older young people may be so disenchanted by their unsuccessful efforts to find work and lack of hopeful prospects that they may resist any help offered and make no attempt to seek official help. In response to this problem, careers officers may make home visits and try to encourage young people to take part in the specialised pre-vocational programmes that they run. These involve some counselling support, practice interviews, role-play exercises, and advice and guidance on job applications.

Careers services are provided by each local authority, but the standard of provision varies. More committed authorities will have special provision for disadvantaged young people, and some have extended the service to adults. They will encourage youngsters who want to cross existing traditional boundaries to employment by offering positive support to girls seeking jobs in engineering and to boys wanting positions in caring work. Such authorities will have done much to reduce the bureaucratic and formal image of the careers service by making it more acceptable and more accessible to users.

The education welfare service

The education welfare service stems from the work carried out by the late-nineteenth-century 'school boardmen' who were appointed to ensure the school attendance of children between the ages of five and 13. Recruited largely from the police force and military sources, these men were generally disciplinarians concerned simply with the enforcement of the law. However, as a result of their investigations they became aware of the poor living conditions and severe poverty in which many families were living and were able to bring this information to the attention of the authorities. The need for child care and welfare, in addition to formal education, began to be recognised.

Today the role of the education welfare officer (EWO) has been greatly extended, but she is still primarily concerned with school attendance. The education welfare service provides social-work support to the school or schools to which EWOs are allocated and which they visit on a regular basis. As well as scrutinising registers in order to identify pupils who are developing problems of irregular attendance, the EWO will talk to teachers or heads-of-year about children who are causing concern because of the problems they are presenting. She will also help teachers to appreciate the difficulties experienced by particular families at home.

Home visits are made by EWOs in order to establish reasons for absence, and records of their involvement will be kept. Consultation and supervision are provided by senior staff who may themselves carry a small case-load.

Most education welfare services are run by local education authorities, but in some cases the service is based within the social-services department.

Under the Education Act 1944, it is the duty of every parent to see that his or her children receive full-time education between the ages of five and 16. (This need not necessarily take place within a school – where the parent is a qualified teacher, for example, it is possible for that person to educate his or her children in their own home. However, education is concerned with more than simply imparting knowledge, and to educate children exclusively at home would be to deny them the social opportunity to mix and make friends with other children of their own age.) The EWO may summon parents to court under section 39 of the 1944 Act if she feels that they are failing in their duty to ensure that their child receives full-time education. Alternatively, she may take the child to a juvenile court, under section 12e of the Child Care Act 1980, if she feels that the parents have done all that they can to encourage a child's attendance but the child has persistently stayed away from school.

These legal measures are taken only as a last resort, when all other forms of help have been offered. However, it is often the case that the actual implementation of the court procedure is itself enough to encourage improved attendance.

Children absent themselves from school for many reasons, which range from difficulties experienced at home to general disaffection with the school. Although not unknown in primary schools, most attendance problems occur within secondary schools. It is part of the EWO's role to ascertain the root cause of the continued absence and to offer help accordingly. If the cause of the problem is felt to lie within the school itself, then the school may be able to provide alternatives and make changes in the curriculum or organisation.

Like other professional workers involved in schools, EWOs have a responsibility to identify children 'at risk educationally' and may recommend a child to be considered for a special-needs statement. In certain cases, a change of school will be beneficial for a child, and the EWO will arrange this.

The education welfare service provides financial benefits in the form of grants for essential school clothing, travel allowances, and free school meals for children from low-income families. EWOs can advise about these benefits and also offer advice to parents on the availability of pre-school provision, special education, and the procedure for school transfer. In addition, they can outline for parents the work of the child-guidance service, the careers department, and other educational support services as well as give information about the type of help offered by other agencies. Sometimes this information is made available at education-welfare adult centres situated within the community. In providing benefits, the education welfare service is the only agency outside the Department of Health and Social Security (DHSS) to supply direct financial assistance to families (although the social services also have limited resources which they can use to help a family if this diminishes the need for a child to be brought into care – section 1 of the Child Care Act 1980).

Finally, the EWO is responsible for checking that school-age children are not being employed illegally, either under age or beyond the maximum hours they are legally permitted to work. As well as responding to allegations of illegal unemployment made by individuals within the community, the EWO will patrol likely areas – such as markets – outside of normal office hours if necessary.

The Franks Report   The 1973 Franks Report is the only official report on the work done by EWOs. It concluded that the most relevant professional training for educational welfare officers is social-work training, although their work is clearly different from mainstream social work because of its educational setting. The report led to the EWO being upgraded from a clerical to a social-worker grade. However, not all local authorities have responded positively to the recommendations of the report, therefore in some areas education welfare officers are still untrained. Qualified EWOs have tended to leave for different employment in another social-work agency, as educational welfare work is still regarded by some as a low-status service.

Social workers attached to schools

In some areas of the country, social workers who are also members of area social-work teams have been appointed to particular schools. This provision is complementary to the education welfare service and the pastoral role which teachers provide within a school. It is aimed at strengthening the links between the social-services department and the education department.

Unrestricted by the demands of timetables or any other school responsibilities, the social worker is able to provide individual counselling for children and/or their parents who may be referred by the education staff. The social worker is well placed to identify signs of stress within school resulting from social, emotional, or institutional problems and to share these observations with education personnel. With access to social-services and other community resources, the social worker can provide help to families to prevent them reaching the type of crisis which would normally qualify them for social-work attention.

The appointment of school social workers is in line with the philosophy of the Barclay Report, in that the service is being taken to the community and established within an everyday setting enabling social work of a more preventive nature to be carried out.

The youth service

Local education authorities employ youth workers to provide a service aimed at encouraging the personal development of young people in an informal setting. There are separate provisions for children between eight and 13 and for young people between 13 and 25.

Some youth centres are based in schools and may be open to the local community on one or two nights in the week as well as to those who attend during the day. Others, operating from community education centres, may be open day and evening. These centres often incorporate a youth club, play schemes, women's groups, and sessions for the unemployed within the same building complex.

Although youth clubs provide essentially recreational activities, they also aim to advance a person's general education. Through involvement in supervised group activities, young people can develop relationships which may encourage them to challenge their existing perceptions of others and of society. Issues such as racism and sexism can be confronted informally

Youth centres may provide girls with an opportunity to be involved in new activities.

in settings unrestricted by timetable requirements. The available advice and counselling offered by youth workers is founded on a trust relationship which is built up through association. Young people are encouraged to make decisions and are supported in accepting responsibility. The youth worker will respond to initiatives that stem from the group and will organise activities accordingly.

Outreach work   This is undertaken to gauge the unmet need for youth work in the area. It involves the youth workers going out into the community and talking to particular individuals, to schools, and to other agencies in order to establish what should be offered to young people. In some areas, special projects have been set up under such headings as 'Girls' work' and 'Asian youth groups' among others, in an attempt to extend resources to hitherto neglected young people. More people are therefore given an opportunity to engage in interests and activities within a supervised setting.

Detached youth workers   These go further towards trying to meet the needs of young people. They may be based in a local centre, but much of their work is done on the streets, in cafés and other meeting places where they attempt to reach more isolated individuals. Some young people may lack sufficient confidence to join a youth club or may simply be unaware of the resources which are offered.

130

Community education

Community education has developed from the adult and youth and community services. It derives from the 1970 Youth Service Development Report and from the 1973 Russell Report on adult education. It aims to provide wide-ranging educational opportunities to all members of the community, particularly those groups who have traditionally been excluded.

Many people's educational experience is restricted to the time they spent at school. For a number of reasons – lack of confidence, ignorance of courses on offer, added responsibilities, or lack of time or money – they may have been unable later to fulfil their educational desires or needs.

Community colleges include all the local further-education, adult-education, and community-education sites within a specified area. They are now in the process of extending services to more people and involving the community in policy decisions. This move has meant that community colleges have had to develop more flexibility with regard to timetabling and the nature of courses offered, in order to respond to felt needs within the community. The main groups identified as having a special need within the community include women, manual workers, mentally handicapped people, ethnic-minority groups, unemployed people, and older adults.

Women Although more men are becoming involved, society still lays responsibility for child care firmly on the shoulders of women. With the general lack of full-time day-care facilities for children under five, many mothers spend much of their lives attending to the needs of children. For some this is an ideal way of using their time, but others may feel the need to develop their particular interests and may feel trapped in what can often be an isolating activity. It is estimated that twice the number of women would seek work or some form of education if adequate day-care facilities were available.

For community colleges adequately to meet the needs of parents – mothers in particular – they need to be able to provide crèche facilities and shorter courses (between 10 a.m. and 3 p.m.) so that children can be taken to and from school. In a stimulating educational setting, women can develop interests, grow in confidence, and prepare themselves for the time when their children have grown up.

Manual workers Most manual workers are unlikely to have participated in any further education and usually they have left school with few or no qualifications. Sometimes this is regretted. Furthermore, during the course of their adult lives, people often discover that they possess talents or interests and an all-too-often frustrated desire to develop them. This is where community education can help. Some people may see no relevance for them in the courses already offered, and it is part of the role of community education to ascertain people's needs and to get together in designing appropriate courses. It is regrettable that some people carry their negative school experiences with them throughout their lives.

131

Community education aims to give everyone the chance to develop new interests.

The mentally handicapped   The Warnock Report recommended that educational provision for mentally handicapped people should be extended, so young people finishing residential school are now encouraged to take up additional education. Link courses to adult residential homes are made, and courses are offered to mentally handicapped adults living in the community. Courses vary in their range from some form of basic education to more sophisticated work in computer workshops. Many mentally handicapped people find the facilities more stimulating and the atmosphere friendlier in a community college than in an adult training centre, say, and in turn their presence contributes to a greater social integration.

Ethnic-minority groups   Members of ethnic minorities have a right to preserve their distinctive identities, culture, language, religion, and social values. Many community colleges have responded by introducing changes in curriculum, procedure, practices, and provision to meet this need.

It is recognised that a high proportion of children from ethnic-minority backgrounds have underachieved at school. This is seen partly as a result of the difficulty some children have experienced in trying to come to terms with the values of two different cultures – those of their parents and those of the wider society in general. This is particularly evident with regard to language. For example, an English child born of West Indian parents may speak one language at home (patois) and another with his friends (a mixture of patois and English), but academically his linguistic proficiency is measured purely in terms of the dominant wider culture. It is, of course, important for everybody that Standard English is learned, as it is the basis of communication in society, but where children have been given no additional help they will inevitably leave school disadvantaged.

For social-work and other caring organisations to reflect the attitudes of the population as a whole, professional representation needs to be made from all the various groups which make up our society. In a deliberate effort to encourage the recruitment of caring practitioners from different backgrounds and cultures, some colleges have developed *access* courses, linked to training courses at polytechnics and other higher-education establishments, and have restricted entry to ethnic-minority members. These access courses aim to enable students to reach the academic level required for professional training.

Most access courses, however, are open to everyone over the age of 21; but those restricted to ethnic-minority members are an example of *positive discrimination*, aimed at counteracting previous less obvious *negative discrimination* which for a long time went unrecognised.

Increasingly, some ethnic groups are involved in providing their own educational courses within the traditional adult educational structure. For example, in some areas the Asian communities run courses in Urdu and other languages as well as wider aspects of their own cultures.

Older adults   Increased opportunities for early retirement and a shorter working week mean that some people have greater leisure time. Education is not simply about obtaining formal qualifications – it is concerned with developing potential within individuals, with the overall aim of enriching and improving their quality of life. Community colleges are involved with meeting intellectual, physical, and creative needs as well as with the acquisition of relevant skills. Well planned pre-retirement courses in particular can enable individuals to adjust to changes in life-style.

The unemployed   There are few more debilitating or demoralising experiences in life than being unemployed, particularly over a long period of time, or having been made redundant at a late stage in life with little hope of re-employment. Without the sense of usefulness and social involvement attached to economic activity, people may become despondent and feel unfulfilled. A wide range of courses aimed either at specific retraining or broader personal development are available to help people back into the job market or at least assist them to live their lives in a more constructive and satisfactory manner.

There are, of course, other groups within society who could benefit from extended educational provision – the above list is by no means exhaustive.

In order to ascertain need, committed community colleges are involved in *outreach* work, talking to individuals and community groups to find out

133

what people want. Some colleges offer a *drop-in* service where people may call at any time during the day, either to participate in a particular interest group (for parents and toddlers or unemployed people, for example) or to seek advice about the availability of educational opportunity. Systems of *open learning* have extended educational provision to more people, with the development of individual work packages as part of course modules and the availability of tutor support. Through open learning, people are able to work at their own pace to complete chosen courses of study. This may be done in the college workshop or at the student's home or place of work. In this way it has been possible for a person working in a remote situation, such as an oil-rig, to continue his education and to consult a tutor by post or by attendance at the college during shore leave.

The inclusion of ordinary members of the public on neighbourhood education management committees enables individual participation and allows the public to actively affect the kind of educational provision being made.

Local-authority housing departments

Although this book is mainly concerned with social work as seen from the perspective of the practitioners, this approach is not possible when dealing with the work of housing departments, as welfare posts have not been generally developed in these. Some authorities, though, have created specialist posts for those working in housing-aid teams, homeless-family units, and single-homeless support groups. The work of housing personnel is outlined later – most of this section is concerned with housing policy and problems experienced by individuals and families.

Historically, housing has been taken for granted and to a certain extent left to individuals to provide for themselves. When the State became involved in housing, it did so initially from a concern with public health. Involvement has been maintained because of the realisation that housing is expensive and its provision can be open to abuse. There has also been a gradual recognition that people have a fundamental human right to decent housing.

Today, local-authority housing departments have many complex statutory obligations to both private and council tenants alike. These include the demolition of condemned property, the provision of new houses, the monitoring of building standards, and the granting of subsidies to individuals or voluntary organisations for the restoration of ageing property. In addition, housing departments advise on people's rights to housing benefit and adjudicate on the assessment of fair rents for private tenants. They also have a responsibility towards vulnerable people within the community – the disabled, the elderly, and the homeless – and since 1980 they have been directed to actively involve the public more closely in decision-making processes. The Chronically Sick and Disabled Persons Act 1970 empowered local authorities to require all new public buildings to be accessible to disabled people and to provide separate facilities for their use.

Council housing
At the end of the nineteenth century, local authorities were empowered to provide housing to meet need, but few made any substantial provision until after the First World War, when the Government committed itself to the policy of providing 'homes fit for heroes'. Government housing subsidies in the form of grants to local authorities were introduced to help provide low-cost rented accommodation. Since that time, subsidies have been withdrawn and then reintroduced at different periods. Today council housing is still subsidised – in 1982, 38% of the cost was not recovered by rents.

Not everyone can afford to buy his own accommodation (although 55% of households in 1980 were owner-occupied) – public provision is therefore necessary, in particular for young families, low-income families, the elderly, and the handicapped. In 1981 there was a shortage of over 800 000 homes in Great Britain. Many existing houses are too expensive, unfit for habitation, or not located in the area where housing is required. Consequently there is a great demand on limited local-authority housing in some areas – particularly in major cities. Where this is the case, allocation of houses is normally made by a points system, but not every authority assesses housing need in this way. In 1984 there were 1.2 million households (family units or single people) on council-house waiting lists.

Rehousing officers Rehousing officers are responsible for registering applicants for housing and collecting information about their current personal circumstances and accommodation needs. So that the allocation of housing resources is fair and people's requirements are met as well as possible, a system of *prioritisation* is used and this, normally, includes the *points system* mentioned above.

The points system Attempts to quantify the urgency with which people need to be rehoused may involve an assessment of the following conditions:

a) *Overcrowding* Points for overcrowding are awarded on a sliding scale calculated on the relationship between family size and the number of rooms in the house at the time when the housing department is first notified of the condition.
b) *Medical* Applicants whose household includes one person who is suffering unacceptable hardship due to the structure of the building (a severely handicapped person having to negotiate stairs, for example) will receive maximum points under this category. Points will also be awarded to those whose medical condition is less severe but where rehousing is likely to result in an alleviation of distress.
c) *Insecurity* This refers to people who have received an eviction warrant or a 'notice to quit' their homes and who therefore need urgent consideration. Fewer points will be granted to others who have no security of tenure (such as lodgers, who may be asked to leave at any

135

moment) but where there is no pressure for them to leave at present.

d) *Social*   A person's social circumstances are taken into account within this category. A range of points may be awarded where people are experiencing violence or fear of violence; harassment (racial or from neighbours or landlord); or relationship difficulties, including family separation and bereavement. Consideration will be made in this category for applicants wishing to move to smaller accommodation now that their children have grown up and left home and for those people who are isolated by distance from friends and relatives. The degree of social hardship and ability to cope will be taken into account.

e) *Property condition*   Maximum points will be awarded to families whose home has been designated 'unfit for habitation', and a varying number of points will be awarded to others according to their house's general state of repair.

f) *Lacking or sharing amenities*   People and families either lacking amenities (such as an inside toilet) or having to share resources (such as bathrooms and kitchens) will be awarded points related to the degree of inconvenience involved.

g) *Environment*   This category relates to factors outside a person's dwelling – for example, where a family with children is living in an unmodernised pre-war block of flats. Environmental points are awarded for the presence of disruptive or distressing features as well as for the lack of essential or desirable facilities (such as play space or a grass area).

h) *Travelling*   Applicants who have to travel long distances to work, to use public facilities, or to receive or give support to relatives will be considered under this category.

i) *Multi-occupancy*   A multi-occupied dwelling is defined by the Housing Act 1969 (section 58) as a 'house which is occupied by persons who do not form a single household'. Such dwellings include hostels, night shelters, guest houses, and homes converted into bed-sits where cooking, lavatory, and bathroom facilities are shared. Some people in this category may have already been awarded points on other criteria (such as social, environmental, or overcrowding), and the extra points they obtain under multi-occupancy will emphasise their plight. This category in particular reflects the intention of some local authorities to phase out the inadequate hostels for the single homeless.

j) *Children at height*   For reasons of safety and access to play space, children need to live at ground level. This category recognises the desirability for families with children to live in ground-floor accommodation and awards points according to the number of children who live above ground level.

k) *Elderly*   The age of an applicant does not necessarily represent housing need, but an elderly person is more likely to experience difficulties and an allowance on the points scale is made for this.

l) *Related issues*   To be considered for rehousing, people must usually be residents of the council area, but exceptions are made for people living in 'overspill areas' beyond the local boundaries and for elderly or Forces personnel who wish to return to their area of origin.

m) *Time and housing need* The above categories combine to determine a person's or a family's housing priority – from them is calculated the applicant's position on a waiting list. Families who are classified as having only a 'medium need' to be rehoused would, under a static points system, have little chance of progressing towards the type of property they desire. However, consideration is also given to the length of time that families have spent waiting for accommodation – extra points are granted yearly on the anniversary of a family's original application for rehousing.

Case conferences On some occasions, when an individual or family is experiencing 'exceptional housing need' which necessitates urgent rehousing, a case conference of housing personnel will be arranged to consider reports from other agencies and decide the course of action. This may result in a family being rehoused ahead of those already on the list, but circumstances occasionally make this step necessary.

High-rise living Between the late 1950s and early 1970s, many housing authorities were engaged in the mass clearance of housing considered unfit for habitation. In the process, long-established communities were destroyed and their homes were often replaced by high-density architecturally innovative housing complexes. Although the buildings looked impressive on the drawing-board, these high-rise and deck-access housing schemes are now acknowledged to have contributed to the social problems of the people obliged to live in them. Many buildings were poorly constructed – among their faults were thin walls and inefficient and costly heating systems. Furthermore, people living in deck-access accommodation had little privacy and lacked an area outside their home which they could call their own.

In response to these problems, housing authorities have where possible rehoused families with children, and other vulnerable groups, and have used the high-rise accommodation to meet the needs of single people and students. In extreme cases, some local authorities have pulled down high-rise and deck-access complexes, some of which were built less than fifteen years ago. Some housing authorities have adapted and renovated existing accommodation to make it more appropriate to the needs of families. This has involved such alterations as removing the top floor of a three-tier block of flats and converting the building into a series of individual maisonette-type units. Such alterations are costly, and different authorities have made varying progress with them.

When much of the high-rise accommodation was being built, housing departments were under pressure to rehouse people from clearance areas quickly, and central government threatened to withhold fundings if rehousing took too long. It is unlikely that housing authorities will repeat the mistakes they have made in the past.

Tenant participation One thing that has been made clear by the experience of many housing departments from the 1950s onwards is that they failed to properly take into account the views of the people in need of housing and the communities within which they lived.

Partly as a consequence of housing departments' failure to consult tenants in the past and partly as a result of the growing recognition of the need for people to be more politically involved in their own lives, tenant participation is now actively encouraged. The Tenants' Charter, first proposed by the Labour Party in 1977 and incorporated into the Housing Act 1980, urges local authorities to make provision for tenant participation and consultation in the decision-making process.

Many local-authority housing departments are engaged in improving the communication between housing staff and tenants. This involves the co-operation of housing officers, councillors, trade unions, and tenants. To facilitate this, local authorities are obliged to display arrangements by which tenants can be consulted on major changes in housing policy. In the past, tenants' associations have been formed only to be disbanded after a particular issue has been fought. Today the aim is to encourage the development of a permanent tenants' association on every housing estate and to encourage communication between them.

Local authorities can provide individual tenant handbooks and can supply other information in local public display cases. Provision is made under the Housing Act 1980 for authorities to make accommodation available for tenants' associations and to provide professional support staff and financial aid in the form of small starter grants. Typically, tenants may be involved in the vetting of repair schedules, gauging the needs of local interest groups (such as toddlers' clubs), and identifying community need. In this way, ordinary people will have more of a stake in where they live.

Local estate offices Some local-authority housing departments have decentralised and have relocated their offices within the community. Where this has happened, housing matters are dealt with by small management teams.

Local estate offices are concerned with the management and supervision of the council housing in their area – hence they are involved in rehousing assessments; allocation of properties; and the problems concerning disputes with neighbours, non-payment of rents, arrears, and eviction of tenants.

Local authorities are usually reluctant to evict tenants, partly because they may have a responsibility to rehouse them. Instead, they will offer advice on income maximisation and may suggest helpful repayment schemes or offer limited practical counselling. If necessary, they will refer a family to the local social-services department. In the past, some housing authorities have been guilty of reallocating ('dumping') families with large rent arrears into one specific area containing the less desirable properties and have so created 'ghetto' estates.

Officers from the local estate-management office will visit homes in response to complaints.

In making services more available and accessible to people, the housing department is demonstrating a commitment to local democracy in a similar manner to the social-services departments who are operating on a patch basis. In some areas, multi-service neighbourhood centres involving social services, housing, education, welfare, and cleansing departments have been established.

Homelessness

There are several reasons why a family or individual becomes homeless, the most common being the result of a dispute between a husband and wife or between a lodger and the family or friends or relatives with whom the lodger is living. Other direct causes of homelessness are eviction, fire, flood, and similar emergencies, and new arrivals into the town or city. Local authorities are obliged to provide help but not necessarily permanent accommodation unless it can be established that the applicant has a '*priority housing need*' and a local connection. Housing officers are involved in the assessment of families as well as having an advisory role.

The Housing (Homeless Persons) Act 1977   This Act was the first official recognition of the problem of homelessness. It included in its definition of 'homeless', in addition to those with no accommodation, people unable to secure entry into their own homes (due to illegal eviction, for example), those threatened with violence in their own homes (such as battered wives), and those living in mobile homes without any legal place to reside (travelling families, for example). The Act also extended the concept of homelessness to include those people anticipating homelessness within 28 days. This time period allows local authorities to work in a preventive way and to make arrangements for families before they actually become homeless, so lessening the trauma to the family.

Priority need Under section 2 of the Housing Act 1977, certain categories of homeless people are regarded as having *priority need* for accommodation and they include the following:

a) those with a dependent child or children;
b) those made homeless through flood, fire, or other disaster;
c) pregnant women;
d) anybody considered *vulnerable* or who is living with someone who is at risk because of physical disability, old age, mental handicap or illness, or 'any other reason'.

If any 'priority need' individuals or families are considered to have *intentionally* made themselves homeless, the authority will not consider rehousing them permanently – instead, housing officers will offer advice and assistance, over a reasonable length of time, aimed at enabling them to secure accommodation for themselves. If, however, the authority is convinced that a person or persons have become homeless *unintentionally*, then the local authority is obliged to make accommodation available to them. Help may initially be provided in the form of temporary accommodation until the family's or person's circumstances can be assessed and classified and their position on the housing list can be determined.

The homeless-families section Some local authorities provide support teams to help families who are homeless. Before such families are considered to be in 'priority need', they may be received into temporary hostel accommodation until a separate individual offer can be made. The length of stay in temporary accommodation may depend to some extent on their willingness to accept offers of accommodation made to them by the housing department which, for a variety of reasons, the homeless family may or may not consider suitable. Vacancies are more likely to occur in areas where nobody wants to live.

Housing problems are often interrelated with other difficulties. For example, a family made homeless by mortgage repossession or council-house eviction could experience related social difficulties in addition to financial hardship. For this reason, homeless-family hostels are sometimes serviced by social-work teams. Social workers may encourage involvement in group work and other activities aimed at building up a family's self-respect and confidence to counter the demoralising experience of being homeless.

The single homeless   The code of guidance incorporated in the Housing (Homeless Persons) Act 1977 states that certain single people should be regarded as having priority housing need. This includes young women threatened with physical abuse and other young people exposed to financial or sexual exploitation. There is no legal requirement upon local authorities to provide accommodation for most other able-bodied single homeless people, although the code of practice recommends some help if it is possible. Some would argue that homeless single people are, by their very circumstances, vulnerable and that more should be done for them under the 'vulnerability' concept outlined in section 2 of the Act.

Housing officers will provide single homeless people with information about the resources available in the area. They may produce a list of recommended bed-and-breakfast hotels known to accept single homeless people and, for someone who is unemployed, provide information on the procedure for obtaining financial assistance from the DHSS. They will also advise on the availability of housing benefit to applicants who are not unemployed as well as to those who are.

In 1985 the DHSS introduced a contested ruling limiting the period that single people below the age of 26 could remain in hotel accommodation while receiving DHSS benefit to eight weeks in a large city and four weeks in a smaller town. Hotel accommodation remains only a temporary solution to the problems of unemployed homeless young people.

The housing officer can also inform about *local-authority hostels*, where they exist. These are usually single-sex establishments, often with dormitory accommodation. Where there are no local-authority hostels, the housing officer can advise on the *voluntary provision* within the area (Church Army or Salvation Army establishments, for example) and comment on the vacancy situation and their charges for overnight or long-stay accommodation.

In certain areas of the country there are *resettlement centres* provided by the DHSS which cater for the needs of people who are described as being 'without a settled way of life'. Sometimes these centres are used on a casual basis by people ready to move on, or they may be used more permanently by people who will have access to food, washing facilities, and medical treatment when necessary. Such centres are located near to large cities, and the DHSS or 'out-of-hours' duty social workers can issue travel warrants to homeless single people wishing to make the journey. The DHSS has recently announced its intention to withdraw from running these centres, and it is expected that another agency will take over the responsibility.

Night shelters   These have come into existence in some major towns in response to the lack of provision for the single homeless. Most of these shelters – usually run by a church or other voluntary organisation with

141

some local-authority or DHSS support – are extremely basic, providing just shelter, food, and sleeping accommodation. Some shelters are mixed, but most have no provision for women. They may be based in a church crypt or even in a disused building. They tend not to refuse anybody who is homeless and they remain open for applicants up to a certain hour of the night, or all night in a few cases. Such hostels are vacated early in the morning, and a user is usually not allowed to return until the doors re-open at a specified time in the evening, although a growing number are remaining open for part of the day, and some provide basic meals.

Teams working with the single homeless Much of the accommodation for the single homeless is inadequate – it is often provided in large unadapted Victorian institutions which are inappropriate for the needs of the twentieth century. Some local authorities are committed to the closure of these institutions and to their replacement by smaller, more intimate, units. Innovative schemes to assist the institutionalised single homeless person to transfer to independent accommodation or smaller hostel accommodation within the community have been made possible where housing departments have set up single-person strategy groups. Housing officers then have a home-making function, helping clients to obtain DHSS assistance and to establish themselves in furnished or unfurnished accommodation within the community. This work is quite labour-intensive for the officer concerned, particularly when helping someone who has for many years been dependent on institutional settings.

Housing aid
Many local authorities run a separate housing-aid service, normally from the city centre, which provides information on all housing matters, particularly those not related to council housing or public tenancies. In other areas, this type of service may be provided by independent voluntary bodies (such as Shelter or the Catholic Housing Aid Society).

Advice may be given on any of the following problems: excessive rent, overdue repairs, harassment, lack of supply services (gas and electricity), and evictions. Housing-aid officers have access to a number of specialists within the authority, some of whom may be employed by social services – these include welfare-rights advisors and housing-benefit advisors. The housing-aid officers themselves will be able to provide most information, but they will consult a specialist where the circumstances are more complex. Similarly, housing officers will themselves undertake basic debt counselling unless the situation requires greater expertise.

Where somebody feels that his rent is too high, the housing officer will advise him on the appeals procedure, help guide the client through the forms, and prepare him for attendance at the rent tribunal. The housing officer is not able to represent anybody at the tribunal – a 'fair' rent will be decided by the *rent officer*.

Housing-aid officers will have small case-loads and, although they will be involved in some counselling, this is of a more practical nature related to a person's housing needs.

Conclusion
Housing services to both private and council tenants vary enormously throughout the country. Although housing problems are by no means confined to the major cities, it is there that the pressure for housing is greatest and the problems most apparent. Many authorities have responded positively, with the development of housing advisory services, homeless-family provision, and support for the single homeless.

The Housing Act 1980 encouraged the participation and involvement of tenants in decision-making, and local authorities are making provision for this. The Act also gave council tenants the right to buy their own homes – at prices lower than the market value, depending on their length of residence. While this move has provided people with an opportunity for home ownership and has introduced individuality to council-housing areas, it has had the consequence not only of reducing public housing stock but also of removing much of the most desirable council accommodation. This aspect of the 1980 Act has contributed to a worsening of the housing problem.

Community work

Community work is discussed separately in this chapter, although community workers are employed by the statutory agencies already mentioned. They are also employed by voluntary organisations. Irrespective of the employing agency, the community worker's role is often (in the words of the Gulbenkian Foundation) that of 'an enabler, a catalyst, an advisor or an innovator of social change according to the needs of a given situation'.

The perspective of their work is different from that of social workers. Some people consider community work as a part of social work, whereas others regard it as a completely separate discipline. Essentially, community workers focus on the needs of the community as a whole, rather than on the needs of individuals. Employing agencies include social-services departments, education departments, housing departments, leisure and recreation departments, and various voluntary organisations. In some cases there are joint appointments made by local voluntary groups and statutory agencies.

The development of community work
The urban-renewal programmes that started in the USA in the 1940s and 1950s did much to influence the development of community work in this country. The public became disillusioned with the bureaucratic nature of government and the lack of public participation in matters affecting ordinary people. This coincided with the recognition, by the early 1960s, that the Welfare State had failed to protect everyone: that poverty and urban decay existed in many towns and cities. Furthermore, from the

breakdown of many traditional communities, increased social mobility, and problems experienced by new communities with mixed ethnic populations, it was clear that people were not sufficiently involved in determining changes in their own environment. For example, there were compulsory purchase orders on family homes to make way for new roads and office accommodation.

Community workers had been successfully employed by local authorities in new-town developments in assessing need and encouraging community involvement. For example some new-town corporations employed community workers *before* families moved in, to help the families settle in the new surroundings. Stemming from this innovation, the need to employ community workers in more established areas was recognised.

Official recognition of community need
The 1969 Skeffington Committee report *People and planning* recognised that public participation 'can improve the quality of decisions by public authorities and give personal satisfaction to those affected by the decisions'. This opinion had already been made in the Seebohm Report (1968), which added that 'designated areas of special need should receive extra resources, comprehensively planned'. Following the Plowden Report (1967), education departments had introduced *educational priority areas* (EPAs) in regions where poverty owing to unemployment, low wages, and poor housing was reflected in a low level of educational aspiration, high staff turnover, and truancy problems in schools. More resources were to be invested in EPAs, and teachers were to receive improved conditions of pay.

In 1969 the Home Office initiated the *Urban Aid Programme* and in the following year set up *Community Development Projects* in 12 selected areas of the country. From about this time, the volume and variety of community work and the number of appointments made within it were increasing rapidly. In 1969 the Gulbenkian Foundation set up a study group to exchange ideas and examine the function of community work and its proper place in both practice and training.

The role of the community worker
The role of the community worker is not always clearly defined and will be determined by the needs of the employing agency and those of the community she serves. These needs may not always be compatible, therefore conflict is seen as an institutionalised aspect of the work – community workers may be involved in the dual task of assessing and developing community needs while pressing their own departments for the allocation of further resources. Some community workers will be concerned with the needs of a small area or neighbourhood and may be based in the local community centre; others will have a wider brief and may be involved in regional planning, new towns, expanded towns, and decaying inner cities.

The community centre is often a focal point for a wide range of local groups and activities.

Whether they work from the 'ground level' or at an administrative regional level, community workers will share common aims:

a) To encourage people to act for themselves *collectively* – they are rarely concerned in helping people solve individual problems.

b) To *share* their knowledge and skills with groups within the community.

c) To *stimulate* neighbourhood interest in the development of *self-help* activities such as childminding and the running of community centres.

d) To *liaise* efficiently with other statutory and voluntary organisations.

e) To *establish priorities* in their aims to strengthen disadvantaged groups in disadvantaged areas who are seeking improvements in services and resources.

f) To *identify* and *assess* – looking at neighbourhoods and collating information with regard to the needs of people, organisations, services, and building spaces.

g) To make *formal and informal contact* with local residents via newsletters, community newspapers, coffee mornings, sponsored fundraising, and social events for the whole community.

h) To do *outreach work* which may include door-to-door visiting of local residents to encourage involvement and to determine need.

i) To offer encouragement to *existing groups* and to facilitate their development – to offer opinions and advice and back-up resources

145

(such as typing and telephone services) which might relieve strain on the group. All of this is designed to encourage the community without inhibiting *self-determination*.

j) To seek to improve the *skills* and *confidence* of group members and their understanding of problems and issues.

k) To help people to *identify needs*, to encourage them to come together in a group, and to support them in their action.

l) To increase learning opportunities.

A National Institute for Social Work survey of community workers in the UK showed that 59% of community workers were employed by voluntary organisations – either national organisations (such as Help the Aged and the Save the Children Fund) or local groups (such as citizens' rights groups, tenants' associations, and consumer groups). The remainder were employed by local authorities – chiefly education departments (19%) and social services (11%). Many of the voluntary organisations received the bulk of their funding via the local authorities.

Whether they worked full- or part-time, the survey defined community workers as '*paid staff* whose primary responsibility is to develop groups in the community whose members experience and wish to tackle needs, disadvantages, or inequality'. Forty-seven per cent of the workers were women, and this represents an above average proportion compared to the rest of public social-service personnel. Thirteen per cent of community workers were from ethnic-minority groups, and these were employed mainly in community-relations councils and other voluntary organisations. Overall, less than one-third were professionally qualified in some way.

Some problems of community work

Community workers are not free agents – they are bound by the limits imposed by the organisation for which they work. This provides constraints for the community worker. Another dilemma frequently experienced by some workers occurs when they are seen by local people merely as 'paid professionals' from outside the community who have no personal investment within the area. This may lead to feelings of resentment. Lack of proper resources is another problem – for example in the field of education, where high fees and inadequate grants act as a barrier to formal education. This will sometimes hamper the efforts of community workers who want to encourage people to further their learning.

There is a tendency for the more motivated more able members of the community to take up leadership roles in groups and organisations, and it is important that the community worker encourages this. At the same time, it is also important for her to get in touch with the less articulate more isolated members of the community so that they too may be enabled to influence what happens around them.

Funding
Community workers in general are paid by their local authority, voluntary organisations, the Manpower Services Commission (MSC), or by the European Economic Community Social Fund.

Urban Aid is a grant of money paid by the Department of the Environment to specific voluntary projects and channelled through the relevant department of the local authority, which itself contributes 25% of the funding. For example, a neighbourhood community project may be Urban Aid funded – 75% coming from central government (the Department of the Environment) and 25% being paid by the local education authority. Some organisations receive money direct from central government – for example, law centres which obtain funding from the Home Office.

Social work, counselling, and advisory groups
In addition to community-work schemes such as neighbourhood and play-group schemes, there are often specific social-work and advisory projects funded by the State – either directly or via the local authority. These projects, run by non-statutory organisations, are set up to meet community needs that are not being properly catered for by existing services and are usually financed on a short-term basis. This funding is periodically reviewed – it can be extended for a specific length of time or withdrawn altogether. Occasionally the work of some projects is taken over by statutory organisations and incorporated into their basic service.

The threat of withdrawal of funding makes working on temporary projects difficult in that future planning is restricted. Some projects are long-established, so the workers may be confident that funding will be renewed (or extended). However it may still be difficult to tempt professional workers into an insecure job situation. The type of projects that are often experimental include those run for homeless or mentally ill young people, drug-misuse centres, and law centres.

Law centres These operate from local offices and are part of the Law Centre Federation. Each centre is governed by a democratically elected management committee made up of local members of the community (which will include professional and ordinary working people). The aim is to provide a legal-advice service to local people on matters that are not covered by Legal Aid. Under the Legal Aid scheme, anybody on a low income (calculated on disposable capital and disposable income) can receive initial services from a solicitor up to £50 free before contributing towards full legal costs according to calculations made on his income. Not all matters may be dealt with by Legal Aid, so recourse to advice centres is essential.

Law centres employ qualified solicitors, advice workers, and sometimes barristers. They deal with a wide range of problems, including matters involving industrial disputes, unfair dismissal, industrial accidents, low pay, and welfare benefits. The law-centre representative may act as an advocate for someone attending a DHSS appeals tribunal. Workers may be involved in helping people with their debt problems or negotiating with gas and electricity boards in order to prevent disconnection of supply. Additionally, the centre may be engaged in running a 'take-up campaign' by publicising information in order to encourage people to claim welfare benefits they are entitled to.

Community drug teams These have developed in response to the growing problem of drug misuse and the absence of specialised help for people with drug problems. They deal with all forms of drug abuse – both legal and illegal – ranging from reliance on prescribed sedatives to dependence on heroin and other 'hard' drugs.

Structured therapeutic communities exist for people with serious drug problems, and, as a preparation for these, people may receive some induction at the local drugs-project centre to prepare them for involvement in a residential setting. It is important to realise that the desire to change one's life-style has to come from the individual and cannot be imposed externally. Local drug-project centres and therapeutic communities may enable people to achieve their desired goals.

Community drug teams work with members of the community who have drug problems, engaging them in group work, counselling, and support. Work is also done with relatives of drug misusers, outlining facts related to drug abuse and encouraging support and understanding. However, the focus of their work is on the individual – he is encouraged to consider the options and alternatives open to him, but without inner commitment there can be no change. Community drug teams employ workers who are experienced in counselling and group work. Former drug users may also be employed.

The police

The police are primarily concerned with law enforcement and crime prevention; however, there is also a strong community-relations aspect to their work. During the 1960s and early 1970s, for reasons of efficiency and expediency in response to manpower shortages, much police work was done by officers in 'panda' cars. The sight of the 'bobby on the beat' became less common, and the day-to-day contact between the police and the public was lost. Police officers became distanced from the communities they served. Since the early 1980s, however, there has been a move to re-establish local policing and foot patrolling. This has been made possible by increased recruitment.

Although community relations is a part of every police officer's general duties, it is often also a specialist function of police work which is carried out by a separate *community-contact department*. This department, headed by an inspector, will be engaged in the two-way process of ascertaining community feelings and transmitting these to other police officers.

Community contact
The inspector, or one of his officers, will endeavour to make contact with the various community leaders, youth workers, and heads of religious organisations and other community groups. Members of this department may also go into schools – both junior and secondary – and local colleges to talk about the history and practice of policing. The idea is to inform about the role of the police, to attempt to break down barriers, and to challenge the stereotype images that tend to develop about their activities – indeed, to present the human element of those involved in police work.

Missing persons
The police are involved in trying to trace people who are reported missing for various reasons. The police may try to find someone in response to a request from a family member who is concerned for that person's safety. Once the police have located someone who is listed as a 'missing' person and are satisfied that he is safe and well and is not being coerced to remain in his present situation, they will report this to the friend or relative who instigated the inquiry and take the reported name off the missing-persons list. The police are not obliged to reveal the whereabouts of any adult who wishes this to be kept secret.

Juvenile offenders
The police are generally reluctant to bring a child before the court, particularly if he has not been in trouble before. First offences are therefore often dealt with by a caution in the presence of the child's parents. There have been occasions, though, when even a series of cautions has not had the required effect and so a court appearance has become unavoidable. In all cases of juvenile crime, the police aim to obtain an in-depth appreciation of the child's social setting, his schooling, and his family circumstances, and these will be taken into account before any decisions are made.

Child abuse
Cases involving child abuse may be dealt with by specialist police officers, or possibly by the inspector heading the community-contact team. A representative of the police will be present at all case conferences to provide relevant and confidential information about the family involved.

Like social workers, the police have a statutory power to remove a child from his home to a 'place of safety' if necessary.(The placement of the child is usually arranged in consultation with the social-services department.) A place-of-safety order taken out by the police expires after eight days, but it does not have to be granted by a magistrate as is the case with a social-services application for a place-of-safety order which then runs for 28 days.

The Department of Health and Social Security (DHSS)

The DHSS is often confused with the social-services department – both may be colloquially referred to as 'the social'. However, they have distinctly separate roles. The DHSS is concerned with recognising *financial need*, assessing and handling claims, and distributing welfare benefits.

At local offices, individuals present claims upon which benefit is calculated. To a limited extent the DHSS staff can advise clients on their entitlement, but the whole system of welfare benefits is extremely complex and time-consuming to work out. Because of the pressure of work and generally low staffing levels, DHSS staff do not have time to examine the intricacies of all claims presented. They are empowered to make emergency cash payments where need is demonstrated. Individual claimants have a responsibility for knowing what they are entitled to, and information in the form of booklets and leaflets is made available in DHSS offices.

Owing to the complexity of the welfare-benefits system, the bureaucratic procedures, and the stigma sometimes felt by claimants, a huge proportion of available benefits remains unclaimed each year. In order to overcome this and to take some of the pressure off counter clerks at local offices, in 1984 the DHSS established a free information and advisory telephone service. People with queries about their personal

Owing to the complexity and volume of claims presented to the DHSS, long delays are often experienced by people seeking financial assistance.

entitlement may phone the operator and ask for the *DHSS Freephone service*. The service will deal with enquiries and make calculations on people's personal entitlement.

DHSS officers also make home visits to people who are unable to make the journey to a local office. If they come across an individual or family whom they consider may need social-work support, they will refer them to the appropriate agency.

Inter-agency co-operation

Child abuse

In 1973 the tragedy of Maria Colwell – the seven-year-old girl who died as a result of sustained maltreatment by her stepfather while officially in the care of the local authority – brought the attention of the general public to the harsh realities of the problem of child abuse. It also highlighted the inadequacy of the collective response of the caring agencies. The public inquiry which followed criticised the professional agencies involved with the family, not only for some of the decisions reached but also for the lack of communication between those agencies. As a result, all local authorities have published guide-lines for those who may be involved in the detection of, or working with, families where non-accidental injury has occurred or is considered likely to occur. Liaison with other agencies is built into the procedure. 'Non-accidental injury' refers to psychological cruelty, physical harm, and sexual abuse.

The non-accidental injury (NAI) register   The names of all children who have been, or are suspected of having been, abused by those in charge of them are placed on the NAI register. Once their names are on the '*at-risk*' register (as it is generally called), the cases are reviewed at regular intervals until such time as all the agencies concerned in working with the family feel that the circumstances have altered sufficiently for the child to no longer be in any danger. This register will be kept in a 'named place' (such as the children's ward in a hospital or in a NSPCC special unit, where this exists) and will be accessible at all hours of the day and night, everyday, to those professionals who are dealing with the family, including the staff of the NSPCC and other voluntary organisations. Parents are not obliged by law to know that their child's name is on the register – it is up to the discretion of the workers involved to decide whether or not this information should be shared with the family. It is feared that in some cases parental knowledge of the fact that their child's name is on the register may result in antagonism towards the child.

According to the Association of Directors of Social Services, 'There are said to be some 50 000 children on "at-risk" registers in this country. Some of these children will be committed to care. Some will be subject to supervision orders. Many will be subject to entirely voluntary supervision.'

151

Once a child is suspected to be the victim of deliberate parental violence, a *case conference* will be arranged to consider what immediate and long-term actions are necessary. All the professional agencies who work with the family will be invited to attend this meeting and will be expected to provide written reports around which discussion can take place. In some cases the emergency removal of a child from his home to a *'place of safety'* will have already been carried out – of necessity, the case conference will then be convened as soon as possible afterwards.

As well as gathering information from all agencies connected with the family, the conference will aim to outline a concerted professional approach towards working with the family. A *keyworker* with primary responsibility for the family will be nominated. Normally this person will be the local-authority social worker but, where the NSPCC has been more closely involved with the family, it may be more appropriate if the NSPCC inspector assumes the role, for the sake of continuity. Similarly, the health visitor may be nominated where she enjoys a trusting relationship with the child and his parents.

A case conference involves the attendance and contribution of a number of different people, each seeing the child and his family from a different perspective:

a) *The senior social worker* may chair the meeting, having specialised knowledge about child abuse and conference procedure.

b) *The child's general practitioner* can provide detailed medical reports on the child and all other members of the family if appropriate.

c) *The health visitor* will be able to comment on the child-care practice within the home, the social setting, and the adequacy of parenting.

d) *The paediatrician* may have had to carry out a detailed medical examination of the child at the hospital – she will report her findings.

e) *The social worker* can provide information about her involvement with the family, their difficulties, their relationships, and their home circumstances.

f) *The NSPCC inspector* may at one time have been involved with the family and can outline the work carried out.

g) *The police* may have been involved in the removal of a child from the home or may have had dealings with the family in the past. This information may be useful to those currently concerned.

h) *The teacher* will be able to comment both on the child's performance in the classroom with regard to learning skills or difficulties in learning and on the way the child relates to other children and adults in the school.

i) *The education welfare officer* (EWO) may have been involved with older children in the family and will report on the children's attendance, as well as on her own involvement with the family.

j) *The probation officer* may attend to give details of her involvement if a member of the family is on her current case-load.

Case conferences enable representatives of various agencies to share knowledge and assess and plan future involvement.

Together, the members of the conference will try to establish how best the child and his parents can be helped and will work towards a situation where the child is no longer at risk.

Case conferences

Case conferences may be called for reasons other than suspected child abuse – for example, to discuss an elderly person in order to decide whether or not he needs to be admitted to an elderly persons' home. Similarly, a children's residential establishment may arrange a case conference to consider whether or not a child should be discharged and allowed to return home. In each case, all the professional workers involved from the various agencies and the staff of the establishment concerned will be invited to attend to offer observations and interpretations of the person's circumstances as seen from their perspective. Sometimes it is appropriate to invite parents or relatives to listen to what is said and to invite them to contribute to the decision that is made. Other agencies who may call a case conference include the housing department and child-guidance clinics.

Case conferences are sometimes held when another agency becomes involved or takes over responsibility – for example, when the Probation Service takes over the responsibility for a juvenile from social services when the youngster has offended and been brought before the court; also,

153

when a family moves to a new area and has been on a NAI register in its previous area.

Case conferences should not be confused with *reviews*, which are usually carried out internally within an establishment or area office without necessarily involving outside organisations. It is statutory that children in care should be officially reviewed at least once every six months, but some are reviewed more often. This procedure gives the main social worker involved (the residential worker if the child is in a home; the field-worker if the child is in the community) an opportunity to outline the work done, consider any existing difficulties, and determine a plan for the future. This will be presented and discussed with senior management and other interested parties.

Although there is not always a legal obligation to do so, other clients are sometimes also reviewed in this fashion – for example, the elderly, the handicapped, and families with difficulties. In addition to social-service departments, other agencies carry out reviews in the same way – for example, probation officers may consider their progress with clients.

Conclusion

This chapter has dealt with the caring services of the statutory agencies other than the Probation Service and the social-services departments. Each agency has its own primary function, too detailed to describe here and beyond the scope of this book. Instead we have sought to outline the social-care functions of these organisations.

The word 'network' was used to describe the relationship of the various agencies in preference to the word 'system', which would have implied the existence of fully integrated services. The statutory agencies developed independently and at different times concerned with their individual spheres of responsibility; consequently even the geographical boundaries of local-authority and non-local-authority services often cut across one another. However, in recent years co-operation and joint planning has increased. This is evident in many fields – nursery centres jointly run by the social-services and the education departments; homeless-family projects combining personnel from local-authority housing, education, and social-services departments; and the inter-agency involvement required to ascertain a child's educational special needs.

During the course of their work, professional carers will make formal contact with workers from other agencies, by phone or letter, or at case conferences or reviews or other meetings. Over a period of time, these contacts will become less formal as each worker strives to reduce bureaucratic delay in seeking help for her client.

The voluntary sector is also part of the caring network and has very strong links with the statutory bodies. The work of the various voluntary agencies will be dealt with in the next chapter.

Appendix 1 – example of a problem presented to the head of the third year in a secondary school

Stephen Terrie is a 13-year-old twin whose brother Michael is also at the school. They have three older sisters who are either still attending or have left the same school. Stephen has a history of sporadic attendance, whereas Michael (who is in a different class) works well and enjoys school. The difference in attitude to work and to school has been most clearly marked since their transition from lower to upper school three months ago.

Monday
Stephen is absent from school all day. His twin brother is unable to offer any reason for this.

Tuesday
Mrs Terrie, the boys' mother, who has expressed an 'anti-school' attitude in the past, calls to see the year tutor, bringing Stephen with her. She begins with an explanation. The previous day, Stephen met his 18-year-old friend in the town centre at 9.00 a.m. and did not return to the family home until 11.00 p.m. When he arrived home, he claimed to have been kidnapped by two men on his way to school. The uniformed branch of the police became involved, and later Stephen was interviewed by the CID. Eventually, at 2.40 p.m., Stephen broke down and admitted that he had made up the story in an attempt to avoid being punished for what he had done.

Response
The head-of-year appreciates the mother's concern, particularly in view of her previous unco-operative attitude towards the school. As a short-term measure, he suggests that Stephen be placed 'on report'. This means that he is given a report card which is to be signed by teachers detailing attendance for morning and afternoon sessions, conduct, and effort made. This card is then stamped daily by the head-of-year and taken home by Stephen and signed by his parents. Thus a detailed up-to-date record of attendance and attitude is obtained. Meanwhile, Stephen is referred to the educational psychologist.

Mrs Terrie is informed that the social-services department could be involved if she would find this useful, perhaps to explore Stephen's relationship with other family members.

At the same time, the year tutor makes himself available to Stephen, saying that he would be happy to see Stephen any time he feels like making an appointment. At present, Stephen is not very forthcoming about why he stays away from school.

Comment
In this case it can be seen that the year tutor does all he can to try to solve

the problem within the school. Problems are often brought into school from outside – from within the family or community – and teachers are restricted in the type of help they can offer.

Appendix 2 – typical duties for a head-of-year

8.20–8.45 Arrive at school. Check mail, notes, letters, court reports, telephone messages, etc. See staff about any outstanding problems. Check staff absences to see if I need to substitute for anyone.

8.45–9.00 Pupils arrive.

8.50 Registration. See as many pupils as possible about chasing up problems/truants. For more difficult problems, tell pupils to come back when I am free.

9.00 Assembly:

Monday – full school assembly.

Tuesday – third-year assembly, led by year tutor.

Wednesday – third- and fourth-year assembly, led by head of upper school. Tutors come to see me.

Thursday and *Friday* – tutor period: pupils see their own tutors. As head-of-year, same as 8.45–9.00.

	Mon.	Tues.	Weds.	Thurs.	Fri.
9.15–10.25	Free*	3rd yr games	Free*	5th yr AC community project	Support†
10.25–10.40			Break		
10.40–11.50	5th yr AC	3rd yr PSE	Support†	5th yr AC	Free*
11.50–12.45			Lunch		
12.45–12.55			Registration		
12.55–14.05	See EWO	4th yr modern studies	5th yr AC	5th yr PSE	3rd yr history
14.10–15.20	3rd yr history	Free*	Free*	4th yr PSE	5th yr modern studies

* Free from teaching. Time spent on phone calls, meetings with parents, social workers, probation officers. See pupils. Write letters.

Sometimes called to classroom to deal with pupils' misbehaviour. Do all my own filing; write up records; do all the jobs I've been putting off for weeks. Write reports for courts or social services.

† Teacher may book me in to go into a class to help with less able pupils, enabling her to work with a smaller group on a specialist topic.

AC = alternative curriculum

EWO = education welfare officer

PSE = personal and social education

15.20 See as many pupils as possible. Some arrive with report cards
onwards checking behaviour/attendance/work. Others arrive with notes from teachers concerning problems related to the day's lessons – behaviour, work, 'no pen', etc. Make phone calls. See parents. See available staff about pupils. Attend meetings (average two or three a week – on personal issues, curriculum, etc.). Try to go to watch my year's teams – cricket, netball, hockey, football, etc. Occasionally make home visits, usually as an emergency – injuries, long-term truancy, both parents working (now quite rare), or parents genuinely unable to get to school.

17.15 Go home – provided there is no union meeting, staff-development course, or parents' evening.

Appendix 3 – annual reports illustrating the scope of a neighbourhood project based in a community centre

Present at annual general meeting

a) Management-committee members:
    Ten local residents,
    Chairperson,
    Vice-chairperson,
    Secretary,
    Treasurer,
    Assistant treasurer.
b) Group representatives:
    Local residents in charge of (six) groups who use the centre:
    gymnasium group,
    local-newspaper group,
    keep-fit group,
    physically handicapped group,
    dance group,
    elderly persons' group.
c) Members of staff:
    Centre manager,

Cook,
Assistant cook,
Caretaker,
Domestic,
Administrator,
Neighbourhood community workers (two),
Youth workers (two),
Adventure-playground workers (two),
Trainee (one).
d) Two representatives from social services management teams.

Written reports presented – abridged versions

Chairperson's report
The year ending in March 1985 was a successful one for the project. Our end-of-year finances were pretty sound, as you will see from the audited accounts, and – apart from the need to abandon the Thursday club – the work of the project has continued and developed throughout the year. I hope you will enjoy reading about some of it in the rest of the report. I am particularly pleased with the way in which there has developed a strong staff team who work well alongside members of the management committee and other volunteers.

However, the whole year was overshadowed by the fight to gain refunding when our Urban Aid grant ran out in March. Right up to the end of March the situation was uncertain. Staff had to be given notice, we had to make application for redundancy payments and contingency plans for the winding-up or radical alteration of the project. Also, it meant that for almost two months all the normal work of the project had to take second place to the time-consuming and expensive business of running our survival campaign. One good spin-off was the close links we made with other voluntary organisations who were also fighting for survival. I hope they will be maintained and strengthened.

So we are now in another year. Our Urban Aid funding is reasonably secure (but not certain) for the next few years. Our priority must be to build up our support at all levels to ensure that, whatever happens, the neighbourhood project will continue to make its contributions to the life of this community.

Centre manager's report
It can be frustrating – you plan all the jobs you need to do in a day, then comes 'Ian, can I see you about something?' or 'Give us a hand with this.' Inevitably, jobs pile up until they become urgent.

Some people think the Centre is just for one group or for one area of the neighbourhood – *it isn't*. The Centre was built because of the efforts of local people who pressurised the council into providing a local centre. The Centre is run by local people who meet every two weeks to plan and run it.

It is *your Centre*. If you don't like it, don't moan – do something about it.

Vandalism has increased this year. This wastes your money. To replace a door costs £50; a new window costs £10. This is your money being wasted.

Thanks this year must go to the following for their help and support in the past years: [various individuals, the brewery, social services, careers services, Probation Service, play resource unit, and area resource centre.]

Ian Jarvis

Cleaner's report

I am the cleaner of the Centre. I just work 20 hours a week, but probably put another 15 on top of that doing voluntary work. I have my ups and downs with the cleaning of the Centre. You can imagine the traffic we have, from the elderly to the children. You get the odd child who thinks the full toilet roll should go down the loo!

I work voluntary in the youth club as the tuck lady. This also means having to go to the cash-and-carry, buying sweets.

I have just taken on another role – helping the retired class on Wednesday afternoons. We do everything: knitting, crocheting, art, dressmaking. It only started last week and it was great. The beautiful things some of the people brought were fantastic, and I can't wait to get going. Anybody who reads this is welcome to come. It is a nice easy-going class with plenty of activity for people who have retired, or who are at home with a couple of hours to spare. You don't have to do anything if you don't want to – just come along for a chat. I'm just waiting now for a class that has something to do with swimming, and maybe I'll be able to fulfil a lifetime dream of being able to swim. Ha Ha!

I might add that if I didn't have the co-operation of my family I wouldn't be able to put in all these hours at the Centre. My husband takes some stick! It goes without saying that we need all the help we can get, and if there are any functions at the Centre please come along – it's your Centre, use it.

Bye for now.

Irene Drummond

Report of the neighbourhood workers.

This year has seen the neighbourhood worker less involved with groups he was once regularly involved with. This is partly because some of them don't need a neighbourhood worker any more, and also because this worker has been only working 16 hours a week since Christmas. His area of responsibility is work with elderly people, the *Splash* community-newspaper group, and a diminishing contact with the street residents' association. The other part-time neighbourhood worker is responsible for work with residents' associations and other adult groups. We both have work to do with the entire project which overlies all our other tasks.

Elderly people in the community

As a project we offer elderly people a range of opportunities:

a) *The lunch club* The worker spent time in the early part of the year producing leaflets (using the offset litho machine acquired by *Splash*) and visiting district nurses, health visitors, doctors, and social workers to publicise this. This led to a small handful of newcomers, but there is need for more work here.

b) *Pensioners' social afternoon* There is a report on this elsewhere. The worker attends as much as possible – to help, talk, and listen.

c) *Help for individuals* The worker is responsible for trying to meet requests for help from individuals. These are for decorating, gardening, welfare rights, and problems of isolation. The difficulty is that it is not appropriate for the worker to spend much time helping individuals himself. He depends on people in the area who want to do this kind of thing – and he must find ways of meeting such people, as well as meeting the individuals who need assistance. Unfortunately this remains a haphazard and only intermittently successful enterprise. Occasionally an appeal to an existing group – residents or an interest group – has brought forward one or two kindhearted offers.

Occasionally heaven sends a person who walks into the office or is referred by the Council for Voluntary Service. At such times we are able to get on with a number of helping tasks – including welcoming people back from hospital (an area where we always do our best to meet requests for help, in order to retain our contact with hospitals).

Residents' associations are beginning to play a part in organising trips and paying attention to the needs of retired people in their areas. The project is indirectly involved here through the support it has given to these associations.

The picture is patchy, but this area of work is strengthening – particularly as the worker now has fewer responsibilities in other areas. Developments described below are also going to have an effect.

d) *Activity afternoons* It is easier to look towards a group activity as a way of meeting people's needs than to consider individual cases. For this reason, work towards the development of retired people's activity afternoons has taken up a good deal of time for a group of people since June. At the time of writing, the first successful session has just been held.

e) *Entertainment* We have only arranged one music hall since the last annual report – which is a pity, as they are so popular.

f) *Local history* Partly springing from interest aroused by *Splash* and through contact of one of *Splash*'s members with local historian Mary Cooper, we arranged for and publicised a short course on the history of the district. This led to a further course planned for the winter.

Conclusion

The range of opportunities and interests is expanding. As it grows, the

160

worker hopes that areas where we are weak at present will gain in strength.

'Splash' community newspaper
The height of its success was at Christmas. Since then, the burden of work has fallen on a few dedicated shoulders. The worker fervently hopes it will begin to attract more support, since he is sure it is one of the most useful services provided in the neighbourhood. Despite the contracting group of producers, it continues to appear regularly and achieves an undoubtedly high standard – much thanks for which must go to the community education worker, John Murphy, who has done most to train previously inexperienced people in the skills of production.

Other groups

a) *Ringley Street residents* have seen a successful year which is entirely their own achievement. The worker no longer 'works' with them.

b) *The anglers*   Until Easter, the worker was still involved in helping to arrange meetings, but his involvement has declined. Any new work with them is the responsibility of the other neighbourhood worker.

c) *Greendale residents*   The worker spent time with this group in the first half of the year – in particular helping them to organise their first clean-up day and giving advice about the organising of meetings and contacting appropriate agencies. There is no space to detail this work. The other neighbourhood worker now liaises with this group.

d) *The gymnasium*   Again a diminished involvement, but in the early part of the year a crisis concerning coaching and management meant increased involvement and time was also spent silk-screening posters with members.

Neighbourhood project
Management-training preparations occupied a considerable amount of time and have been indirectly productive in that plans laid earlier have been incorporated into the training course organised by the law centre. Refunding problems in April meant the aborting of this work. Time has also been spent on standing in for the centre manager, staff meetings, and management meetings. The refunding crisis in February–April was a disturbing experience to us all. For many months we did not know if the project would survive, and we still carry scars from that period. Hopefully we will be given the time to heal them.

Norman Bates

The other half – a report by the second neighbourhood worker
I've now been working on the project as a neighbourhood worker for a bit over two months and find the work interesting, varied, and exciting. I'm impressed by the number of groups around the area and by how much they've managed to achieve.

Some groups/things I'm involved with:

a) *The anglers* need very little help, being a very well run group. I've mainly carried messages between the club and the Recreation Department and parks police. I'm also trying to find a minibus for an angling holiday.

b) *Greendale residents* are another going concern. I've liaised between the group and the Centre, and produced a questionnaire on repairs for them.

c) *Mums and toddlers* The mums have expressed a wish to be involved in educational activities. I took three mums and kids to an 'Education for women' day at the polytechnic, which they found interesting and useful. As a follow-up, a worker from TUBE (Trade Union and Basic Education – part of the Workers' Educational Association) is coming next month to discuss with the mums the setting up of an educational course at the Centre.

d) *Middlewood residents* (just formed) have so far had two meetings. I'm giving support and encouragement, doing leaflets, and attending meetings.

e) *The recreation group* seems to be having a few difficulties, so I attend meetings and have suggested a new money-banking system.

f) *Individual/one-off counselling* Welfare rights, hospital visiting, discussions with local people on their local needs (e.g. bowling club, Hillier Street).

g) *The project.* Yes, and sometimes the project management committee, or staff group, needs some help sorting things out too. Help has taken the form of discussing problems with people, bullying people for Annual Report contributions, and typing.

Reg Evlyn

Administrator

Before I came to the project, I used to work in an efficient and tidy office in the centre of town. Misguided as I was, I thought the set-up at the project would be the same. Needless to say I was wrong!

At this moment I am surrounded by crisps, drinks, and toffees for the summer playscheme; 20 reams of paper for *Splash* (a user group); jumble for a sale being held to raise money for a retired people's activity afternoon; and (somewhere underneath it all) my work.

The work, however – when I get to it – is fascinating. No two days are the same, no day goes by without a problem, and the time passes so quickly that without a phone call from my husband or my two starving children I forget what time it is.

It is difficult to be as efficient as I would like, and at first that used to worry me. I realise now that it's the people who use the Centre that matter and that – as long as I keep up to date with the books and wages – the filing system I planned to introduce and the tidiness of the place can afford to wait a little longer. Luckily I have had a lot of help. Cath, our office trainee, apart from her regular duties, provides endless cups of tea and chatter, and for the first few months of my job I was blessed with a volunteer named Mehrnaz, who with her accurate typing and happy personality made life at the project a lot easier.

Nevertheless, it has taken a long time to get used to the complexities of the funding arrangements and the way in which money is allocated and budgeted for the various areas of work, and it is only now, after eight months as administrator, that I am aware of the amount of careful thought that has to go into every decision. It is no easy task to provide services on a limited budget such as ours, especially when each section of the work seems as important as the others. All I can do is express my admiration for both the management committee and the volunteers for the amount of work they are prepared to put into the project so that they, alongside the staff, can provide this area with the basis of the community it so desperately needs.

It seems a long time since the days I spent in my tidy and efficient town office and the certainty of finishing at 5.00 p.m. on the dot, but somehow I'd rather suffer the trials and tribulations of working in a Centre such as ours and go home each night tired but satisfied.

K. Ellwood

Exercise 1 – role-play – an example of a case presented to a head-of-year

8.50 Mrs Knell and her daughter Wendy (aged 15) arrive at the head-of-year's office without an appointment. Mrs Knell slams down a tin of glue, saying that last night she went into her daughter's room and found Wendy semiconscious. Mrs Knell would like to know 'Is the school going to do anything about this?'

Roles

1. *Wendy* This was the first time you had used solvents at home, but you have sniffed glue outside the home several times.
2. *Wendy's mother* Angry and desperate, expecting the school to be able to provide a solution.
3. *Head-of-year* You decide on the head-of-year's response.

Task
Role-play the scene (10 minutes).

Exercise 2 – role-play – an example of a problem presented to a form tutor

Jenny Best is 16 years old and in the fifth form of a comprehensive school. During the second year she had attendance problems for a few weeks, around the time that her mother remarried. Since then she has worked well, and she is now preparing to take her O-levels.

She has always been overweight and, since she broke her leg four weeks ago, has recently depended on her stepfather to bring her to and pick her up from school.

One morning when he brings her to school, her stepfather rather angrily points out to the form teacher, Miss Martin, in front of Jenny, that he has had 'enough of Jenny's behaviour at home', which is rapidly deteriorating. Mr Best is asking for some kind of help from the teacher.

As soon as her stepfather leaves, Jenny breaks down and starts to cry.

Roles

1. *Jenny*

   a) You are anxious about your forthcoming exams. Your teachers expect you to pass them, but you feel that you will not be able to do enough work in time.
   b) You are worried about your weight. Being immobile with a broken leg is adding to your problem.
   c) You have recently discovered that your stepfather is having an affair with another woman. Your mother is aware of this.
   d) You are the oldest of three children, but your brother and sister are too young to talk seriously with. Since you have been studying for your O-levels, you have lost contact with your best friend and do not really know whom to talk to.
   e) You like Miss Martin and have done so since she taught you English in the second year.

2. *Miss Martin*

   a) You like Jenny and feel that she is a good student, capable of doing very well provided she continues to work hard.
   b) You have other teaching duties (a class in ten minutes).
   c) You could see her for some time after school.

Task

Role-play the talk between Jenny and Miss Martin.

Exercise 3A – a points system for housing allocation

Devise your own points system for housing allocation, based on the categories already outlined in this chapter. You can decide on which category should be allocated the highest number of points – for example, start with 100 points and apportion them between the categories you decide upon.

Exercise 3B – allocation of a one-bedroomed dwelling

Apply your points system to the following applicants for a one-bedroomed dwelling and establish a priority waiting list:

a) *Mrs Silcock* (49) lives alone in a bed-sitter. She has no separate kitchen and shares the bathroom with six other people. The bed-sitter is damp and in poor condition. Mrs Silcock has recently had a stroke and would like to move nearer to the hospital where she attends regularly for physiotherapy.

b) *Mr Worrell* (35) is single and currently in prison. He would like accommodation on his release in four weeks' time. He has the prospect of full-time work locally.

c) *Mr Zambos* (32) is single and living at home with his mother and father in a three-bedroomed flat. He would like to move nearer to the city centre, where he works as a shop manager. At the moment it takes him an hour and a half to get to work each morning by public transport.

d) *Ms Fadel* (46) is a voluntary patient in a psychiatric hospital where she has been staying for three months. She is being encouraged by nursing staff to leave the hospital and is ready to move out but has nowhere to live. She would like self-contained accommodation near to her parents, who live in a small council flat.

e) *Mr Thorburn* (27) is unmarried and a tenant in a one-bedroomed multi-storey flat. He has a full-time job and is studying for A-levels at night school. He would like eventually to go to university. He finds the noise and music from the surrounding flats distracting and would like to be transferred to a quieter area.

f) *Mr Grogan* (28) is legally separated from his wife but is still living in the three-bedroomed family home with her and their three children. He sleeps on the sofa in the living room and shares all the facilities of the home. Mrs Grogan is distressed and has repeatedly asked him to leave, but he claims that he has nowhere else to go.

g) *Mrs Hutchins* (59) is a divorcee who lives in a three-bedroomed house. This is now too big for her needs, as all her children have left home. She would like a smaller dwelling – preferably a ground-floor flat, as she has arthritis and climbing stairs is difficult for her.

Exercise 3C – allocation of a three-bedroomed dwelling

Apply your points system to the following applicants for a two- or three-bedroomed dwelling and establish a priority waiting list:

a) *Mr and Mrs Connelly* own their own three-bedroomed house. Their daughter is physically disabled and now too heavy to be carried upstairs. They would like ground-floor accommodation with bathroom facilities at ground level.

b) *Mr and Mrs Lynch* and their two sons and daughter are tenants of a three-bedroomed house. The family is the victim of racial harassment, and recently youths physically assaulted their home, breaking a window and damaging the front door. They would like to move away from the area, particularly because the children are becoming distressed.

c) *Mrs Hanson* is a young single mother who cares for her six-year-old daughter in their two-bedroomed council flat. Mrs Hanson has recently been violently attacked by the child's father and fears further violence. She feels that the only way she can be safe is to move out of the area altogether.

d) *Richard (Lord) and Dianne (Turner)* are a young couple lodging with Richard's parents. Dianne is expecting a baby within the next two months, and they have been asked to leave before the baby arrives.

e) *Mrs Carroll* is a single parent and lives with her young twin sons in a two-bedroomed council flat. The neighbour below keeps complaining unduly about noise from their flat. She writes abusive letters and shouts foul language along the corridor. Mrs Carroll is very anxious and has been prescribed sedatives by her doctor. She would like to move to another area.

f) *Mrs Eduh* is a widow who, together with her adult daughter, lodges in a one-bedroomed flat. Mrs Eduh has arthritis and finds the stairs difficult. They are sharing facilities with the landlord, who now would like them to leave as he intends selling his house.

g) *Mrs Thompson* has been living in another part of the country in army accommodation with her husband and two children. The couple's marriage has now broken down, and she would like to return to her city of origin and obtain two-bedroomed accommodation for herself and two children.

Questions for essays or discussion

1. There is often much 'stigma' attached to those who suffer from mental illness. Why do you think society feels so differently about physical and mental illness?

2. Compared with other EEC countries, pre-school provision in the UK is low. In countries like France and Belgium, 90% of three- to five-year-olds have full-time places in nursery schools or their equivalent. What advantages – particularly to the socially disadvantaged child – can be had from nursery provision?

3. If you were a detached youth worker, how would you set about your task of reaching young people isolated in the community?

4. There are very few black policemen in this country. Why do you think this is so and what can be done to improve recruitment from ethnic-minority members of society?

5. Some people argue that it is important for professional carers – social workers, teachers, and community workers – to actually live in the area in which they work, in order to more fully understand the families whom they are seeking to help and to identify with the needs of the community. Consider the advantages or disadvantages of this proposition.

6. Consider the statement 'All single homeless people are vulnerable by their very circumstances and should be offered support.'

Further reading

1. *Community health and social services*. Brian Davies (Hodder, 4th edition 1984). An account of the structure of the community health services and their relationship to the social services.
2. *Shelter election briefings and information*. Shelter, 157 Waterloo Road, London SE1 8XF. Up-to-date facts and figures reflecting the state of the current housing situation with the various arguments and counter-arguments on housing policy issues.
3. *The FAC book – a history of the Moss Side Family Advice Centre* (Manchester Free Press, Youth Development Trust, 1981). An account of the creative contribution made by ordinary people to the life of the community.
4. *What health visitors do*, June Clark (Royal College of Nursing of the UK, 1981). A close look at the practice of the health visitor.
5. *Special education, the way ahead – children with special needs*, John Fish (Open University Press, 1985). A look at the main issues concerning the development of special education.
6. *Inside the British police – a force at work*, Simon Holdaway (Blackwell, 1983). A readable comprehensive review of our modern police force.

5   The voluntary sector

Introduction

Thousands of *voluntary organisations* make up what we know as the *'voluntary sector'*. This term refers to all the *non-statutory organisations* which contribute in various ways to social welfare. Unlike *statutory* organisations, voluntary bodies are not set up by means of *statute*, and the majority are not controlled by central or local government. Many of them have *charitable status* and are non-profit-making.

There are something like 350 000 different voluntary organisations in the UK today. About 40% of these are *registered as charities*. This means that the *Charity Commissioners* in England (or the Inland Revenue in Scotland and Northern Ireland) have been satisfied that they meet at least one of certain conditions – namely that they benefit the community in some way, advance education or religion, or relieve poverty – and do not engage in political activity. The advantages gained by being a registered charity are tax and rate relief and being able to receive money in the form of covenants at beneficial rates.

It is important not to be confused between voluntary bodies and voluntary work performed by *volunteers*. A voluntary body is a non-statutory organisation. Some happen to be staffed by unpaid volunteers, but others use no volunteers at all – they employ only salaried staff. It is the status of an *organisation* that makes it voluntary, not the status of the staff working within it. Many statutory agencies use volunteers too – an example is the social-services departments' use of volunteers to visit the elderly living in the community. Although these volunteers are unpaid, they may receive all or part of any expense incurred in travelling or subsistence.

Having said this, most voluntary bodies do rely on volunteers to perform a wide variety of tasks. Two examples may make the situation clearer:

i) 'Age Concern' employs salaried staff at its central office and elsewhere, but recruits volunteers to work with old people in its local branches.

ii) 'Mind' (the National Association for Mental Health) employs salaried staff for its national-organisation functions, but volunteers are used at local level to counsel distressed people who seek help.

Many voluntary bodies employ professionally qualified workers in salaried posts, just as statutory services do. Two examples are CQSW-qualified staff working for the NSPCC or Family Service Units (both voluntary organisations) and trained nursery nurses working in voluntary-sector playgroups.

We can further differentiate between the voluntary and *private* sectors in social care. Voluntary organisations are non-profit-making. Private bodies are profit-making – they therefore cannot register as charities, and their income is derived from fees charged to the users of their services. However, private concerns can be inspected by statutory local or central-government inspectors – an example is the inspection of the rapidly growing number of private homes for the elderly.

Sometimes the voluntary sector is referred to as the *'voluntary movement'*. This is an over-simplification, because it implies that there is a consensus as to the general purpose, or philosophy, of this large array of groups. In fact, they thrive on diversity.

Origins

Back in the mid nineteenth century, when the first voluntary organisations were founded, they were known as *'charities'*. The word is derived from the Latin word *'caritas'*, which means 'regard, esteem, affection, love'. Dr Barnardo's was founded in 1866, the Church of England Children's Society in 1881, and the NSPCC in 1884. Even as early as 1861, there were no less than 640 charities in London alone, and there was a great deal of confusion and overlapping of services – so much so that in 1869 the Charity Organisation Society (COS) was formed in order to conserve efforts and plan more rationally.

The growth of voluntary initiative was at first piecemeal and haphazard, as a variety of small organisations were started by a few wealthy people. This happened during a period of great economic prosperity for the rich. The situation of the poor, however, worsened under the harsh Poor Law of 1834, as its provision of 'poor relief' actually had the unfortunate effect of punishing and stigmatising recipients.

In many well-meaning, philanthropic, and (very often) Christian people, this social and economic climate led to the awakening of an altruistic concern to ease the plight of the poor. It is no surprise to find the various denominations of the Christian church very active in the foundation of many of the first major charitable concerns. The Church of England and later the Salvation Army were greatly involved. 'Good works' were thought to be of paramount importance to those motivated by their Christian faith.

Most of the early individual charitable pioneers were either wealthy businessmen or people of independent means. There were some who were not driven solely by altruistic motives, as, with the growing disparity between rich and poor, there was much concern to maintain the social order and avoid civil unrest and conflict.

The range of activity

The above is a simplified and somewhat generalised outline of the historical background of voluntary organisations. The work of such organisations today is much more varied and diverse. Some are formed to cater for a particular social need – 'Help the Aged', for example. Some provide for a minority group in society – 'Gingerbread' for one-parent families, for example. Others act as *pressure groups*, attempting to influence Government policy – for example, 'CHAR', the campaign for the single homeless. Still others are *self-help* groups that provide mutual support for people who share a common problem – 'Alcoholics Anonymous', for instance.

Despite gloomy predictions that the present depressed economic climate would cause many voluntary groups to founder, the voluntary sector appears to be in a lively and healthy state. In fact over the past twenty-five years there has been phenomenal growth in the voluntary sector, with more new groups being formed than at any other time.

Today there is a bewildering diversity of voluntary bodies, which range from large groups catering for many thousands of people – NACRO (the National Association for the Care and Resettlement of Offenders) or SCODA (the Standing Conference on Drug Abuse), for example – to the specific groups catering for a much smaller client population – such as the Brittle Bone Society or 'Wireless for the Bedridden'.

Some are organised on a national basis, disseminating information and services across the country; others are tiny, catering for the interests of a very small group in a particular locality. Whatever the diversity and range of activity, we can be sure that the total number of people involved is very large, and that our society would be very different without the massive amount of hard work and goodwill they contribute.

Relationship with the statutory sector

The Beveridge Report of 1942, which led to the official creation of the Welfare State, spoke of voluntary groups as being *'society's conscience'*. Such groups can keep in touch with changing needs in society and respond to them as they arise. Their smallness, and the resulting flexibility of organisation and management, often means that they are better placed to defend and champion the interests of minorities in society than are the statutory services.

It is wrong to think of the voluntary and statutory services as being in competition. Obviously, as new legislation was introduced to officially establish statutory social services (especially after the Second World War), many voluntary organisations, whose functions had been superseded, ceased to exist. There was no need for them to continue, to merely duplicate provision.

It is more correct to think of the statutory and voluntary services as providing *different kinds of assistance*. The Seebohm Report of 1968 stressed that voluntary services were not a secondary type of support to statutory services but the source of a different quality of help, as can be seen in their 'developing citizen participation in revealing new needs and in exposing short-comings in the [statutory] services'.

There is often less *stigma* involved in someone being in touch with a voluntary group, or with others who share the same problem, rather than with a statutory social-work agency. Furthermore, being on the case-load of a statutory social-work agency can cause a person to be dependent, to lose initiative, and possibly bring about an 'us and them' situation – the providers and the provided for. This can clearly be unhealthy.

The relationship between the voluntary sector and the statutory services is, at its best, one of partnership and complementation, rather than competition. A good example of this is how the NSPCC works with social-services departments to safeguard the interests of children at risk and to take preventive measures.

In a similar way, volunteers should not compete with salaried staff but work in co-ordination with them. The 1969 Aves Report, produced by the National Institute for Social Work (NISW) and the National Council for Social Services, examined the role of the voluntary worker in the personal social services. It defined the role of the volunteer as being *complementary* to the work of employed staff.

Finally, it is interesting to question whether the healthy revitalisation of the voluntary sector since 1960 is due to an increase in general public concern or to a growing frustration with statutory services, officialdom, and bureaucratic 'red tape'.

Some examples of voluntary organisations

It is obviously impossible to give a comprehensive review of the voluntary sector – this would involve a massive, if not impossible, task. There is the added problem of the speed at which the situation changes. What follows is therefore an account of some of the more important and innovatory voluntary organisations – some very old and well established, and others quite recent arrivals on the voluntary scene. Details of some other well known voluntary organisations are given in appendix 2 to this chapter.

The National Society for the Prevention of Cruelty to Children (NSPCC)
A particular concern in the second half of the nineteenth century was the predicament of many children who were either exploited for their labour potential or mistreated, neglected, or abused. Three of the large voluntary organisations which still care for children today were formed at this time: Dr Barnardo's in 1866, the Church of England Children's Society in 1881, and the NSPCC in 1884. Dr Barnardo, as well as founding his own charity, was one of the founder members of the NSPCC. From its origins in Liverpool in 1883, it started work in London and its organisation soon spread to provide national coverage for England, Wales, and Northern Ireland. (In

Scotland, its sister group is the Royal Scottish Society for the Prevention of Cruelty to Children.)

The NSPCC marked its centenary in 1984, and in these hundred years it has protected over nine million children. Today, approximately 50 000 are helped each year. About 8% of these are thought to be actual cases of non-accidental injury (child abuse). Other cases involve neglect, sometimes long-term; children regularly left alone at home all day or for many hours; the problems experienced by one-parent families; and families suffering from poverty or other deprivation. It is much better understood today how a poor physical environment – bad housing and inadequate financial or material resources – will pressurise a family and often lead to marital tension and break-up. All of this inevitably means that children will suffer.

The role of the NSPCC has changed considerably over the years. At first it was an investigative and prosecuting organisation which frequently resorted to the courts to get protection for children. Today, it is *not* a prosecuting society – very few of the cases in which it is involved actually go through the courts. The NSPCC is actually in a unique position for a voluntary body – it has the authority to take legal action on behalf of a child, and it also has access to the 'child-abuse' (or 'at-risk') non-accidental injury register which (as mentioned in chapter 4) contains details of families where children have either been abused or are at high risk of being abused. Naturally, the NSPCC works closely with other agencies such as the police, social-services departments, and health services. Many of its staff are professionally qualified, having the Certificate of Qualification in Social Work (CQSW).

In its earlier days it worked more with children, in isolation, but today the NSPCC is very much concerned with helping the whole family to over-come problems and difficulties. It does *not* wish to see families split up, with children taken away and placed in care: it is concerned to help families stay together and work through their difficulties with help and support. Obviously, in a few desperate cases, children will have to be removed for their own safety – the safety and welfare of the child will take precedence. However, it is *prevention* of abuse which is stressed today, and the Society hopes to put far more resources into this in the future.

The NSPCC employs over 200 salaried *inspectors* – each one works in a particular area. The work of the inspector is still central to the Society's activities, and it employs both men and women to provide a 24 hour avail-ability service throughout the country. Cases for investigation will be referred to the inspectors from concerned members of the public, relatives, and other agencies, but about one-third of all cases are referred by the parents themselves, realising that they need help. The inspector will spend most of his time visiting families in their own homes.

However, the inspectors are only one aspect of the NSPCC's work. There are now 14 '*special units*' which provide a 24 hour highly skilled family service which includes psychological and psychiatric assessment for parents or children. The special units also maintain the child-abuse

172

NSPCC special units encourage the whole family to relate freely in an informal atmosphere while staff offer support.

register. The units seem to have been successful – reports from their areas indicate that they have significantly reduced the rates of fatality, serious injury, and re-injury. Sometimes the units will host *case conferences* where representatives of all agencies involved with a family can meet together to discuss progress and plan ahead. NSPCC research based on special-unit registers reckons that one child dies every week in Britain as a result of abuse and that at least 5100 receive non-accidental injury each year.

The Society also runs 65 playgroups containing a large number of children who have been or are at risk of being abused or who are deprived. In these groups, play is seen to be therapeutic because it stimulates children whose development has often been hampered by a poor home environment.

Four *day-care centres* (originally called '*family centres*') in Leeds, Manchester, Northampton, and Shotton (North Wales) are specially designed to 'treat' the whole family. Central to this is the involvement of the parents in the activities of their children as much as possible. Numbers are kept low so that familes can receive as much individual attention as possible from NSPCC staff.

In a few areas, *child-protection teams* have been formed, and the Society plans to extend them nationally. Such teams work in small geographical areas and, through the medium of group work and day-care facilities, there is a stress on educational work with families and fellow-professionals.

In 1964, the 'Emergency Relief and Welfare Department' was established by the Society. This can provide such items as clothing, bedding, and other household articles in emergencies. Some financial assistance can also be offered, as well as small grants from a *welfare fund* which helps to pay outstanding bills. At Christmas, supporters of the NSPCC provide thousands of toys for needy children. In the summer, holidays and outings are arranged.

Over 80% of the Society's funds come from the public, most of it as a result of the NSPCC's own fund-raising activities. The 16% provided by central and local government in the form of grants is only payable for specific purposes. Volunteers are very much involved in the NSPCC – they are recruited at both headquarters and local-branch level, and the work the Society carries out would be impossible without them.

Children are important supporters also. In 1891 the League of Pity was founded, and in 1980 this became the *NSPCC Young League*. There are about 40 000 child members, and it raises one-seventh of the Society's income.

The Pre-school Playgroups Association (PPA)

During the Second World War it was necessary for women to be employed in jobs that were normally carried out by men. With men away abroad, women worked in munition factories and in many other traditional male work-roles. As a result, young children had to be catered for outside the home, and so day-nursery provision was made widely available. However, with the end of the war, this provision shrank. There were more day nurseries in 1945 than there are today. In March 1984 there were 753 local-authority day nurseries in the UK, providing places for 32 852 children.

Given this unsatisfactory situation, many people felt concern about the lack of pre-school provision for the under-fives. One person, Belle Tutaev, a mother, wrote to *The Guardian* newspaper to appeal to other mothers of young children to provide, in co-operation with others, for their children's play and general pre-school experience. This letter, published on 25 August 1961, proved to be the stimulus for the start of the playgroup boom of the 1960s. There are now something like 15 000 groups in England and Wales alone. The co-ordinating body for the majority of these groups is the Pre-school Playgroups Association (PPA), founded in July 1962. The PPA moved into its first centralised office in 1964, and since then its growth has been extremely rapid.

In 1974, the annual general meeting of the PPA agreed on a 'statement of aims'. This reads, 'PPA exists to help parents to understand and provide for the needs of their young children. It aims to promote community situations in which parents can, with growing confidence and enjoyment, make the best use of their knowledge and resources in the development of their children and themselves.' Central to this is the encouragement of the formation of playgroups and the active involvement

174

Playgroups provide an opportunity for pre-school children to benefit from supervised group play.

of parents in providing them. The PPA is a registered charity and has about 350 voluntary area organisers and branches. It has a small salaried staff at its headquarters in London.

Despite the hard work of the PPA, there still exists an enormous need for full-time day care for the under-fives. Even the legal position of playgroups is not clearly defined. However, they are covered by the Nurseries and Child Minders Regulation Act 1948. Under this Act, they have to be classified as either *day nurseries* (if in non-domestic premises) or *childminders* (if in a private house). The Act stipulates the amount of floor space there should be per child, the number of toilets and handbasins necessary, and the adult/child ratio of the group. Planning permission is required, along with the fire department's approval.

Playgroups are either managed privately (by one person or a partnership) or by the community – in the form of a group-elected committee. Most fall into the latter category. A good playgroup is thought to consist of no more than 20 children (at a time) aged from three to five years, with three to five adults assisting in leadership. As the PPA stresses, it is very much a situation of adults and children learning and growing together through the medium of *play*. It means that parents are greatly involved in the growth and development of their children as well as interacting with other parents. The PPA is also keen to involve teenagers in participating in playgroups.

Since the 1960s, the value of play has been increasingly recognised. It provides new experiences for children alongside other children, as well as adults. It helps them to learn more about their environment and their own place within it. It encourages them to think, to use their imagination, and to indulge in their own fantasies and dreams. It is also a good preparation for school and benefits a child more than if the child had remained at home where there would be little contact with other children and adults.

Good facilities in a playgroup should involve sand, water, clay, dough, paint, and junk. Books and spoken stories should provide further stimulation, and there should also be aids for physical activities – climbing frames and slides, for example. Plants and other living things are an important part of a child's learning, and creative pursuits like painting, cooking, and singing should be included. Finally, a good playgroup might also provide opportunities for outdoor play.

There are more children in playgroups than in any other form of pre-school provision. One of their limitations is their *part-time* nature – on average, playgroups are open for just over 2½ days per week, and naturally this limits the aims of a parent wanting full-time work.

Almost 20% of the groups affiliated to the PPA are *parent-and-toddler groups* for parents and children under three years. There has been a rapid growth in the number of these groups since the mid-1970s. Compared to playgroups, they are less formally organised and are not usually run by a committee. Under DHSS regulations, they do not have to *register* with the social-services department – this is because children in a parent-and-toddler group will always be with at least one parent and not necessarily with someone employed as a playleader.

Both playgroups and parent-and-toddler groups usually enjoy a good relationship with the social-services department and other local agencies and groups. The social-services department is often a source of good advice to groups, or to those intending to set up groups.

Permanent fund-raising activities are necessary in order to equip a playgroup, but grants from the local authority can be received for various purposes – a playleader's salary, rent of premises, or the initial cost of setting up a group, for example.

The PPA has proved a very successful venture. It has meant that parents have had opportunities to become far more involved with their children's growth and development, and the involvement has developed parents' confidence and organising skills. It is an excellent example of a *self-help* voluntary organisation which has provided an educational service and also furthered the social interaction of many thousands of children and adults.

Women's Aid Federation (England) (WAF(E))

Male violence towards women has always existed. Traditionally, women have had to suffer it silently – there was little publicity about it, and it was regarded as a taboo subject as far as conversation was concerned. A heightened social conscience and better informed public opinion in the 1960s caused the problem of male violence to become more exposed. The media began to talk of 'battered wives' or 'battered women', and women themselves started to act to deal with the problem that made so many of their lives an unbearable misery.

After writing a book (*Scream quietly or the neighbours will hear*), which dealt in some detail with male violence towards women, *Erin Pizzey* opened the first '*refuge*' for women victims in Chiswick, London, in 1971. Since then the number of such places has grown dramatically, but it is admitted, even officially, that provision is inadequate to deal with the need.

Women's Aid Federation (England) was founded in 1975 to encourage the provision of refuges, to help female sufferers of male violence, and to generally educate the public as to the nature and extent of the problem. Provision for women in Wales, Scotland, and Northern Ireland is organised separately.

In its publication *How we work* (1983), the full objectives of WAF(E) are set out by the organisation itself as follows:

i) 'To provide temporary refuge, on request, for women and their children who have suffered mental or physical harassment.

ii) To encourage the women to determine their own futures and to help them achieve them, whether this involves returning home or starting a new life elsewhere.

iii) To recognise and care for the emotional needs of the children involved.

iv) To offer support and advice and help to any woman who asks for it, whether or not she is a resident, and also to offer support and after-care to any woman or child who has left the refuge.

v) To educate and inform the public, the media, the police, the courts, social services and other authorities, with respect to the battering of women, mindful of the fact that this is the result of the general position of women in our society.'

The organisation has not sought charitable status. It relies on volunteers at both national and local level – without them it could not function. Some funding comes from local authorities but, because cuts have been made under current economic policy, Woman's Aid groups have had to resort more and more to their own fund-raising. This often makes the security of a project very uncertain.

There are over 130 Women's Aid groups in England. Most run refuges for women and children. Some run other projects as well, such as 'half-way houses', advice centres, drop-in centres, and educational and publicity facilities. Some have their own workshops – for printing, for example.

Referrals come either directly or through the social-services department, the Probation Service, citizens advice bureaux, the Samaritans, or the police. Many women hear of Women's Aid's facilities through friends or relatives. Mental and sexual or other physical abuse are dealt with. In some areas '*rape crisis centres*' exist where volunteers will counsel the

177

Women's refuges can offer immediate support to women in need.

victims of rape, sexual assault, or harrassment. Many of these groups have close links with WAF(E) and some are actually run by Women's Aid.

Refuges provide temporary accommodation for women for however long they need it. During her stay, a woman will be helped to make plans for her future and consider the various alternatives (such as going back to the marital home, finding new accommodation, or moving out of the area altogether). WAF(E) stresses, however, that only the woman herself knows what is best for her and her wishes must be respected. Persuasion, or influence, is not used. The address of the refuge will be secret – to avoid interference from men and to ensure that women have a 'breathing-space'. There is a national '*open-door*' policy which ensures that no woman is ever turned away – if a refuge is full, then a referral will be made elsewhere.

As a result of social surveys, it is thought that at least 25% of *all violent crime* is inflicted by men *on women in the home*. However, much of this violence goes unreported for various reasons:

a) Women fear further violence from men if they go to the authorities.
b) The police are reluctant to get involved in what they regard as 'domestic' incidents and, because of this, women are often reluctant to contact them.
c) Some women may regard violence as an accepted part of a relationship with a man.
d) Many women feel a sense of shame at being the victim of violence.
e) Women may fear that they will be separated from their children, either

temporarily or permanently, if they contact the authorities.

f) Some religious-minded women fear betrayal of their marriage vows and, consequently, their partner.

The legal safeguards for women have improved over recent years, but they are still felt to be inadequate by many people. Under the Domestic Violence and Matrimonial Proceedings Act 1976, a woman can apply to a court for an *injunction*. This is an order of the court which forbids someone to do something – in this case, it can forbid a man to assault, molest, harass, or even go near a woman. An injunction can also *order someone to do something* – it can order a man to leave the home, even if he owns it or the tenancy is solely in his name. To apply for an injunction, it is no longer necessary for a woman to start separation or divorce proceedings.

It is also possible now for a judge to attach a power of *arrest* to an injunction, and the police have a *duty* to investigate such a case. If an arrest is made, the person can be held in custody for up to 24 hours. In order to attach a power of arrest, the judge must be satisfied that a woman has suffered *actual bodily harm* (a visible bruise or wound) and that she is likely to do so again. This has limitations, because women have to undergo visible physical harm before any legal protection can be afforded.

A woman made homeless by having left the matrimonial home must be provided with accommodation by the local-authority housing department if she falls into certain categories of *priority need*. These are

i) if she has dependent children – all those under 16, or under 19 if in education, training, or unemployed school leavers;

ii) if she is pregnant;

iii) if she is at risk through disablement or old age.

Critics of this provision rightly point out that a woman rehoused is often forced to accept substandard housing and given no alternative.

Women's Aid is a good example of a self-help organisation which acts in several different roles. It is a *pressure group* for change; it provides *direct* help and support; and it also educates the public on various issues. In 1975 the (central) Government Select Committee on Violence in Marriage recommended that there should be sufficient refuges to provide at least one family place per 10 000 of the population. If this had actually been put into practice, there would be 1000 refuges in England and Wales today, not the 150 that actually exist.

Councils for Voluntary Service (CVS)

A *volunteer* could be described as someone who, without pay or compulsion, does something which will usually be of benefit to somebody else. At its best, volunteering is extremely satisfying and usually enriches the quality of one's life. A huge number of people are involved in it at the present time, and all kinds of opportunities are offered to volunteers. They work in both voluntary and statutory organisations. The social-services departments, the Probation Service, and other statutory services use large numbers of volunteers. At the other end of the spectrum, tiny local voluntary organisations may survive on the efforts of just a couple of volunteers.

In almost all areas of the country there exist independent voluntary organisations which co-ordinate the activities of most of the other voluntary organisations in the locality. These are usually designated in their operating areas as the *Council for Voluntary Service*. (Before the mid-1970s they were called 'Councils for Social Service'.) They are not new organisations – many were founded in the early years of this century. There are over 200 such bodies in the United Kingdom, and they in turn are co-ordinated by the National Council for Voluntary Organisations. The NCVO was founded in 1919 and until recently was called the 'National Council for Social Service' (NCSS). It has charitable status and describes itself as 'the central voluntary agency for the maintenance and promotion of voluntary social action'.

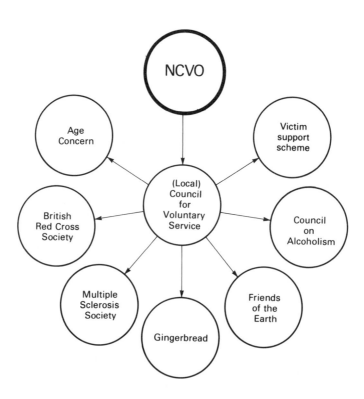

The NCVO co-ordinates local Councils for Voluntary Service, and these in turn co-ordinate the activities of a wide range of different groups.

The *local* Council for Voluntary Service has three major functions:

i) It co-ordinates the efforts of a host of local voluntary organisations – large and small. These may include the British Red Cross Society, citizens advice bureaux, 'Mind', the Spastics Society, and the Friends of the Earth. Some local groups may even be provided with office space in the CVS building. Otherwise, the Council helps share information between groups, publishes useful material or directories of local projects, allows the use by other groups of services such as reprographics, and gives advice. All this help is given to conserve energy and not duplicate provision. It will also act as a pressure group for, or advocate of, local voluntary bodies which are affiliated to it.

ii) It continually reviews existing social-welfare provision, identifying areas of unmet need and initiating action to respond to and meet them. It frequently brings new organisations into existence, establishes working parties, carries out local research, and seeks out funds for new projects.

iii) It organises what is usually known as a *volunteer bureau*. This recruits, interviews for suitability, and refers to local voluntary agencies all who come forward wishing to volunteer. Some time later, when the volunteer has been successfully placed, the bureau will 'follow up' the volunteer – that is, assess the suitability of the person to the agency and vice versa. As well as constantly recruiting new volunteers, it will also be seeking new openings for voluntary work. It will place volunteers with both voluntary and statutory organisations.

The number of people volunteering is increasing at present. This is probably related to the high rate of unemployment, but unemployed people coming forward must ensure they do not work voluntarily for too many hours, as this can affect their 'availability for paid work', and thus their social-security benefit.

Unpaid work found through the CVS could involve adult literacy teaching; counselling or advice; hospital work; fund-raising; outdoor practical work; and work with children, the elderly, the physically handicapped, the mentally handicapped, or the mentally ill. Some people offer their services as drivers, and some people offer special skills such as music, first aid, or craft-work – all can be utilised. The CVS will usually be able to match up the skill with a placement!

The person at the head of a CVS will usually be paid and may be known as a 'Director' or a 'General Secretary'. He will require great organising skills. The actual *Council* (or management committee) will normally be made up of unpaid representatives of the local statutory agencies or community bodies. Local church denominations are often involved, and lately the great expansion of the Manpower Services Commission has led to MSC-sponsored workers becoming involved in the Councils.

Volunteers can be of any age. They may, after being placed with an agency, undergo training to better equip them in their role. The gains for the individuals in voluntary work will often be considerable and may include:

a) stimulation and a broadening of interests, owing to their involvement with other people;
b) the building up of confidence, and an increase in personal and inter-personal skills;
c) the satisfaction derived from helping others;
d) a prolonged period of volunteering may form a good basis for future training and a career in social work.

Conclusion

The voluntary sector has changed out of all recognition since the mid nineteenth century. From the charitable concern of a few people, we have moved to a situation where thousands of people get personally involved in sharing. It is now a very professional and skilled field of activity. The Wolfenden Report of 1978 – *The future of voluntary organisations* – was the first ever major review of voluntary organisations in a Welfare State. It emphasised the changing nature of society and the voluntary sector. It pointed out the voluntary sector's pioneering role and its domination of advice and advocacy services, and it valued the opportunities given to people to involve themselves in the community.

An example of the growing professionalism was the setting up in 1973 of the national *Volunteer Centre*. This followed a recommendation in the 1969 Aves Report – *The voluntary worker in the social services*. The Centre's role is to promote voluntary effort and to encourage the growth of information, research, and training.

While it is generally felt that this is sound progress, we must not forget that the real strength of the voluntary sector lies in its independence, spontaneity, and the simple desire to give energy and services without wanting any material reward.

Appendix 1 – a typical 12 hour duty day for an NSPCC social worker

9.00 Arrive at office and read through mail. This includes an anonymous leter making allegations of a child being neglected. (This kind of letter is commonly received. It contains only an address – the name of the family is not mentioned.) In response to this, check through case files, the 'at-risk' register, and with other agencies (social-services department and health visitors) to see if the family is known. It is known, so decide to visit the home tomorrow to assess what risk there may be to the children.

Read through case-conference minutes from the previous week.

Receive four phone calls from clients already being worked with, requesting help with such matters as housing and financial assistance from the DHSS.

Time spent between calls in getting up to date with case recording.

11.30 An office interview with two students who are completing a project on the work of the NSPCC. Give them information, statistics, etc.
 In response to a telephone call, agree to give a talk next week on our work at a local college of further education.

12.00 Lunch.

1.00 Office interview with a rather isolated couple who have two children. The wife is worried that she may injure her baby of six months. This child has spent three periods in hospital, and there appears to be a poor bonding relationship between the child and mother. The family has large financial debts of some £2000, despite the husband being employed (on a low wage). The result of the discussion is that I agree to contact a health visitor in order to find out what parent-and-toddler groups there are in their area, and I also agree to visit the family in two weeks' time to assess what progress has been made.

2.30 Case discussion with a social worker, health visitor, and probation officer. We all work with the same family and we discuss co-operation and the family's progress. We agree on a joint strategy.

3.30 Contact a health visitor about a recent case referral. She will contact me after she has visited the family home again.

3.45 Telephone referral received about a two-year-old boy with a 'black eye'. Check out the case and find that the social-services department is officially involved. In fact the boy is in hospital under the terms of a 'place-of-safety' order, so it is unnecessary for us to become involved.

4.15 Telephone call from a neighbour making allegations that two children aged ten and twelve are being left alone for long periods. Write out referral and pass to the team leader for allocation to a member of our staff.

5.00 Switch telephone to my home, as I am evening duty officer.

5.30 Arrive home.

6.00 Telephone call from an NSPCC volunteer offering baby clothes. I suggest she delivers them to our 'charity shop' for sale to the public.

6.30 Telephone call from the police. They have visited a home where a young boy (aged six) is saying that his mother's 'boyfriend' has burnt his neck with a cigarette on several occasions. I agree to meet the boy and his mother, along with the police, at the casualty department of the local hospital.

7.00 Arrive at the hospital – hear what the police have to say about their visit to the house. There are four very faint marks on the child's neck. Speak with a doctor who has not been able to be definite about the cause of the marks – they could be (as the mother insists) spots of some kind. The police arrange to interview the mother's boyfriend. The child is not admitted to hospital, and I give him and his mother a lift home. I arrange to visit them the following day.

9.00 I return home to await any further calls.

Appendix 2 – some well known voluntary organisations

Name	Address and telephone	Object
General and advisory		
National Association of Citizens Advice Bureaux	Middleton House, 115–123 Pentonville Road, London N1 9LZ (01-833 2181)	To provide free, impartial, and confidential advice and help through local CABs to anybody on any subject.
National Council for Civil Liberties (NCCL)	21 Tabard Street, London SE1 4LA (01-403 3888)	To defend and extend civil liberties within the United Kingdom.
Samaritans Incorporated	17 Uxbridge Road, Slough, Berks SL1 1SN (0753 32713/4)	To help the suicidal and despairing.
The Volunteer Centre	29 Lower Kings Road, Berkhamsted, Herts HP4 2AB (04427 73311)	To promote voluntary action in the health, social, penal, and probation services and in voluntary organisations. To disseminate information about volunteering. To encourage and promote the training of voluntary workers.
Women's Royal Voluntary Service (WRVS)	17 Old Park Lane, London W1Y 4AJ (01-499 6040)	To help government departments, local authorities, and voluntary bodies in organising and carrying out welfare and emergency work for the community through a nationwide network of local groups.

Children

Dr Barnardo's
Tanner's Lane,
Barkingside, Ilford,
Essex IG6 1QG
(01-550 8822)

To provide care and treatment – both residential and non-residential – for any child in need, especially those who are physically or mentally handicapped or emotionally disturbed.

Child Poverty Action Group (CPAG)
1–5 Bath Street,
London EC1V 2PY
(01-253 3406)

To promote action for the relief, directly or indirectly, of poverty among children and families with children.

Church of England Children's Society
Old Town Hall,
Kennington Road,
London SE11 4QD
(01-735 2441)

To offer a comprehensive child-care service to any child or family in need.

National Children's Home
85 Highbury Park,
London N5 1UD
(01-226 2033)

To provide supportive help for children and families in need, through preventive work, fostering, adoption, and housing provision and day care.

Families

Family Service Units (FSU)
207 Old Marylebone Road,
London NW1 5QP
(01-402 5175)

To provide services for severely disadvantaged families.

Family Welfare Association (FWA)
501/505 Kingsland Road,
London E8 4AU
(01-254 6251)

To promote the mental health of families in distress and the professional development of social-work practice.

Parents Anonymous
6–9 Manor Gardens,
London N7 6LA
(01-669 8900)

To help those parents who are tempted to abuse their children and those who have done so.

185

Appendix 2 – *continued*

Name	Address and telephone	Object
One-parent families Gingerbread	35 Wellington Street London WC2E 7BN (01-240 0953)	To provide emotional support, practical help, and social activities on a day-to-day basis for lone parents and their children.
National Council for One-parent Families	255 Kentish Town Road, London NW5 2LX (01-267 1361)	To improve the financial, legal, and social position of Britain's 950 000 one-parent families.
Children in care National Association of Young People in Care (NAYPIC)	c/o Bradford Council for Voluntary Service, 9 Southbrook Terrace, Bradford BD7 1AD (0274 22772, x30)	To improve conditions and provide advice for young people in care and to promote their views and opinions.
Adoption and fostering British Agencies for Adoption and Fostering	11 Southwark Street London SE1 1RQ (01-407 8800)	To promote good standards of practice in adoption, fostering, and social work with children and families.
National Association for the Childless	318 Summer Lane, Birmingham B19 3RL (021-359 4887)	To counsel people with infertility problems, support the childless, and help them find a fulfilled life-style and to assist overseas adoption.
National Foster Care Association	Francis House, Francis Street, London SW1P 1DE (01-828 6266/7)	To improve the quality of the foster-care service in the UK

The elderly

Age Concern England ⟨⟩ " Scotland .

60 Pitcairn Road
Mitcham, Surrey CR4 3LL
(01-640 5431)

To promote the welfare of elderly people and those who work with or for the elderly.

Help the Aged

16–18 St James Walk,
London EC1R 0BE
(01-253 0253)

An international organisation aiming to relieve the distress of the elderly caused by poverty, sickness, bad housing, loneliness, national disaster, or political upheaval.

Dependent relatives

Association of Carers

Medway Homes,
Balfour Road,
Rochester, Kent ME4 6QU
(0634 813981)

To provide support for those who care for elderly and physically handicapped relatives in their own home, and to act as a pressure group for improved state support.

The physically disabled

Chest, Heart, and Stroke Association

Tavistock House North
Tavistock Square,
London WC1H 9JE
(01-387 3012)

To work to prevent chest, heart, and stroke illnesses and to help those who suffer from them.

Disablement Income Group (DIG)

Attlee House,
28 Commercial Street,
London E1 6LR
(01-247 2138)

To secure for all disabled people the provision of a national disability income and to promote research into the socio-economics of disability.

PHAB (Physically Handicapped and Able-Bodied)

Tavistock House North,
Tavistock Square,
London WC1H 9HX
(01-388 1963)

To further the integration of the physically handicapped into the community by encouraging opportunities for the handicapped and able-bodied to meet on equal terms, so that barriers of fear, ignorance, and prejudice can be destroyed.

187

Appendix 2 – *continued*

Name	Address and telephone	Object
RADAR (Royal Association for Disability and Rehabilitation)	25 Mortimer Street London W1N 8AB (01-637 5400)	To improve the environment for disabled people.
The mentally handicapped Mencap (Royal Society for Mentally Handicapped Children and Adults)	123 Golden Lane, London EC1Y 0RT (01-253 9433)	To increase public awareness of the problems faced by mentally handicapped people and their families and to secure for them the provision they need.
The mentally ill Mind (National Association for Mental Health)	22 Harley Street, London W1N 2ED (01-637 0741)	To promote mental health and to help the mentally disordered, to promote research, and to press for improvement in statutory mental-health services.
National Schizophrenia Fellowship	79 Victoria Road Surbiton, Surrey KT6 4NS (01-390 3651/3)	To secure improved community-care facilities for schizophrenics, to sponsor research, and to encourage mutual support among sufferers and their families.
Travelling families National Gypsy Education Service	82 Evesham Road, London E15 4AJ (01-555 3648)	To promote educational provision for gypsies.

The homeless

CHAR (Campaign for Single Homeless People)
5–15 Cromer Street, London WC1H 8LS
(01-833 2071)

To campaign with member organisations and homeless people for better housing and services for people without homes or families.

Church Army Housing Ltd
Welford House, 112A Shirland Road, London W9 2EL
(01-289 2241)

To provide housing for the homeless and those in unsatisfactory housing.

Homes for Homeless People
Smithfield House, Digbeth, Birmingham B5 6BS
(021-622 1502)

To work on behalf of all single homeless people in providing accommodation for them and in drawing attention to their plight.

Salvation Army
101 Queen Victoria Street, London EC4P 4EP
(01-236 5222)

To provide homes for the aged, homes and nurseries for children, hostels for working men, centres and homes for the treatment of alcoholics and drug addicts, and a large number of other projects for a variety of social needs.

Shelter (National Campaign for the Homeless)
157 Waterloo Road, London SE1 8UU
(01-633 9377)

To ensure that every household has access to a decent home.

Prisoners

Howard League for Penal Reform
322 Kennington Park Road, London SE11 4PP
(01-735 3317)

To educate as to the prevention of crime and constructive methods for the treatment of offenders.

PROP (The National Prisoners' Movement)
PROP, BM-PROP, London WC1N 3XX
(01-542 3744)

To protect and extend the rights of prisoners and to act as a pressure group to achieve this.

Name	Address and telephone	Object
Ex-offenders		
Apex Trust	1–4 Brixton Hill Place, London SW2 1HJ (01-671 7633)	To help ex-offenders into suitable employment and to campaign for equal opportunities in the job market for them.
NACRO (National Association for the Care and Resettlement of Offenders)	169 Clapham Road London SW9 0PU (01-582 6500)	To help voluntary bodies who aim to prevent crime and promote the care of offenders. To help resettle offenders.
Alcohol-related problems		
Alcoholics Anonymous	11 Redcliffe Gardens, London SW10 9BG (01-352 3001)	A network of self-help groups of people who aim to support each other to stay sober and to help other alcoholics to achieve sobriety.
Al-Anon Family Groups	61 Great Dover Street, London SE1 4YF (01-403 0888)	To provide mutual support among the family and friends of problem drinkers.
GLAAS (Greater London Alcohol Advice Service)	91–93 Charterhouse Street, London EC1M 6HR (01-253 6221)	To co-ordinate and develop alcoholics' support services, and to provide advice and information for anyone living in London.
Drugs		
Release	169 Commercial Road, London E1 6BW (01-377 5905)	To provide information and advice – especially legal advice – to drug users.

SCODA (Standing Conference on Drug Abuse)	1-4 Hatton Place, Hatton Gardens, London EC1N 8ND (01-430 2341/2)	An umbrella organisation for the voluntary projects working in the drugs field.
Gambling Gamblers Anonymous and Gam-Anon	17-23 Blantyre Street, Cheyne Walk, London SW10 0DT (01-352 3060)	Gamblers Anonymous is a self-help fellowship of those who want to do something about their gambling. Gam-Anon is for the wives/husbands of compulsive gamblers, in order to find mutual support and understanding.

Note This is not a comprehensive list of voluntary organisations. New groups can be created at any time, in response to a particular need which arises – the situation is, therefore, constantly changing. For more information, consult:

a) *Charities digest* (published annually by the Family Welfare Association – FWA),
b) *Voluntary organisations – an NCVO directory* (published at regular intervals by Bedford Square Press).

P.P.A - Pre-school Playgroups Association

Exercise 1 – local voluntary organisations

a) Select a local voluntary organisation. (Do not choose the local branch of a national organisation.) It may be worth scanning local newspapers to see if they carry any stories about its work.
b) Arrange to visit its office and interview one or more people working for it.
c) Write up an account of what it does and how it is organised and financed.
d) Interview a number of local residents to find out whether they know of its work. If they have had some contact with it, what is their impression of how well it functions and the services it provides?
e) Finally, write up your assessment of the organisation.

Exercise 2 – national voluntary organisations

a) Study the list of voluntary organisations in appendix 2 to this chapter. Choose one and write a *report* about its activities. This will involve making direct contact and asking for information to be sent to you. (Be sure to enclose a stamped addressed envelope when you write to any voluntary organisation for information.)
b) Find out how it is organised and funded.
c) Find out if there is a local branch or office in your area and contact people who work for it. Has it set up any projects locally? What does it do in your area? How is it organised and funded?

Exercise 3 – the Citizens Advice Bureau

The Citizens Advice Bureau (CAB) has been described as 'the GP [general practitioner] of the voluntary sector'. Imagine that you are a volunteer at your local CAB. Today (a Tuesday) is an average day, and ten people come in with a variety of queries, as below. Many of them have to be referred to other agencies, either statutory or voluntary; others you may be able to offer advice to yourself. Work out what you would do in each case.

a) A man with what he describes as 'shoddy goods' – a pair of shoes he bought two weeks ago, which have split and are unwearable. He had his receipt for them and returned to the shop to complain, but was told they could not replace them or refund him.
b) A married man who says that he and his wife have experienced substantial problems in their relationship over the past few months. He now feels desperate and realises that they need some help and advice urgently.
c) A young woman who has been living in a private rented flat and was told last night that she must be out of it, removing all her property, by the end of the week. She has no formal agreement with the landlord and no rent book.

d) An old man, weary from lack of sleep, is extremely angry about his neighbours – a young couple who play loud rock music 'day and night', keeping him awake 'until the early hours'. He has repeatedly complained to them, but, despite promises that this will change, things remain the same. The situation is intolerable for him and he is now 'at the end of his tether'.

e) A couple with a 14-year-old son are convinced he is 'glue-sniffing' – they are extremely worried about him – but their angry confrontations are met by adamant denials. He behaves oddly at times, his mood fluctuates rapidly, and he has appeared as if drunk but without the smell of alcohol on his breath. They are desperate for some kind of advice and assistance.

f) A man (about 40) has been denied access to his two young children (aged four and seven) on the past two weekends. His ex-wife is refusing to communicate with him, and he wants to know quickly what he should do.

g) A very agitated single mother with one child complains that she has not received her latest Girocheque from the DHSS. A visit and phone call to the local office have not helped – she feels that she has been 'fobbed off' when told her money will arrive by the weekend. She has no money, not even for food, and no friends or relations who are able to help.

h) A young man (aged 18) has received what he feels are serious threats from a group of youths he used to 'hang around with'. He has thought of contacting the police, but fears the consequences if the group finds out that he has done so. What can he do?

i) An Asian couple who have just moved into town are keen to receive help with speaking English. They feel that poor English has limited their social life, and they want to improve the situation.

j) A single man of 28 has just arrived in the area, having heard that there is work to be found here. He does not have any address to go to, has no friends or relations near, and is asking for help in finding accommodation.

Questions for essays or discussion

1. With the coming of the Welfare State after the Second World War, some thought that all voluntary activity would be taken over by paid professionals working for statutory caring agencies. This has not happened. Why do you think voluntary effort is still very much in evidence?

2. What advantages does the volunteer have over the professional in the caring services?

3. Since the deaths of Maria Colwell and, more recently, Jasmine Beckford, much attention has been given to non-accidental injury (NAI) to children.

a) Why do you think parents inflict physical violence on their children?
b) What can be done to change this situation?

4. The NSPCC inspector occasionally has to take parents to court for cruelty towards, or neglect of, their children. How might this affect the way in which the inspector will subsequently work with the family?
5. What do you think are the underlying reasons for male violence towards women? Should any help be offered to the men who are violent? If so, what?
6. Increasingly, volunteers in the caring services receive some form of training. Choose two of the following and explain what kind of training you think volunteers working with them should receive:

a) the mentally handicapped,
b) young children in a playgroup,
c) the physically disabled,
d) the elderly and infirm,
e) offenders.

Further reading

1. *Working for free – a practical guide for volunteers*, Sheila Moore (Pan Books, 1977). Covers the whole range of possible volunteering.
2. *The voluntary sector in˙ British social services*, Maria Brenton (Longman, 1985). A comprehensive and up-to-date review of the voluntary sector.
3. *Scream quietly or the neighbours will hear*, Erin Pizzey (Coventure, 1976). A book which examines male violence towards women.
4. *People power*, Tony Gibson (Penguin, 1979). A practical guide for those involved in setting up groups within the community.
5. *The volunteer bureaux directory* (Volunteer Centre). Published regularly, this lists all volunteer bureaux.

Most voluntary organisations publish material about their work. You can find a selective list of such organisations with addresses in appendix 2 of this chapter. Enclose a stamped addressed envelope if you write for information.

6 Residential social work

Introduction

Whereas most field social-work staff are professionally qualified, only a small percentage of residential workers – estimated at around 4% – have received any social-work training. The situation is slightly better for residential staff working with children and young people, where about 20% of workers are appropriately qualified. The lack of training within the residential sector compared to field-work reflects the traditional regard (or non-regard) given to the respective ways of working. However the philosophy of residential care has altered over the past few years – it is now more purposeful, and its enormous potential for effective social work is increasingly being recognised. The role of residential workers, particularly those working with children, is widening to include that which was formerly undertaken by field-workers. In some authorities, qualified social workers from the field are moving into residential posts in recognition of the scope available for responsible efficient practice.

Residential establishments cater for a wide range of client groups – children, the elderly, mentally handicapped, mentally ill, physically handicapped, single homeless, offenders, and alcohol- and drug-dependants. The establishments themselves vary and include small group homes, larger homes (some with specialised units), hostels, and self-contained communities which are often set in rural areas. Many of the very large Victorian institutions still being used are in the process of being run down in favour of more appropriate community-based accommodation.

Local authorities provide most establishments, but many are run by voluntary agencies – either independently or in conjunction with their local authorities. Some are run by private concerns, and this is particularly noticeable in the provision of homes for the elderly.

The function of the residential establishments varies according to their speciality. Some are concerned with observation and assessment, others with emergency admission and/or short stays, and other homes may offer a specific period of residence. Some homes may have a combination of functions, and others will provide long-term permanent care.

It is not necessary to outline the role of each individual type of establishment for, despite serving different client groups, many homes share a similar objective and purpose. However there is a distinct difference between the needs of children and those of the more physically dependent clients who may be elderly or handicapped in some way. The residential provision for these two categories of people differs also from the needs of ex-offenders in probation hostels or those adults living in therapeutic communities where rehabilitation is sought. The remainder of this chapter will focus on the following four areas: children and young people, physically dependent people (particularly the elderly), ex-offenders in probation hostels, and adults with special needs in community settings.

Homes for children and young people

Over the past ten years, the pattern of child care in residential establishments has changed significantly. Previously it was not uncommon for a child to be received into care at an early age and remain in a residential setting until he reached the age when the local authority could legally give up responsibility. At 18 or 19, the child was then discharged from care. This process itself created problems of dependency – some youngsters were often ill-equipped to deal with the demands of living on their own. Residential institutions had met their material and physical needs, but their initiative and independence had not been adequately developed.

Today there are fewer children coming into care (101 200 in 1977, 93 200 in 1982), and the duration of their residential experience is being purposely reduced. Many authorities are striving to limit the period to a maximum of two years.

At the end of their period in care, children should be ready to return home to their families or to substitute foster or adoption homes. For those older children who cannot be rehabilitated at home or placed with a substitute family, the aim of the establishment will be to prepare them for independent living.

More alternatives are being sought to prevent younger children experiencing institutional care. For example, preventive work involving the collective use of day nurseries, family centres, and sponsored child-minding is aimed at supporting families and avoiding breakdown, and the idea behind the current expansion of the fostering and adoptive services is to provide a more appropriate ordinary family experience for young children where care is unavoidable.

As a result of changes in child-care philosophy, residential provision for children is now mainly catering for older children – usually for specific time periods and to meet particular needs. Consequently, residential work with children has become more specialised.

Formerly, field social workers arranged admission into care – the residential staff took over responsibility after the child had been admitted. Nowadays, residential staff may be involved in pre-admittance interviewing, either at the child's family home or at the children's home when the child attends for an introductory visit. This is not, of course, possible in emergency cases, but usually one home will have responsibility for unplanned admissions.

Once the child becomes a member of the home, one of the residential staff will be designated his *keyworker*. Residential social workers will act in the role of keyworker to two or three children – the aim is to develop a

Time spent alone together allows trust to develop between the keyworker and the young person in care.

special trusting relationship that ensures that the child benefits from a warm concern that encourages confidential communication of needs and assists the child to develop the confidence required to take an interest in and determine his own future. Children in care who have had disturbed family experiences usually have never had the opportunity to form very close relationships, so initially they may respond to the keyworker in a distressful and unco-operative manner. Nevertheless, perceptive skilled involvement by the residential worker will enable a consistent relationship to develop.

Residential staff will liaise with field-workers when a child is due to be rehabilitated with his own family. Usually, the keyworker will be involved in working with the child's parents either by inviting parental involvement with the child at the residential establishment or by visiting the parents in their own home. It is usually more appropriate for field social workers to see the family, because of an ongoing commitment, but sometimes it is more useful for the residential social worker to be the main link with the family.

Where the children's home is working towards preparing a child for a substitute family, the residential social worker will be engaged in a relationship with the potential foster parents. She will arrange introductory visits and will accompany the child on visits to their home.

It is not always possible to find alternatives to residential care for some children – their own home may remain unsuitable and there may be a lack of prospective substitute families. Some children are damaged and disturbed to such an extent that they are considered 'hard to place'. Such children may have to remain in residential care, where the residential workers of the home will be concerned to meet their needs within an institutional setting. All possible assistance and guidance will, of course, be given to the children.

Preparation for independent living for children who are ready to leave residential care is provided by specialist establishments. Youngsters are helped to develop life and social skills – including cooking, budgeting, and home management. Residential workers will also advise, inform, or assist with job-seeking, social security, housing benefits, and training courses at local colleges.

Roles of workers in children's homes

Houseparents The basic-grade residential social workers who work in ordinary children's homes and homes for mentally or physically handicapped children are known as 'houseparents'. The post is graded according to the size and nature of the establishment, and people are appointed on a scale according to their qualifications and experience. Houseparents are paid a salary and can progress through the grades until they are ready to become senior houseparents or to move into management. Basically they do the work of a parent – attend to children's needs, listen to them, be readily available to offer help, and make sure they have things ready for school. They are also concerned with the routine running of the establishment.

Admission to care It can be distressing and disorientating for a child to be suddenly transferred from his own home to a residential setting; so, where possible, some homes will encourage the child to make introductory visits before he is formally admitted. As we have already mentioned, it is important that a child has the opportunity to develop a special relationship with one member of staff, and soon after admission a keyworker will be found to suit the child. Some homes will wait for three or four weeks to see if a 'natural relationship' takes place before designating one of the houseparents as the child's keyworker.

Keyworkers The keyworker will attend the initial *planning meeting* with the field-worker and the officer in charge to help establish short-term and long-term aims for the child. The use of *life-story* work enables the child to talk about his history and his plans for the future. The keyworker may use the personal information gained as a light lever to explore other, more sensitive, issues with the child. The purpose is, of course, to assist the child in every way possible. On some occasions the keyworker may be called upon to provide a report or attend juvenile court along with the child.

Night-worker/houseparent There is always a need for someone to be on duty throughout the night in children's homes, in case of emergency. This role is closer to that of a domestic than that of a social worker, as in the main it consists of cleaning and tidying duties. However,the person employed needs to be calm and reliable and capable of knowing when it is necessary to ring for the senior. Such a post might offer some useful experience and insight to a person interested in making a career in residential work.

Senior houseparents Large homes may employ senior houseparents (or a senior houseparent). The duties attached to the post will include management functions.

The management team This consists of a third-in-charge, a deputy, and an officer-in-charge.

The third-in-charge will have specific responsibilities such as ordering food and planning meals or ensuring that medical equipment is available. In addition, the third-in-charge may liaise with doctors, accompany children to the surgery, and make sure they attend dental appointments. On the whole, any direct managerial role means that there is rather less direct 'face-to-face' contact with the children.

The deputy (second-in-charge) usually is concerned with working out staff rotas and generally assisting the officer-in-charge. In most homes the deputy will provide regular supervision to the houseparents and will act as officer-in-charge during the OIC's absence.

The officer-in-charge (*OIC*), as head of the home, is concerned with the day-to-day policy of running the home. There is much freedom of power in this role – together with the other managers, the OIC can determine the quality of residential care. She is free to encourage outside involvement and links with the wider community in addition to deciding on what activities should take place within the home. For example, the OIC may wish to involve volunteers from outside as extra pairs of hands, each to be responsible for one particular child or to accompany houseparents taking groups out, particularly at weekends or in the evening. The officer-in-charge may confer with the other management staff on a regular basis with the object of allowing them to contribute informally on the policy of the home, to examine their own practice, or to express any anxieties they feel about needs that are not, in their opinion, being met.

Teamwork

A residential children's home requires co-operation to achieve continuity and consistency of care. Regular team meetings are held to facilitate this. Homes are run on a shift basis, normally 6 a.m. until 2 p.m. and 2.30 p.m. until 10.30 p.m., with a half-hour change-over period in between. During the change-over, staff are able to share information and discuss individual children and any significant events which have taken place during the shift.

Reviews

All children in care need to be reviewed every six months by law, but many homes hold reviews more frequently. The keyworker, the officer-in-charge, the placements officer from social services, the field social worker, and a representative from the school are normally present to read reports and discuss the child's future. When an important decision is to be reached about a particular child, a *case conference* is held – all the residential staff, as well as appropriate professionals from outside, will be present. Every effort will be made to ascertain the child's own views and feelings, so that they may be presented at reviews and case conferences.

Homes for physically dependent people – elderly persons' homes

Residential homes for elderly or physically or mentally handicapped people have much in common with regard to the philosophy and practice of care given. Homes vary in their functions, and many provide a range of services in addition to full-time care. For example, elderly persons' homes (EPHs) may provide *day care* to non-residents from the community between 10 a.m. and 4 p.m. during days of the week, *rotational care* for two weeks in every six for people with difficulty managing by themselves but still able to function in the community, and *short stays* for elderly people while their carers are away on holiday. Homes for the mentally handicapped may also provide regular *respite care* for people in the community who are being cared for by relatives. *Day care* may be provided within the establishment, although residents may attend another home for variety and the chance to meet new people in a different setting.

Elderly persons' homes (EPHs)

Elderly persons' homes were first provided by local authorities following the National Assistance Act 1948 (part III). For many years they catered for the more able and generally younger older person, functioning more like hostels or hotels than the homes of today. Over the past ten years the clientele of local-authority EPHs has changed, and now the majority of residents are more dependent and frailer, many being either physically handicapped, mentally confused, or both.

This change in type of resident reflects the increased proportion of the elderly in the population as a whole, and additional demands for residential care are brought about by the unavailability of geriatric beds in hospitals. Many of today's residents would have been cared for in hospitals in the past. However, the new development of specialised sheltered housing and the recent huge growth in the number of private homes for the elderly indicate that the more able-bodied elderly person is once again likely to be catered for.

Many local-authority EPHs have been criticised for failing to provide stimulation and participation for their residents. Others, particularly those which have introduced group-living practices, have done much to reduce the dependency of residents – they have increased the residents' involvement and, consequently, the quality of their lives.

Group living within the establishment
Group living involves residents being allocated to small groups (five or six in each) with the purpose of helping them to take some responsibility for the quality of their lives and to engage in *mutual care*, i.e. support of other residents. The role of the residential worker in such homes is not to do everything for residents but to encourage and enable them to perform tasks by themselves.

Charlotte Towle, in her social-work book *Common human needs*, refers to six basic human needs present in client groups of all ages which have to be acknowledged by any caring regime in order that lives of residents are not diminished:

  i) the need to make decisions,
 ii) the need to explore and find out,
iii) the need to make relationships,
 iv) the need to take risks,
  v) the need to take responsibility,
 vi) the need to give as well as to receive.

These are now outlined with reference to EPHs.

Group living fosters mutual care and involvement.

Making decisions It is administratively easier for caring staff to make decisions on behalf of residents – to decide on meal times, bed times, and what activities should go on throughout the day. By doing this, some establishments can ensure a smoother running of the home – but this is achieved at the cost of the residents' independence. Order and routine are necessary in any group-living situation, but people should be allowed to contribute to decisions affecting their lives. Mass bingo sessions, constant television, and everybody rising at a certain hour of the morning for communal breakfast will suit some people but not everyone. It is far better that people should be able to opt out of group activities that they are not keen on, decide on their own meal times and bed times, and instigate activities that are of personal interest to individuals and to small groups.

Exploring and finding out Society sometimes views old age as an illness – a time of inactivity and rest. Many old people with reduced physical capacity are very alert mentally, still crave stimulation, and have the capacity to develop new interests as well as maintain old ones. Dancing, music, painting, and embroidery are just a few of the hobbies that may interest residents, and raised garden beds and the provision of special implements can make gardening accessible to most residents, including those who are wheelchair-bound.

Some elderly residents of EPHs who are neglected by relatives or visitors may have little opportunity of getting out of the establishment.

New surroundings are often a sufficient stimulus in themselves and can act as an antidote to residential living.

Those homes which have transport may take residents to local centres of interests, on day trips to the seaside, or on shorter journeys to local community colleges to take part in any activities available.

Making relationships This need applies to relationships not only with the staff and other residents within the home but also outside the home as well. Homes which encourage community involvement with local children from schools or youth groups via open-days and garden fêtes enable residents to form relationships with people from the community. This is further encouraged when residents themselves are involved in community activities outside the home.

Group living itself and the interdependence it fosters help people to form deeper relationships with one another, based on trust, respect, and mutual support.

Taking risks It is all too easy for residential establishments to create dependence within the first few hours following admission. If people have things done for them from the moment they become members of a home, they learn to rely on and expect help at all times. Where staff patiently encourage residents to manage by themselves whenever possible, the sense of achievement created – however small – can be built upon. It may be convenient or tempting to agree to a resident's request for a wheelchair, but time spent on encouraging him to move on his own with the use of handrails, a Zimmer frame, or sticks will enable the resident to maximise his own resources and be ambulant longer.

Establishment rules should be kept to a minimum, to allow residents as much independence as possible. It is obviously necessary to restrict the smoking habits of someone mentally confused, so that his cigarette smoking can be supervised. However, there is little justification – apart from convenience – behind the rationale of getting all residents ready for bed at an early hour of the evening.

There are, of course, risks attached to allowing mentally confused elderly people to wander into the community, and for this reason some homes keep their front door permanently locked. The erection of secure fencing would overcome this problem and allow all residents more freedom of movement between the home and the grounds.

Taking responsibility People need to be allowed to take responsibility for their own actions and to be given choices. Group living enables them not only to take responsibility for themselves – to manage tasks like preparing light meals, making cups of tea, washing-up, and table setting – but also involves them in support of other residents. Living in groups means that roles need to be allocated and responsibility shared. Even people with restricted physical ability or slight mental confusion can cope with a fair range of tasks, including collecting meals, serving out, cleaning away, washing-up, and returning used crockery, and can in this way contribute to their own care. Elderly people can more meaningfully increase their involvement in the running of their home if they are consulted regularly on policy issues, the type of activities to be planned, the establishment of any rules and procedures, and ways of improving the home.

Giving as well as receiving   Where residents are always the recipients of caring and have no opportunity to return help, they are likely to feel that they are a burden to others. To be denied the chance to help others is to be diminished in terms of personal human capacity. Group living, with shared interdependent roles, enables residents to give and receive help from others. The simple achievement of making tea for oneself and other group members at a chosen time of the day may take a little time but can nevertheless be a satisfying procéss for the person responsible. The opportunities for this type of practice will be facilitated in homes where, for each small group of elderly residents, there is a raised electric socket and an automatic kettle established in a firm base close to a small fridge which should be easily available and accessible.

Where group living is practised and residents are involved and engaged in mutual daily care, the therapeutic effect of an active life can be detected by the clients' interested attitudes and the confidence they display in coping.

Roles of workers in elderly persons' homes

Under DHSS regulations, elderly persons' homes are officially designated as 'category-A' or 'category-B' homes, according to the dependency of the residents. Category-A homes are for 'highly dependent' people, and category-B homes cater for the more able residents. In practice there is little difference between the clienteles of local-authority EPHs, and most cater for the more dependent resident. The size of the establishment and the number of residents determines the staffing grades and the pay structure of the managerial staff.

EPHs may have been purpose-built or have been established in large Victorian houses which have been specially adapted. Modern establishments may lack the warmth and character of the older buildings but, being specially designed, will not be hampered by existing structures such as stairs and large rooms. It is not, however, so much the physical nature of the establishment but the philosophy of the home which determines the standard of care. In some homes, care staff will be involved in a supportive enabling role; in others, their work will be more practically directive. Inevitably the roles of staff overlap, for the members are all part of a large family community, but each member has particular tasks and responsibilities.

Domestic staff   The domestic staff are not officially part of the care staff, since they are engaged to perform necessary cleaning duties. However, they will interact with residents during the performance of their job and it is important for them to be friendly and tolerant in their work.

In an emergency – for example when a resident has fallen or is in difficulty – they may offer assistance or call upon one of the care assistants.

The inclusion of domestics at staff meetings helps reinforce the mutual dependence of staff, the feeling of involvement, and the need to work as a team. For people with no social-work experience, the job of a domestic may provide a useful opportunity to gain insight into the working of a residential home.

Care assistants Care assistants attend to the basic daily needs of residents who are elderly, infirm, or handicapped in some way. Much of the work of the care assistant may be physical – bathing and dressing residents and helping them to eat, in addition to various cleaning tasks and food preparation. Where group living is practised, the care assistant will be involved in an enabling role – reminding residents to go to the toilet in order to control incontinence and assisting or standing by as the residents engage in mutual care.

The clients' personal, emotional, and spiritual needs have also to be considered within the day-to-day running of the home. Because of other pressing duties, care assistants do not always have the time they would like to relax with residents and spend moments getting to know them better. However, care assistants can use all moments of personal contact with clients to establish supportive relationships.

Volunteers Some residential establishments encourage the use of volunteers within the home. Volunteers do not do the work of a care assistant but assist them by carrying out simple complementary tasks. By taking trolleys around, serving teas, or helping an elderly person with handicrafts, they help reduce the load of the care staff (whose work can never be said to be done).

The management team The management team will be made up of a third-in-charge, a deputy, and an officer-in-charge. Their roles will be interdependent, although each will have specific responsibilities. They will help shape the policy of the home.

The third-in-charge Care assistants may be promoted to become third-in-charges – or 'thirds', as they are often referred to – although few would have had any training for a management role. Sometimes experienced staff are brought in from outside the establishment to take up management posts.

The third-in-charge will be concerned with the day-to-day running of the home and may have special responsibility for ordering supplies. She may stand in for the deputy or even the officer-in-charge in cases of absence.

205

The deputy (second-in-charge)   The second-in-charge is also concerned with the routine running of the establishment and will probably have specific duties such as the distribution and checking of medication. She may be in charge of offering supervision to the care staff and be responsible for students on work placements. As part of the management team, the deputy will contribute to the planning of the establishment, perhaps devising ways of increasing residents' participation and setting up group-living schemes.

The officer-in-charge (OIC) has overall responsibility for the establishment and may often not share any of the practical duties that are delegated to other management staff. The OIC will liaise with doctors, consultant geriatricians, psychiatrists, social workers, and senior management staff within the social-services department. She will be involved in planning admissions, assessing priorities among those people on the waiting list, and holding reviews and case conferences on residents.

The purpose and function of the home will be determined by the social-services department, but the regime and quality of care will be the result of the policy of the management team and the work of the care staff.

Reality orientation therapy (ROT)
To enable elderly mentally handicapped and confused residents to cope better with their surroundings and to improve the quality of their daily life, various reality orientation procedures are used. This practice is aimed at engaging people more fully in everyday situations. Simple devices such as large clearly visible clocks, colour-coded rooms, large signs over toilets, and daily notices on notice-boards help residents keep in touch with the 'here and now'. Other innovations such as the provision of seasonal flowers and fruits, displays of local photographs, and group outings help make surroundings meaningful. Familiarity can be further increased if residents bring in personal items such as chairs, pictures, and vases to keep in their own rooms.

Elderly-persons support units (EPSUs)
Some authorities are operating schemes for supporting frail and handicapped elderly people in ordinary houses as a direct alternative to building more residential establishments. These schemes are known as elderly-persons support units (EPSUs).

Some people have been admitted to elderly persons' homes because of inadequate support services in their area; but, however good the care provided by residential establishments, it is much more satisfactory for individuals to remain in their own homes within the community if that is what they want.

An EPSU may be established in any suitable building. It will be equipped with cooking facilities and have a dining area, various small lounges, a hairdressing room, a specially equipped bathroom, and even a room for 'messy craft activities' (such as painting or horticulture). It

Reality orientation therapy (ROT) helps elderly residents to be more aware of what is happening around them.

functions rather like a community/luncheon centre. Services such as home helps, home wardens, and 'meals-on-wheels' can be provided from the centre, and rooms can be allocated for visiting district nurses or chiropodists. Essentially it services homes within a short distance, and it can be linked to these residences by a 24 hour alarm/communication system.

The service need not be restricted to elderly people – it may be extended to other community groups in the area who may need rooms for meetings etc.

Probation hostels for offenders

The penal system

Many people who leave youth-custody centres or prisons will reoffend and return to prison at a later date. With a few exceptions, the rehabilitative function of penal institutions is almost non-existent – inmates experience hardship, humiliation, and boredom during their sentence and, not surprisingly, they are often ill-equipped to cope with the outside world on release. It is difficult for them to find work, as employers in general are unwilling to take the risk of employing ex-offenders (there are the rare exceptions, of course), and they may experience difficulty in obtaining accommodation. Without the security of a job and a decent home, the tendency to become further involved in crime is increased. This pattern of behaviour is known as *recidivism*.

British prisons are badly equipped; overcrowded; and negatively concerned, primarily, with security. In these respects, conditions for prisoners in the UK fall behind those of nearly all their European counterparts, where weekend leave and constructive rehabilitative measures form part of a more positive policy towards offenders.

Probation hostels exist in order to assist the rehabilitation of offenders. Until ten years ago they were provided only for young people under 21, but since then they have been open to older offenders. These establishments may be *statutory*, or they may be hostels run by *voluntary* agencies. They cater not only for people leaving prison but also for people who are 'in danger of imprisonment'. Both types of hostel become *approved* after satisfactory inspection by Home Office officials. They are not a free service, and residents pay rent in the normal way.

Approved probation hostels

These are run by a management committee of not more than 12 members of whom two at least must be men and two at least must be women. This committee will include the local chief probation officer, other probation officers, and lay members of the community (general practitioners, vicars, and teachers, for example). One of the members will be appointed chairman, and a secretary and treasurer will be chosen. The committee exists to ensure that the hostel is run in a way that will incline it to promote the welfare of residents.

The selection of residents   This is undertaken by the warden and staff, subject to the approval of the committee. They will consider applications presented by probation officers on behalf of people currently in prison awaiting discharge and those who have been placed on probation where a 'condition-of-residence' order has been made. *Bail* places will also be available – some people will be referred from the court as a temporary and short-term measure instead of being remanded in custody.

Aims of a probation hostel   These are as follows:

a) To provide *alternatives to custody* for those offenders who are in danger of imprisonment.
b) To take risks in selection – that is, to consider taking more serious offenders.
c) To provide *care*, *control*, and *containment* in order to reduce the need to reoffend.
d) To create opportunities for residents to develop their use of *leisure, life, and social skills*, in order to improve their chances of *employment* and eventual *resettlement in the community*.

e) To provide an acceptable *contract* which ensures a constructive use of residents' time at the hostel. In this way, the hostel indicates its willingness to encourage residents to undertake purposeful activities, and this should be reciprocated by the residents themselves. A contract requires commitment on both sides.

A new development in hostels is the *dispersed hostel*, which may take the form of several three-bedroomed houses located in different parts of the community. This has the obvious advantage of 'normalising' accommodation and assisting integration into the community.

Some voluntary hostels provide for both offenders and non-offenders, and some specialise in the care of people suffering from mental illness, alcoholism, or drug addiction. Many are concerned with assisting young homeless ex-offenders and may be run on the following lines.

Four models of hostel provision

The containment model   Establishments based on this model will be less discriminating in their selection of clients and will provide only basic food and shelter for a short period of time. The aim will be to help provide some stability and group support for anyone in need.

The 'melting-pot' model   Hostels run on these lines will be more selective of clients – clients will be expected to benefit from interaction with others who have different backgrounds and needs. There may be an underlying assumption that personal development will happen automatically through involvement with other clients and staff. Residents will be seen as being capable of *self-direction*, so social-work interaction will be kept to a minmum.

The interventionist model   A serious considered selection of clients will be undertaken before they are admitted to any hostel based on this model. Such clients will need more social-work input, and a sensitive assessment of their needs will be carried out. They are likely to have personal problems and to benefit from more intense supervision.

The family model   Hostels run on the family model are usually smaller establishments where the warden is seen as a parental figure at the head of the household. Positive family-based experience may help clients to rehabilitate more naturally to the outside world.

Roles of workers in probation hostels
Establishments vary enormously in their practice, and the roles of the staff are often interchangeable. They will have a general responsibility to assist the reintegration of residents into the community by encouraging them to use the facilities of the hostel in order to manage better when they leave and to reduce the tendency to turn to crime. The warden will be helped in

his duties by the deputy warden and other assistant wardens, one of whom may be employed part-time to cover some of the weekend shifts. The emphasis will be on working together as a team.

The warden   The warden will have overall responsibility, but she and the staff will aim to develop close one-to-one relationships with small groups of residents. Staff meetings will be held to share information about residents and to develop team identity. The warden will be the sole representative of the hostel on the management committee and will be responsible to chief probation officers for the policies of the establishment. She will often be a senior probation officer and may hold the court orders of those clients at the hostel who are on probation. As a probation officer, the warden will have the separate responsibility of ensuring that the terms of the court orders are adhered to by probationers. The warden also provides supervision to other members of staff and will assist in the development of treatment programmes for clients. Her other major responsibility will be to provide the court with social enquiry reports for the hostel residents due for sentencing.

The deputy warden   The role of deputy will be a combination of administration, management, and social-work tasks. The deputy is likely to be a qualified probation officer and will undertake some of the duties of the senior, whom she will support. The deputy will, of course, act as warden when the senior is absent. Many of the cash transactions will be undertaken by the deputy – the collecting of rent, distribution of expenses, and the recording and balancing of books. She will also assist residents in using other agencies (such as the DHSS and the housing department), both in terms of personal development and for the solution of practical difficulties.

Assistant wardens   These are unlikely to be professionally qualified, but they may be graduates who have demonstrated a commitment to and an understanding of social work. In addition to administrative record-keeping, they may also be involved in the distribution of extra allowances when, for example, they want to encourage and enable some of the residents to participate in educational programmes provided by the local National Association for the Care and Resettlement of Offenders (NACRO) education unit. These units are establishments in major towns to provide basic numeracy, literacy, and practical skills; cookery; carpentry; and other learning experiences aimed at equipping offenders with skills that will ultimately enable them to acquire a job and independence.

Assistant wardens may also be required to provide court reports for residents who are on short-term bail awaiting trial. When on duty, they will be expected to provisionally accept new referrals and to provide information. The bulk of their time will be spent counselling residents as part of specific treatment programmes and engaging them in group work, social-skills training, or drama workshops – all designed to increase personal awareness and encourage self-confrontation. The aim is to help residents resolve their personal problems.

Domestic and clerical staff   These will obviously have their own specific duties, but as members of the staff of the hostel they will be included in team meetings and be kept informed. Their opinions will be sought, both formally and informally, by the wardens.

Use of volunteers in approved hostels   Residents of approved probation hostels who have had negative experiences at the hands of those in authority in prisons, for example, may have developed anti-authoritarian attitudes. Probation officers may be seen by the residents in this light, so a volunteer – being free of this taint – may be in a better position to form relationships with residents. At the same time, some of the residents – especially those who have spent some time in prison – may be openly distrustful because they are unused to genuine offers of friendship and they may reject advances made by a volunteer.

Working with offenders can often be difficult and unrewarding. However, because the outside world will, in due course, be the only world the present hostel resident has to live in, it is important that he has somebody to communicate with outside working hours who can assist in his struggle to be re-established in the community. The volunteer can be an important agent in this purpose.

Therapeutic communities

These are self-contained communities normally based on philosophical or sometimes religious principles aimed at encouraging the personal growth of residents who, for a variety of reasons, have been unable to cope with living in ordinary society. The aim is to engage people in fulfilling activities to enable them to participate and co-operate purposefully in the work of the community and to gain strength and confidence from their involvement in the mutual support generated. For many communities, the ultimate goal will be the rehabilitation of members back into the community with increased self-esteem and control over the problems they brought with them. Other communities – for example, those catering for mentally handicapped adults – provide a permanent home for residents that allows individuals to lead as full a life as possible within a protective caring environment.

Therapeutic communities exist for the recovery of the mentally ill (e.g. the Richmond Fellowship), for emotionally disturbed adolescents (e.g. Peper Harow), for mentally handicapped people (Rudolph Steiner homes and the Home Farm Trust), for drug misusers (e.g. Phoenix House), and for other people with special needs (e.g. the Langley House Trust for offenders with behaviour problems).

Example of one type of therapeutic community – for drug misusers
This is not a typical example of a therapeutic community – the regime is deliberately designed to be harsh and hierarchical in order to help individuals overcome their deep-rooted dependency on hard drugs. To be able to do this, their self-discipline needs to be restored to the level where they can make a choice about their behaviour.

Part of the time will be spent exploring the emotional reasons why they have embarked on such a destructive life-style – forced abstinence is not sufficient to end the habit. For example, some people return from a prison sentence and begin using drugs when faced with difficulty. Unless the personal reasons for dependency can be explored, there may be no change. It is hoped that the sense of community among the residents will evoke and reinforce some of the lost feelings of self-worth – if, indeed, for some, they ever existed. The community is open to anybody who has a serious drugs problem, and some people attend as a condition of a probation order.

On arrival, a drug misuser will need to have undergone a period of detoxification, as withdrawal is not undertaken at the community. He will be stripped and searched for drugs or alcohol and, once admitted, he will be expected to take a pride in his personal appearance. (At one time men were not allowed to grow beards or moustaches.) He will be allocated to a senior member of the community who will explain the way of life to the new member, who will be expected to comply with the existing standards of behaviour. Apart from one initial phone call and a letter, the new resident will relinquish contact with the outside world.

New members will be given the responsibility to join in group activities and community programmes. These will involve drama therapy and psychotherapy as a means of increasing self-awareness. Practically, new members will be involved in daily chores and work schedules. They will receive weekly counselling from senior members and groups of their peers and, at an early stage, they will be expected to relate their *life story* to the rest of the community. After they have been there for six weeks or so, they will be required to give a seminar to other community members on one particular aspect of the community that they feel strongly about, as an indication of their acceptance of the regime and its philosophy. After this, they may be ready to move on from their induction to the next stage of the programme.

The next phase may involve the new member being part of a group where he will be expected to consolidate relationships. Peers will be expected to help and counsel each other without senior supervision. Residents should be able to demonstrate a growing commitment to the running of the community and be ready to hold positions of responsibility. Minor privileges may accompany this change.

Depending on progress, the third stage may be reached after a period of six months or so, when residents will be able to take time off from community involvement to engage in social activities, voluntary work, skills training, or further education outside the community setting.

Privileges are granted as responsibilities increase.

The final 're-entry' stage may be reached after 12 or 18 months, when the resident has shown himself to have matured, having overcome earlier difficulties. It is important for the resident to have been engaged in valid activities for at least 40 hours per week, thereby having experienced a 'working' time structure equivalent to that practised outside the therapeutic community – the transition back into society will thus be made more smoothly.

Conclusion

Residential care has changed greatly over the past few years, and the trend continues towards caring for people within the community – either in smaller group homes or by assisting families to care. As a result, some residential establishments are being closed, and those that remain are becoming specialised in the provision they offer. Recently there has been an increase in the number of homes provided by private concerns.

In order to ensure that the standard of care is maintained in the private sector, the DHSS sponsored a working party, convened by the Centre for Policy on Ageing, to report on current practice. *Home life: a code of practice for residential care* was published in 1984 and outlined the principles of care basic to all residential establishments. It emphasised the right of residents to live as normal a life as possible and to have the respect of those who care for them.

Some people may experience residential care for only a short period of time, whereas others may spend the rest of their lives in care. In the past, residential establishments were used to incarcerate unwanted members of society and thus remove people with problems away from society's view. There was a tendency to damage rather than enhance individual functioning. Today, residential care can be more purposeful, when aimed at enabling and developing people's ability to live to their full capacity.

Whatever changes occur in fashions of care, there will *always* be a need for some form of residential provision.

Appendix – system-induced old age

Elderly persons' homes run on traditional lines have been criticised for the unimaginative way in which they are run and the lack of stimulation they provide for residents. These 'routinised' establishments, with their pre-occupation with order and administrative convenience, neglect individual development, and this poor quality of care leads to institutionalisation.

The chart on page 214 illustrates how the philosophy of the home determines the various practices which in turn can be seen to hasten an elderly person's physical and mental decline. This process is referred to as *system-induced old age*.

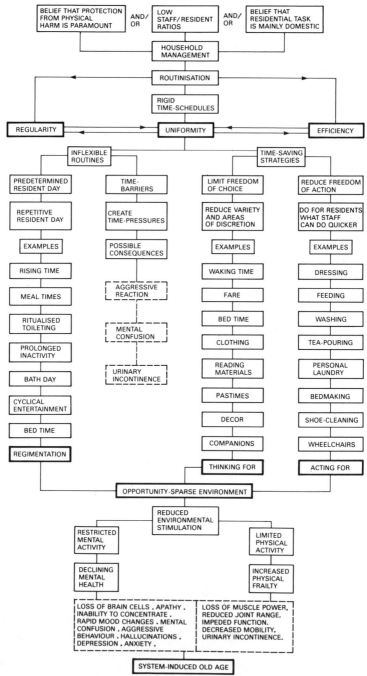

Traditional residential care – a benign guardianship

Exercise 1 – assignment – kibbutzim

The family home is considered by most people to be the best place in which to bring up a child, and residential living is felt to be artificial. Yet, in other societies – notably in Israel's kibbutzim – all children are looked after in residential accommodation, although they have regular daily contact with their natural parents. Find out what you can about the kibbutz system and consider any advantages it may have over conventional family life.

Exercise 2 – role-play – a hostel meeting

Setting
A weekly hostel meeting at which all staff and all residents are expected to be present. Normally these meetings are used for problem-solving and discussing current hostel issues, new regulations, and planned social activities.

Roles
Staff (four): Warden
Deputy warden
Assistant warden
Domestic
Residents (eight – for manageability)
Visiting probation officer
John

Problem
John (19) appeared in court three weeks ago charged with burglary (with three similar cases taken into consideration ('TICs')) and was placed on bail assessment of four weeks at the hostel. In the meantime, John's probation officer is preparing a social enquiry report (SER) for the court.

At John's hearing in a week's time, the court will consider the probation officer's SER and the report from the hostel before deciding on what sentence it will give. The weekly hostel meeting has now to decide whether the hostel should indicate to the court that it would be willing to grant John a full-time place in the event of the court deciding on a probation order instead of a custodial sentence.

Attitudes

Warden
You are aware that John was involved in a fight on his first night at the hostel and believe that he provoked the disturbance. You have heard reports that John has been stealing from other residents and that he is not pulling his weight by carrying out allotted work. You are uncertain whether John should be allotted a place.

Visiting probation officer:
You have travelled 50 miles to attend the meeting. You know about John's background – that he has been unemployed for two years and was turned out by his parents six months ago. Since then he has lived with an older man (30) in his small bedsitter. During the time spent living with his friend, John committed the offences for which he appeared before the court. His friend has also been charged.

You feel that John would benefit from living with a group in a supervised environment where he can face his problems. You feel that any current forms of anti-social behaviour are an expression of his uncertainty and fear that he may be sent to a youth-custody centre. You would like the hostel to offer John a place in the future, as this would strengthen your recommendation to the court that he be placed on probation.

Deputy warden
You have got to know John quite well and appreciate that John is worried about being 'sent down'. He is a bit boisterous and used to getting his own way. He missed the last hostel meeting, but claimed to have run out of money and to have been forced to walk back from town. He does not seem to do his share of jobs, but he has quite willingly spent many hours in the hostel garden and has tidied the front garden area. You feel that John would benefit from the hostel and would like to offer him a permanent place.

Assistant warden
You are concerned that a number of the residents' possessions have gone missing over the past three weeks and that John is being accused of taking them. John denies stealing anything but admits to borrowing 'with the intention of returning' several items – toothbrushes, soap, and some cassette tapes. These have now been returned to their owners, but two tapes are still missing! You are a little suspicious of John and feel that he may well disrupt the harmony of the hostel.

Domestic
You have complained to the deputy warden about the state of John's room, which you find constantly untidy. Also, you find John 'a bit cheeky' and generally disrespectful.

Residents

1. *Terry* You were involved in a fight with John on his first day and have remained distant ever since. You do not particularly like him and feel that he is not to be trusted. You have lost two cassette tapes recently.
2. *Joe* You like John and think he is 'a good laugh'. However, a few of your belongings have 'walked' since he arrived, including a favourite T-shirt. You suspect John.
3. *Levi* You like John and have become quite friendly with him. Although he is quite aggressive to others, he is very considerate to you.

You think him trustworthy, and good fun to have around. You hope he does not go to a youth-custody centre, as this would embitter him.

4. *Bill* You feel that John does not do his share of the work. You know he has already broken some hostel rules, bringing alcohol into the bedroom and shouting at a passer-by from the hostel window. You think he is 'a good laugh'. As far as you are aware, nobody has reported John for breaking the rules and you are unsure about raising the matter at the meeting.

5, 6, 7, and 8. *Other hostel residents* Choose your own role, either in support of or against John being offered a place.

John

You want to be offered a place – you don't like 'silly rules' but enjoy living in a group situation. You don't like being pushed around. If you were allowed to remain in the hostel and were put on probation, you think you would no longer commit offences. You were strongly influenced by the friend you used to live with, who encouraged you to take part in the burglaries.

Task

Role-play the meeting.

Exercise 3 – a problem in a hostel for the mentally handicapped

Peter Harris is a resident in a hostel for the mentally handicapped. He is in his thirties and suffers from epilepsy. Most of his life has been spent in residential care. He does not cut his own toe-nails, nor does he like anybody else doing this for him – he has to be held down by staff when it becomes necessary to perform this task. Recently, a member of staff accidentally nicked Peter's cheek with an electric razor while she was shaving him. Since this incident he has refused to allow any member of staff to go near him to shave him. He now sports a short stubbly beard.

The officer-in-charge would have no objection to Peter having a beard, but anticipates problems arising when it is due to be trimmed. This would be dangerous without Peter's co-operation.

What should the members of staff do to regain Peter's confidence and co-operation?

Exercise 4 – a problem in a hostel for the mentally handicapped

Alan and Jane are a mentally handicapped couple living in a hostel for the handicapped. Alan is a relatively capable man in his late thirties, and Jane is 29 and suffers from Down's syndrome. Their main interest is playing music tapes. At the weekend they go shopping together, and if they can afford it they go to the local pub. They spend a lot of time in Alan's room, and staff at the hostel have recently realised that the couple's relationship has a sexual element to it. Alan and Jane deny this.

Following discussions with the local GP, Jane has started taking the pill – although Jane and Alan continue to deny their sexual relationship. Jane's parents are both dead, but she has a brother and sister who are extremely protective towards her. They would be horrified if they felt that Jane might be sleeping with Alan and would certainly be unhappy about the situation if they were informed.

The question of sexual counselling, the rights of the individual, and the rights of relatives now need to be considered.

a) What should the hostel staff do?
b) Why do you think Jane and Alan deny any sexual involvement?

Exercise 5 – a problem in an elderly persons' home

Mr Graham is a resident (aged 75) of an elderly persons' home and over the past few months he has developed a special friendship with another elderly resident, Miss Burgess (72). They spend a good deal of time in each other's company and hold hands when sitting together in the lounge. Staff have noticed that Miss Burgess tends to encourage Mr Graham's affections but does not return them.

During one particular evening it is noticed that Mr Graham is not in the lounge and neither is he in his own room. Nobody remembers seeing him during the last half-hour. After a short search, Mr Graham is located – in the bedroom of one of the more confused female residents, who is partially undressed.

As officer-in-charge, how do you deal with this?

Exercise 6 – a problem in a children's home

You are the officer-in-charge of a children's home. One boy is enjoying attending a local judo club, where he is achieving some success and making friends. Other children from the home would like to join the club, but the boy does not want anyone else from the home to attend, as he does not want to be associated with them or the home. How will you handle this situation?

Questions for essays or discussion

1. Media attention and the formation of NAYPIC (the National Association of Young People in Care) have meant that the rights of children in care have begun to be recognised. How would you organise a children's home to ensure that the children have more control over their own lives?
2. What do you understand by the term 'institutionalisation'? How can establishments combat this and encourage individuals to participate more fully in day-to-day events?
3. With reference to any client group, consider the notion that adult

residents should be encouraged to develop sexual relationships with consenting partners of their choice and that staff should allow this to happen.

4. Care assistants are extremely busy and have been described as 'Jacks of all trades'. Should they concentrate on physical care or the emotional care of residents?

5. Of the six human needs outlined in this chapter, which do you think is the most important and how would you, as a member of staff, help this need to be met?

6. You are a houseparent in a short-stay children's home. Two girls, Amanda (aged six) and her sister Sylvia (aged eight) are due to stay with you when their mother (a single parent) goes into hospital for about ten days. How would you plan their admission to care in order to minimise any disruption?

Further reading

1. *Common human needs*, Charlotte Towle (Allen & Unwin, 1973). A standard text on good social-work practice.
2. *Home life: a code of practice for residential care* (Centre for Policy on Ageing, 1984). A well-presented book giving guide-lines for residential provision.
3. *The politics of mental handicap*, Jane Ryan and Frank Thomas (Pelican, 1980). An interesting look back at the way in which society has treated mentally handicapped people, and a look towards the future.
4. *Towards independence*, Kay Wood (Church of England Children's Society, 1980). A study of 12 adolescents living in bed-sit accommodation with social-work support, examining their progress after leaving care.
5. *Residential life with children*, Christopher Beedell (Routledge & Kegan Paul, 1970). A comprehensive account of residential work with children.
6. *Residential work*, Roger Clough (BASW/Macmillan, 1982). A comprehensive introduction to residential social work.

7 Ways of doing social work

Introduction

We have said that the most important aim of social work is to help clients to help themselves. There are various ways in which the social worker can assist clients to make progress. These are sometimes called *'methods of social-work intervention'*, making the point that in some way the social worker 'intervenes' in the life and situation of the client. Whatever 'method' or social-work theory the social worker is using, he will aim to bring about some kind of change in the client's position. Good, or effective, social work is not simply 'doing things for' the client, it is more 'doing things alongside' the client – working with the client in co-operation, to bring about positive change.

It is often difficult in social work to separate *theory* and *practice*, as people tend not to conform to laws or rules that try to describe their behaviour – every individual is unique, as is implied by the very definition of the word.

Much of the theory and practice of social work has originated within other disciplines – notably psychology and psychiatry. Now that social work has matured and become more sophisticated, an increasing number of ideas about how the job should be done have come from inside the discipline itself.

New cases will be referred to a social worker from a variety of different sources. The first task will be that of *making an assessment* of the case. Because medicine originally had a strong influence on social work, this was sometimes known as making a *'diagnosis'*, but this word is seldom heard nowadays.

Making an assessment will involve looking in depth at all factors involved in the case, whether it concerns an individual or a family. This process, of course, requires a great deal of *information-gathering*. It may also mean discussing the case with colleagues and other professionals who might be associated with it. This could take the form of a *case conference*, more details of which can be found at the end of chapter 4.

Following assessment, a *work-plan* will be made – involving the client or family as much as possible. As work with the case proceeds, periodic assessments will take place in order to evaluate *progress* (or the lack of it). These periodic assessments may lead to the evolving of a new work-plan, and this might require that the problem should be approached in a different way.

Traditionally, approaches to social work have been divided into:

a) *casework*,
b) *group work*,
c) *community work*.

This division is no longer useful, as it is an over-simplification. New developments have caused several different methods to arise within each major approach, and it is more accurate to view these three as different *settings* within which social work is carried out.

This chapter will explore several different ways of *doing social work*. Based around three different case-studies, it will examine, in turn, three different methods of working with (or intervening in) each case.

Note The cases are *not* intended to be *typical* of a social worker's case-load – they merely serve to illustrate different ways of doing social work. They are composite portrayals, based on situations that could occur.

Case-study 1

John, a 16-year-old who has recently left school, has no job to go to. He has become frustrated and depressed – partly as a result of being unemployed, but also because of the tension that exists between his parents, who are on the verge of separating. Years of hostility (punctuated by violence) between his parents have taken their toll on him.

After a particularly bad row between his mother and father, John has taken (over the previous three weeks) to staying out of home as much as possible, and on some nights he has not returned. When his mother questions him about where he has been, he becomes very aggressive, and in desperation she contacts a social worker. She tells the social worker that she feels that John may get into trouble with the police – she describes some of his friends as 'undesirable', because, she says, they have 'been before the court on several occasions'. With the added pressure of marital problems, the mother feels 'near the end of her tether'. The social worker, after speaking with her for about an hour, says she would like to visit the whole family at home. This is arranged to take place in two days' time.

Unfortunately, when the social worker arrives at the house, John's father is not there, having stormed out earlier, saying to his wife that John is 'her problem' and she will have to 'sort it out'. The mother is tearful and distraught. In addition to John and his mother, John's two sisters, aged 12 and 14, are present.

Following this meeting, the social worker writes to John's father suggesting that she should meet him on a certain day, but he fails to turn up. After making an assessment of the case, the social worker decides on the best plan of action in the given circumstances. She decides that there are three possible ways of intervening: counselling, casework, and family therapy.

Counselling
Counselling is basically a way of helping someone to explore a problem.

As well as listening, counselling involves the observation of non-verbal communication.

The aim is to help a person (or persons) to feel that they can either cope or live with the problem or find a solution to the problem. The basis of counselling is the growth of a relationship between the counsellor and client which is built on trust. Counselling involves *listening* effectively, because, without a good understanding of the situation and the feelings of the person (and/or persons) concerned, the counsellor will be unable to respond appropriately. A major requirement for listening effectively is a good understanding of *non-verbal communication*.

After making her assessment of John's case, the social worker begins to see him alone, twice a week, and to start to help him explore his feelings and problems. After an initial period of distrust and suspicion on John's part, they begin to make progress together, and John begins to understand more clearly how he thinks and feels toward his own behaviour, his home, and his family. Counselling gives him time, and the 'friendly listening ear' of a sensitive adult. As a result, his behaviour changes – he becomes more aware of his mother's predicament and he begins to support her in what becomes an increasingly difficult situation where his father is concerned.

Casework
This is sometimes known as *'social casework'* or *'psycho-social casework'*. It is generally understood to have a wider meaning than counselling, but sometimes it is used loosely to signify the same or a similar method of approach. It basically differs from counselling in that it

involves seeing and working with clients in their social setting. It is concerned with the clients' physical environment, the quality of their accommodation, their financial situation, and family and social relationships.

Casework is an approach which originally came to Britain from the USA and it has its origins in medical and psychological understandings of people's problems. The individual *case reports* and *case records*, along with the development of *case conferences*, originally gave it its name. It is sometimes called 'one-to-one' working.

The social worker in John's case might have decided on this approach and so would have gathered much information about John as an individual and about John within his family and wider social setting. It might have involved helping John to foster more positive interests and social and leisure pursuits in order to divert him away from any tendency towards drifting into crime or delinquency. It might have involved seeing the whole family on occasions, in order to better assess John's progress.

In effective casework, the social worker will bring a knowledge of psychological theory to bear in order to make a better informed intervention.

Following developments which differentiated *'brief'* and *'extended'* casework, a new approach became known as *task-centred casework*. This originated in the USA in the mid 1970s, and is dealt with more fully later in this chapter.

Family therapy

The social worker might have decided that neither individual counselling nor casework were sufficient to deal with the problems presented by John's case. Assessment might have shown his problems to be fully rooted within his family relationships, and the social worker might therefore have felt that *family therapy* would be more appropriate or effective. (This is sometimes also known as *'conjoint family therapy'*.)

This therapy treats the whole family, not just the member presenting a problem (in this case, John). Only very rarely is one particular individual solely responsible for problems – in fact, one person can take on the role of 'symptom-bearer', where his or her 'problem behaviour' is a consequence of more fundamental family discord.

One of the advantages of family therapy is that it sees a whole family in operation, or in interaction. It requires the use of skill, intuition, and sensitivity on the part of the social worker to understand clearly the nature of a particular family's dynamics – the relationships between various members of the family, and the blocks and hindrances to constructive interaction.

It will often take time to become effective. At first, meetings between the social worker and the family may be strained or artificial. However, the skilled practitioner will be able to help family members relax and encourage them to be more open and honest with each other. Much of the approach involves helping people to gain more insight into themselves and to better understand how their behaviour affects other members of the family.

In sculpting, the physical representation of family relationships can provide insights for family members.

A technique called *sculpting* is sometimes used as a device for clarifying relationships between family members. All members of the family in turn have the opportunity to visually represent their own perceptions of their relationships with the others. This will include non-verbal communication such as gestures, facial expressions, and posture. This often enables people to see more clearly their own position and the position of others within the family.

In John's case, gaining the trust and co-operation of his father might have been very difficult, if not impossible, and the social worker would have borne this in mind when considering the usefulness of family therapy.

Case-study 2

Joan is an elderly lady of 77 who lives with her daughter's family. The family consists of her daughter, her daughter's husband, and their two children – a boy aged 18 and a girl aged 15. Joan is finding that mobility is becoming increasingly difficult, and her condition of incontinence is becoming worse. This has put great pressure on the whole family. On one particular day, tired of assisting her mother upstairs, Mary, the daughter, leaves her mother to her own devices and Joan has a bad fall. The health visitor who visits Joan feels that the family needs the contact of a social worker, so she makes a referral to the local social-services department.

224

Joan does not suffer from dementia – on the contrary, she is rather a lively and intelligent person. Recently, however, she has become depressed – a reaction to what she sees as the family's insensitivity to her problems. Her son-in-law works away from home most of the time, so Joan's daughter and the two children bear the brunt of responsibility for her.

When the social worker makes her first visit to Joan, she realises that the family is in a state of crisis – time has taken its toll on the goodwill which had once existed in the family and they now feel that they cannot go on much longer. When making her assessment, the social worker considers three different ways of approaching the problem: crisis intervention, residential care, and task-centred casework.

Crisis intervention

Crisis intervention is not so much a distinct method of social-work intervention as a way of examining the situation of a person who is in a state of crisis and is undergoing much distress. It originated in psychiatry rather than social work, and it has often been applied in working with the bereaved. One of the factors central to it is that people in a state of crisis are usually more amenable to change. It therefore uses this openness to change as a basis towards reaching a desirable solution.

In Joan's case, the social worker attempts to help the family members to see that change can be positive, and to encourage the growth of co-operation in reaching for a better solution to their problem. This will involve not apportioning blame to anyone in particular (Joan cannot avoid the ageing process!). She might well see Joan alone on some occasions, but will certainly want to see all the family members together in order to encourage them to see that the crisis involves them all, as does the finding of a solution.

Crisis intervention in this case will involve explaining the various alternatives to the family's present situation. It may involve practicalities such as introducing aids and adaptations to the home. Here are some possible examples: a chair-lift for the stairs; rearranging rooms so that Joan can sleep downstairs and receive help with toileting; obtaining outside assistance with laundry services; and generally trying to spread responsibilities for assisting Joan more evenly among family members. This last will have the effect of involving the children more, thus reducing the pressure on the mother.

Fortunately, in this case, the family wants Joan to remain with them at home – they do not wish to have her placed in residential care for the elderly. However, it is something which the social worker feels should at least be considered.

Residential care

Again, residential care should not be regarded as a distinct method of social-work intervention – more accurately, it should be regarded as a social-work setting which may involve several different approaches, for example casework or group work.

One of the reasons why the social worker considers it in Joan's case is because the family is deemed to be in a state of crisis. She may legitimately feel that a brief period in a residential setting – that is, respite care – may at some stage provide both Joan and the family with a desirable (if not essential) break from each other, to give them the opportunity to 'recharge batteries' and return to the situation with more energy. It would not, however, be wise to use the resource immediately, before the family has had a chance to formulate plans to deal with the current problem.

A period of separation may have the effect of actually strengthening the bond between Joan and the family, but the social worker would have to be aware that the opposite effect may unfortunately occur. The period of assessment is therefore extremely important. Equally important is that the social worker should have a good intuitive understanding of the likely consequences of her intervention.

Task-centred casework (TCC)

This is a modification of traditional *social casework*. It is an attempt to 'sharpen' it by tackling problems experienced by clients by means of specific achievable *tasks* which may be performed within a time-limit. Assessment is very important, and the approach usually involves the concept of a *contract* drawn up between the social worker and the client. One of the strengths of TCC is that it concentrates on the client's own conception of his or her difficulties as the key to reaching a solution. It is similar to crisis intervention in that it holds that a breakdown in coping with problems can trigger off desires for change within the clients themselves. If used effectively, it will increase the clients' ability to cope in the near and distant future.

In Joan's case, the social worker would make an assessment which would break down the crisis that is facing the family into its component parts. First, she would examine Joan's mobility and incontinence problems, then go on to examine how much and in what way these have caused wider difficulties in the family. Next, she would encourage Joan and other family members to set simple and achievable tasks to help solve the problems. As one task is achieved – for example, rearranging rooms in the house to accommodate Joan downstairs – it would generally have the effect of increasing the family's confidence and capacity to deal with others, for example Joan's toileting difficulties. As tasks are fulfilled, so family relationships would tend to improve, and this would lead to an enhanced quality of life for all involved.

Ideally the tasks should be shared as equally as possible (within practical limitations) throughout the family. Joan's son-in-law would also be encouraged to take a greater part on his return home from working away.

Task-centred casework involves periodic assessment as tasks are achieved, or the setting of new tasks if problems occur along the way. Another strength of the method is that, from the very start of a 'contract', the end is in view because all parties are fully aware of the tasks they have set in co-operation with the social worker. Contracts can be written or orally agreed as the approach is adapted to a particular case.

Case-study 3

Jim is a 28-year-old divorced man living alone in lodgings. He has a gambling problem which has caused his marriage to end in divorce. Money for the family had been scarce even when Jim was in work, but financial problems had got worse as his gambling habit increased. He and his wife parted two years ago. He has now been unemployed for a year and he is severely depressed. He has no social contacts apart from those in the local betting-shop. He has recently sought the help of a social worker because he has begun to think that only suicide could bring an end to his problems. Obviously subconsciously he does not really want to end his life – only his problems – otherwise he would not have sought help.

The social worker, having made an assessment of Jim's case, considers three possible ways of tackling the problem: group work, behaviour modification, and social- or life-skills training.

Group work
The social worker is aware of a group run by a colleague for people with problems concerning gambling. He refers Jim to this group, and Jim, being desperate, is keen to take part in whatever is offered.

The initial focus of the social worker is to help the group to get to know Jim and to encourage Jim to share his problems with the group as a whole. Trust is an essential ingredient if this is to happen effectively, and so too is a relaxed atmosphere.

Other group members are encouraged to share the various, often very personal, methods they have so far used to deal with the temptation to gamble. From the start, the social worker is pleased to observe that this gives Jim hope and an increased confidence that he can overcome his problem.

The group is an ongoing one – it does not set a time-limit to its existence. However, after a period of some months, Jim may feel that he has accomplished something and will therefore try to manage without this form of support and assistance.

Behaviour modification
The social worker might have felt that behaviour modification would provide a more direct solution to Jim's gambling problem. Behaviour modification has its origins within psychology, from what is usually called '*social-learning theory*'. Central to this theory is the concept that behaviour is *learnt* in a social setting; therefore, when behaviour causes problems (in this case Jim's gambling), it can be *unlearnt*. In other words, the client can learn new forms of more appropriate behaviour, in order to cope with life without gambling. As a social-work approach it has a narrow focus, which appears to contribute to its success. Behavioural

227

techniques can be used only if the client is willing to co-operate – in Jim's case, he would have to earnestly desire to give up gambling.

Gambling, like other forms of compulsive habit-forming behaviour – for example smoking, overeating, and drug addiction – is rewarding to the person who does it. The social worker using behavioural techniques must first of all have got Jim to look at those particular aspects of gambling which he finds especially enjoyable – for example, many gamblers are thrilled and stimulated by the tension and excitement they feel in a crowded betting-shop when a race is about to be run.

The behavioural therapist would have helped Jim to work out in detail the stages that lead up to his actively placing a bet – the time of day, the mood he is in, where he is in relation to the betting-shop or telephone (if he is in the habit of telephoning bets), and so on – until he had a clear picture of all the behavioural steps leading up to the actual moment when Jim's money goes across the counter. This information would then be used to design a 'programme' in which alternative behaviours are set up which are incompatible with Jim's placing a bet. For example, if it were discovered that Jim gets the urge to gamble when he is alone and feeling miserable in the morning, it might be suggested that at that time each morning he arranges to attend an adult-education class in a subject that he is interested in. Other alternatives would also have been important – such as avoiding walking past the betting-shop, not listening to the racing on the radio or television, and not buying racing papers.

Jim could also have been helped by deliberately calling to mind some of the more unpleasant experiences he has undergone as a result of his giving in to the temptation to gamble.

Jim would have been asked to keep a detailed record on a chart showing the number of times he felt like betting and the occasions when he managed to avoid giving in to this temptation. The social worker would have used this record to encourage Jim's effort – he would have rewarded him with praise and have offered suggestions of ways in which he could treat himself with the money he had saved. Most people in Jim's situation have lost their self-respect and consequently lack faith in themselves. This often causes them to give up if they have had a bad day – especially if there is no one near them to dissuade them – so measuring success in small steps and using record charts to point out the client's success is a very effective way of eventually overcoming the problem. Encouragement is an essential component of behaviour modification.

Social- or life-skills training
The behaviour-modification approach in Jim's case would have focused on the particular behaviour patterns which led to compulsive gambling, but the social worker might have decided on a different way of tackling the issue. Jim is often bored and frustrated at having nothing to do during the day, owing to his being unemployed. He has now been unemployed for a year, and as time passes he is becoming more despondent about finding another job. His confidence is constantly being sapped, and he is now at

228

the stage where he does not even bother to look for jobs in local newspapers and Jobcentres.

Rather than focus on his gambling 'problem', the social worker might have thought that, if he could increase Jim's chances of getting a job and in so doing help Jim to inject more discipline into his life-style, then it might well have the effect of diverting him from gambling.

The social worker might therefore have initiated a programme of *social-skills training* (sometimes known as *life-skills training*). It could have been very basic, but it might have had a powerful effect in increasing Jim's sense of self-worth and given him a sense of purpose. Jim could have been helped in looking for jobs, in scanning local papers and Jobcentre displays. He could have been helped to use the telephone more effectively and to address other people more pleasantly and positively. *Role-play* could have been used to simulate a real interview to equip Jim with more confidence. Jim could have swapped roles in the scenario and thus have been helped to see other aspects of the interview situation. All this would have been aimed at helping Jim to feel better within himself, which in turn should encourage him to use his own initiative.

A note about the case-studies

In each of the above three case-studies, three possible ways of working were provided. We want to stress here that, in social work, very rarely is there only *one* correct way of working with individual clients and their problems.

Other social-work approaches

Certain ways of working with clients have either not been mentioned or have not been fully expounded so far. They are dealt with here.

Debt counselling or welfare-rights work

Over the past few years, much more attention has been given to the financial resources of clients and the way in which these will affect other aspects of the clients' lives. In fact some social workers have become specialists in this field, and specific courses are run to equip carers with the necessary skills. The work of certain pressure groups such as the Child Poverty Action Group (CPAG) has encouraged this focus. This particular group publishes an annual *National welfare benefits handbook* which is invaluable for the amount of information it contains and its clarity of presentation.

The recipients of State benefits are not the only people that are assisted by social workers – the area of work has broadened to become known as *'debt counselling'* and can involve dealing with any kind of financial problem.

Most social workers do not specialise in this type of work – they incorporate it in their range of skills. They would only refer a case to a specialist if the problem was particularly difficult or complicated.

Radical social work

The increasing interest among social workers in welfare-rights work to some extent reflects the evolution of a growing commitment in the 1970s to a socialist approach to, and critique of, social policy and social work. This was partly owing to the greater number of younger entrants to social work, often with degree qualifications, who had a heightened sensibility of political constraints on people in society. From the mid-1970s, a large amount of written material began to emerge about a socialist approach to social work. From this has developed the concept of *'radical social work'*. This is not synonymous with a socialist approach, but the two are closely related.

Radical social work is not a distinct *method* of social-work intervention: rather it is a *style* of working or an *ideology* which informs the way in which carers will intervene. The basic philosophy is that the problems of clients are rooted in society – in the unequal distribution of wealth and other resources – rather than in supposed individual inadequacies. The radical therefore looks to change society, while standing alongside the client as 'brothers in arms'. This philosophy has meant that certain social-work interventions – for example, casework in its several forms – have been heavily criticised or rejected altogether, while others – for example, community work and welfare-rights work – have been supported.

Community work

Again, 'community work' is not a distinct *method* used in social work but it is a very important way of working which does involve specific skills.

A *community worker* can be employed by a wide range of agencies, both statutory and voluntary. The focus of his work may be with young people; with certain special-need groups (drug users, for example); or with whole communities, where the 'client' population will be a typical cross-section of society. He may have a specific task – for example, the setting-up of play provision on a large council housing estate – or a general role – work in an area of a large city, assessing local facilities and resources and deficiencies and helping to meet social needs as they arise.

Skills required by a community worker will include

a) the ability to relate to a wide range of people who will vary in regard to age, ethnic origin, interests, and political persuasion;
b) a good understanding of political issues – both locally and in a wider, sometimes national, context;
c) a thorough knowledge of local resources, groups, voluntary initiatives, local-authority departments, and a wide variety of other organisations;
d) some competence in *group-work* skills, as much of the job involves working with a variety of different groups of people – for example, council tenants, children, young people, old-age pensioners;
e) an ability to organise a range of different activities – for example,

fund-raising events, or clubs catering for a wide diversity of interests;

f) good diplomacy – the community worker will have to liaise with a wide range of different people, including various professionals, employees of local-government departments, and those working for a large number of voluntary groups and organisations.

This diverse range of skills obviously indicates that community work is demanding. Another aspect of the work is that it often entails working a long week – community workers usually have to make themselves available for weekend and evening work. They have to be careful to take sufficient breaks, to avoid 'burn-out'.

Group work

Group work is so important that it requires more detailed comment than was allowed in the above case-studies. In the UK, it started to become properly established as a method used in social work in the 1960s. It was imported from the USA, where it had been developed by psychologists and psychotherapists. Today, in the UK, an increasing number of social workers are becoming involved in its use.

The growth in intermediate-treatment provision in recent years has provided an encouragement to group work, but it is a mistake to regard intermediate treatment as synonymous with this method – IT is much more besides.

There are several different types of group. We can single out four important ones:

i) *Problem-solving groups* Social workers frequently run groups which will help members who share a common problem to work through difficulties in co-operation with others. Discussion will take place, and the social worker will be keen to see a build-up of confidence in the participants.

ii) *Educational groups* The function of many groups will be to teach members something which will be of use to them. We can include here *social-skills training*, in which there has recently been a tremendous growth.

Social-skills (or *life-skills*) *training* is well suited to group practice. Social workers can bring together, for example, groups of unemployed teenagers and work through the various problems and testing situations they are likely to meet in their efforts to find a job.

Role-play can be used, as we illustrated in our sample case-study concerning Jim, to familiarise young people with job interviews. This can be an excellent group activity, involving all members of the group.

iii) *Self-help groups* People who share a common problem will often form a group in order to provide mutual support. They can then work through their problems in co-operation with others. Examples of these are groups for the wives of men serving prison sentences; groups for the parents of drug abusers; groups for the parents of handicapped

231

children; and other groups too numerous to mention. 'Alcoholics Anonymous', of course, is a well established, international, self-help group.

Social workers can be instrumental in helping people to come together to start a group. Once it is established, the social worker will withdraw from involvement completely so that it does literally become a self-help group.

iv) *Activity-based groups* These will include many intermediate-treatment groups. A wide diversity of activities takes place in activity-based groups (as the name implies) – for example, car repair or motorcycle building for groups of young ex-offenders, or those at risk of offending, and outdoor pursuits (also known as 'Outward Bound') involving a group sharing the experience of living in the countryside for a weekend or a few days. Some of these can be very tough and tiring for all involved. Some activity groups may be designed to help young people use their leisure time more constructively, to stimulate or cultivate an interest – groups may go ice-skating or to the theatre, for example.

There are different styles of group leadership. An 'authoritarian' leader will be very directive, but a 'democratic' leader will endeavour to involve all group members, as much as possible, at the same time. The style of leadership used will depend on the aims and objectives of the group and the task in hand.

Group work has become very popular because it is seen to be effective, although this is obviously very difficult to measure. In some ways group work simulates everyday life, thus the method is more natural than the one-to-one methods of social-work intervention. (We spend much of our time with groups of other people – even if only with our family.) Groups often provide a more intense experience, because several people together generate more energy as they interact. Learning from others is a natural way of learning, and social workers believe it can be therapeutic.

Group work is not 'easier' than, say, casework – it can involve more time and hard work, especially at the 'setting-up' stage. However, if it is done well and it has the desired effect on the individuals concerned, the reward is considerable.

Six-category intervention analysis

This is the work of John Heron and was developed at the University of Surrey in the 1970s. Intervention analysis is a useful *analytical tool* – it is *not* a method of social work. Heron analysed intervention in the helping professions and said that it could be examined in terms of six different categories. Whenever a social worker is working with a client – especially in a one-to-one situation – he will be using interventions in one or more of the following categories, which are divided into two groups of three. The first group are *authoritative* interventions, meaning that the social worker is being fairly dominant or assertive. The second group are *facilitative*, meaning that the social worker is being less obtrusive.

The categories are:

Authoritative

i) *Prescriptive*   This involves giving advice, being critical or judgemental, and generally aiming to direct the client's behaviour.

ii) *Informative*   Here the social worker is acting as 'teacher', in giving new information or knowledge to the client.

iii) *Confronting*   The social worker challenges the client, possibly by giving her direct 'feedback' about her behaviour.

Facilitative

iv) *Cathartic*   This aims to help the client to release emotion – sometimes painful emotion – often signified by physical signs like crying, laughing, and trembling.

v) *Catalytic*   The social worker here seeks to enable the client to learn and develop through self-discovery and self-direction. The onus for doing the 'work', in a one-to-one situation, is on the client.

vi) *Supportive*   This is extremely important in all social-work intervention, as it affirms the worth and value of the client as an individual. The social worker approves, confirms, and validates the client.

Heron says of the above analysis that it aids 'the development of self-assessment and self-monitoring in the helping professions'. It helps social workers to analyse what they do, and to find out which particular parts of practice are helpful and which are not.

Heron makes the point that, in his experience, practitioners tend to be more skilled in the authoritative interventions than in the facilitative. He finds the least competence in cathartic intervention. All six categories are of equal importance – that is, none is 'better' than the others. The skilled social worker should possess expertise in all and be readily able to switch from one way of working to another.

It is important to remember that the six types of intervention are of value only if they are rooted in compassion, care, and concern for the client.

The unitary (or integrated) model of social-work intervention

The development of this model sprang from disillusionment with the traditional tripartite division of social-work methods into *casework*, *group work*, and *community work*. Social-work theorists and educators were keen to have more integration between these different approaches and also to go further and relocate 'problems' traditionally seen as being located in the mind of the individual. *Social situations* became the focus for change, rather than 'pathological' individuals.

This work developed originally in the USA in the early 1970s. Allen Pincus and Anne Minahan (working together) and Howard Goldstein

233

were instrumental in developing the model, but others have put forward similar theories. It was based on *social-systems theory* which stresses the *interrelatedness* of people, agencies, and institutions in our society. The model of society that it proposes highlights how one institution is dependent on others for all to be able to function together and for society to be able to continue to exist.

When applied to relationships between people and organisations in our society, systems theory involves four levels of social system:

  i) *individual personality system* (the individual),
 ii) *interpersonal dyad system* (two people in interaction),
iii) *interpersonal social systems* (these can be families or groups of people relating together),
 iv) *socio-cultural social systems* (this can refer to very large identifiable groups of people – for example, the homeless, or single-parent families, or whole communities, or even countries).

It can be seen that these systems include everyone from the individual to the nation State. All these groups of people or systems interrelate (or interact) with each other and influence each other. Changes in one system will affect others, possibly causing changes in those too.

The unitary model suggests that, if social workers see individuals as being part of a larger interacting social system, they will be aware of a wider range of variables, will see complex problems more clearly, and will be aware of a greater range of possible solutions to people's difficulties. The model criticises *casework* for its concentration on individuals and their problems, because this focus may not be the best way of finding a viable solution. It may be more effective to look for a potential answer beyond the contact between social worker and client.

The model proposed by Pincus and Minahan recognises that, for individuals to live, they depend upon all kinds of people, agencies, and organisations in society. They require material and emotional support. Those people or organisations that provide this are known as *resource systems*. The family is obviously crucially important in providing these resources, especially in an individual's early life.

Social workers should ensure that clients make the best possible use of the resource systems around them in society. In order to help social workers focus their intervention with clients, Pincus and Minahan identify four basic systems which interact:

a) *The change-agent system*   This refers to *who* is going to bring about change in a client's situation. It will be the social worker and also the agency employing him. If positive change is not occurring for a client, it may be the agency that requires changing. This illustrates the radical and wide nature of the unitary model – it considers all possibilities.

b) *The client system*   This refers to the person, family, group, organisation, or community which has 'engaged the services' of the social worker because assistance is required.

c) *The target system* This describes those people whom the social worker (or *change agent*) needs to influence in order to do his work and help to bring about change. Frequently the client system and the target system will be the same, but there will be exceptions – for example, when a social worker is attempting to get a family rehoused because of deplorable living conditions, the 'target system' may well be influencial employees of the local housing department.

d) *The action system* Social workers do not work on their own: they involve all kinds of other people – for example, clients' families, friends, and other professionals – in their efforts to find a solution. All these people, together with the social worker, are known as the 'action system'.

Assessment is central to the unitary model. Effective assessment will involve gaining a thorough knowledge of the client and her friends, relations, and other social contacts. When examining the 'presenting problem', the social worker may well realise that the client should not be the 'target system' for change. Many social workers have found the model beneficial for 'sharpening' their practice, and useful in helping them to look more deeply into 'problems'. It has also been discovered to be a good 'team-building' activity when a complete social-work team takes up and uses the model.

Unitary social work is a useful *assessment tool* in that it involves a thorough investigation of the client's entire situation – i.e. all social contacts etc. It involves identifying four systems concerning the client's present situation. These four systems are interrelated. Part of the assessment process involves considering where the problem to be dealt with actually lies (the *target system*). It may be that the 'target system' is not the client but someone or something else – for example, other people significant in the client's situation, the client's social setting, institutional care, etc. The following case involving two social workers illustrates this.

Susan is 14 years old. For the past two years she has been living in residential care in a small community home ('Abbeycliffe House'). You are a social worker in a social-services-department local office. You have recently taken over as Susan's social worker from a social worker who has left the office. Before meeting Susan for the first time, you read through the case file. In it you come across the following passage which is part of the previous social worker's assessment of the case:

'Abbeycliffe House is ideally suited to Susan's needs, but she has so far proved difficult and unco-operative. Jim Kelly (officer-in-charge) has been very patient with her and has gone to great lengths to help her settle. She has not responded positively to this. Her behaviour has often been disruptive, upsetting other young people in the house. I believe Susan's new social worker should focus his energies on modifying her behaviour and attitudes.'

Clearly, for this social worker, Susan's behaviour is 'the problem' – he has identified her as the target system.

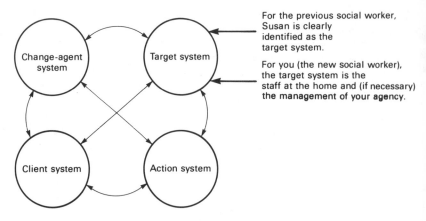

The unitary or integrated model of social-work intervention

Some time later, you have now met Susan three times at Abbeycliffe House and have gained a very different impression of her situation. As a result, you have made your own assessment. You find her quiet and you suspect that she is depressed. When seeing her along with the officer-in-charge, you have detected an intolerance in him for her. He has spoken curtly and impatiently to her. When speaking alone with her, you feel that she is unhappy at Abbeycliffe House and that it is not well-suited to her needs. You do not think you should focus on her as 'the problem' (*target system*): rather, you identify the target system as

a) in the short term, the officer-in-charge and other staff at the home, who you feel are acting inappropriately towards Susan;

b) in the long term, the management within your own organisation, as (if things do not work out well) you may have to insist that Susan is moved to a home which would cater better for her needs.

The influence of the unitary or integrated approach continues to grow in social work in the UK. It is taught by many schools of social work in polytechnics and universities – some of them even make it the core of the curriculum, around which other social-work methods are taught. This also applies in social-work practice, where several different methods – for example, counselling, task-centred casework, group work, and behaviour modification – can be implemented within the unitary model.

Conclusion

The different ways of 'doing social work', which involve theory and practice, form a difficult and complex area of study. This chapter has set

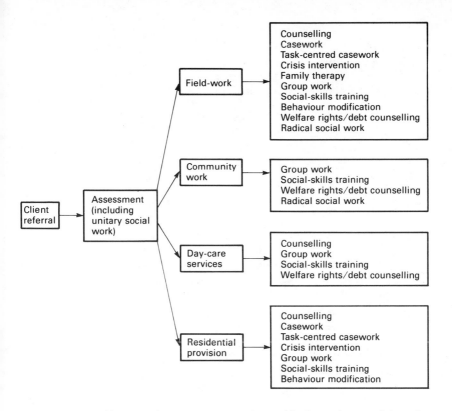

The methods of intervention most commonly used in the various social-work settings
(*Note* Six-category intervention analysis is not mentioned, as it is an analytical tool rather than a method.)

out to make it simple and accessible. In so doing, it may not always have done justice to the intricacies of the discipline, and we ask the reader to excuse this.

We want to stress that effective social-work intervention must use a range of approaches, and thus avoid limitation and resistance to change. Fashions in social-work methods are constantly in a state of flux, as in any area of life. *Effectiveness* and its measurement in social work will always be problematic. Social workers ultimately exist to do themselves out of a job! Whatever means or criteria are used to measure effectiveness, one thing is certain: social workers should remain flexible in their use of different methods or approaches and should adapt these to the client rather than vice versa.

Exercise 1 – role-play – a social-work visit

Read case-study 1 on page 221. You are to role-play John's family situation from just before the social worker arrives at his home – i.e., start with John's father leaving the house in an angry mood. Role-play through until the social worker leaves the house.

Roles
Father
Mother
John (aged 16)
Sister (aged 14)
Sister (aged 12)
Social worker

Think beforehand about the roles and what kind of personality you are going to take on. Think perhaps of some key things you intend to say as the role-play progresses. Allow 30 minutes for the role-play.

Following the role-play, a discussion could take place examining what went on and any general issues raised with regard to family relationships etc.

Exercise 2 – setting up a group

Groups are important tools in social work. By talking to people in your local community, by reading local and community newspapers, and by speaking to key workers in your area – community workers, or community-centre wardens, or youth workers, for example – isolate a particular problem in the area (anything you like, as long as it has a social component). Then plan the setting-up of a 'pressure group', or 'self-help' group, or whatever type of group would be most appropriate for dealing with the problem. Ask yourself questions like:

a) How would you contact people you wanted to interest in your group?
b) Would you hold meetings?
c) What publicity would you need?
d) How would the group be organised?
e) Would it be a short-term or an ongoing group?
f) What activity would the group need to involve itself in?
g) Where might you get funding from?

Exercise 3 – case studies

Read the following two case-studies. At the end of each, you have to decide which of the ways of doing social work explained in this chapter would be most appropriate to use. Don't worry if you feel that more than one kind of 'intervention' would be appropriate – explain why you think this is the case. When you have decided, explain how you would actually set about using the technique(s) chosen to work with the client. Plan out your first meeting, using the method(s) you have decided on.

a) The Afford family

As a duty officer in a social-services-department local office you are meeting Mrs Afford for the very first time. She is distraught, and you gain the overwhelming impression that she is overburdened at the present time. She tells you that three weeks ago her husband died, leaving her with her three children – two girls, aged 17 and 14, and a boy aged 12.

Sarah (the 14-year-old) and Paul (the son) were both proving to be difficult a considerable time before their father's death, which was completely unexpected – the result of a serious accident at his workplace. Sarah spends a great deal of time out of the home, with a group of young people on the estate where the family lives. She seems to come home only to eat and sleep. She is insolent to her mother, who realises that Sarah was dreadfully upset by her father's death, being especially close to him. Paul spends most of his time indoors. What worries Mrs Afford is that he appears lethargic and depressed – not at all usual for him. She has great difficulty rousing him for school in the mornings and suspects he has played truant on occasions – going off on his own to amuse himself. Her older daughter, Jacqui, presents no problem, and Mrs Afford describes her as having been 'supportive' since her father's death.

Mrs Afford does not feel she can cope any longer on her own, and her only relations live a long way away. She feels unable to share her problems with friends or neighbours, as she is worried that she will be thought of as 'inadequate' and a 'poor mother' (her own words).

After speaking with Mrs Afford for just over an hour, you feel that you have a fairly full understanding of her situation. You must now make an assessment as to how you will work with her and her family.

b) Neil – a young offender

You are a probation officer in contact with Neil, aged 18. He has just appeared in court and was placed on probation for one year. He had committed a serious burglary at an electrical-goods warehouse, and you realised that there was a possibility of a custodial sentence. You are pleased that the court did not sentence him to youth custody but allowed him to remain in the community instead.

Neil lives with his mother (a single parent). He is an only child. His mother has struggled to manage financially over the last ten years, since Neil's father left. The home is in a poor physical condition. His mother has found Neil difficult to discipline since he was about thirteen, and she feels that the lack of a 'father figure' in the home has contributed to this. She certainly shows Neil affection, but his attitude to her is inconsiderate, and he can be arrogant and aggressive.

He leads his life outside of the home, spending almost all his time 'hanging around' with friends. He is unemployed, having dropped out of a Youth Training Scheme some eighteen months ago. He says he would like very much to work as a welder, but he does not have much idea about how to find a job. Scrambling bikes are a great interest, but he cannot afford one of his own and so cadges rides on friends' bikes.

Neil seems to find his contact with you valuable, and you feel it is important to build on this now. In three days' time you are to see Neil again. Plan your future contact with him.

Exercise 4 – role-play – SSD office duty

Think about what constitutes good counselling – effective listening, observing non-verbal communication, and helping the client relax, for example.

Situation
You are a social worker on office duty in a social-services-department local office. Mrs Salter – an extremely distraught woman of 35 – comes in, desperate for advice and assistance. She is married with two young children (aged six and four) whom she has left in the care of a neighbour. The problem focuses around her husband's consumption of alcohol. She describes him as always having been a 'heavy drinker', but she fears that he has become dependent on alcohol over the past few months. He is in work, but from week to week he has given her less and less money with which to buy food and other necessities. She has had to borrow from family and friends to 'make ends meet', and the situation now is critical. She has confronted her husband about the problem in an increasingly assertive way, but he either evades the issue or becomes aggressive. (He is not violent.) Mrs Salter has a great deal of sympathy for her husband (she describes his job as 'very demanding and exhausting', for example) and says that he needs help, but she is at a loss and cannot go on.

Task
In pairs, role-play this meeting and see what develops. The social worker, while helping Mrs Salter to become calmer, will be considering how to make contact with her husband and whether or not to visit the home, as well as encouraging Mrs Salter to share her feelings and attempting to encourage a build-up of trust between them.

Following the role-play
Discussion could cover any issues raised and then lead to a more general consideration of effective counselling and what it involves.
Note Other ways of working can be role-played. The group can fairly easily invent case material with which to work.

Questions for essays or discussion

1. In working with people as a carer, do you think it is important that

clients should *want* to change? Can anything be achieved if they resist the idea of personal change?

2. Measuring how effective we are as carers is extremely difficult in that there are so many criteria which we could choose to apply – for example, that clients are better able to manage their own problems, have more self-confidence, are able to form relationships more easily, have some control over an addiction, and so on. As a carer, how would you measure your effectiveness if you were working with one of the following:

   a) the elderly?
   b) the mentally handicapped?
   c) children?
   d) offenders?

   Does your answer encourage you to feel that effectiveness *can* be measured, or is this an impossible task?

3. Some people think that social workers should concentrate on relationships and the interpersonal skills of clients rather than on practical and financial problems. Do you think that debt counselling and welfare-rights work should be an integral part of a generic social worker's skills? Give reasons for your answer.

4. You are leading a group of teenage offenders as part of an inter-mediate-treatment scheme. The group meets once a week to share and discuss their problems. As a group worker, what qualities and skills would you require? How would you deal with a member of the group who is always seeking attention?

5. When using task-centred casework as a social-work method, it is important to set time limits on your contact with the client at the very outset. What advantages do you think there might be to setting a time limit? Are there any disadvantages?

6. Do you agree with the basic philosophy of 'radical' social work: that the problems of clients are often not of their own making but have their origins in the society of which they are members? Can you think of examples to support your answer?

Further reading

1. *Invitation to social work*, Bill Jordan (Martin Robertson, 1984). An interesting and accessible introduction to social work.

2. *Counselling young people*, Ellen Noonan (Methuen, 1983). A thorough basic grounding in what is involved in counselling, especially of young people.

3. *The casework relationship*, Felix P. Biestek (Allen & Unwin, 1967). A clear explanation of the principles of social casework and the casework relationship.

4. *Working with families*, Gill Gorrell Barnes (BASW/Macmillan, 1984). One of the 'Practical social work' series – a good review of

work with families and the complexities involved.

5. *Crisis intervention – studies in community care*, J.K.W. Morrice (Pergamon, 1976). Provides an explanation of the theory of crisis intervention and its practical application in a variety of settings.

6. *Basic groupwork*, Tom Douglas (Tavistock, 1978). A useful book for those who are interested in working with groups in a range of settings.

7. *Behaviour modification*, Brian Sheldon (Tavistock, 1982). A guide to behavioural psychology and its application to social-work practice.

8. *Learning to help – basic skills exercises*, Philip Priestley and James McGuire (Tavistock, 1983). An excellent social-skills handbook focusing particularly on interviewing and group-work skills.

9. *Radical social work and practice*, edited by Mike Brake and Roy Bailey (Edward Arnold, 1980). A stimulating introduction to radical-social-work issues, across a range of social-work settings.

10. *Integrating social-work methods*, edited by Harry Specht and Anne Vickery (Allen & Unwin, 1977). Subject matter for the more advanced reader, as it is difficult in parts. Sets out the unitary (or integrated) model and also examines casework, group work, and community work within this context.

11. *Social workers – their role and tasks*, the report of a National Institute for Social Work working party chaired by Peter M. Barclay ('The Barclay Report') (Bedford Square Press, 1982). Useful reading – it is comprehensive and up-to-date.

In addition there are two very helpful series of books, both stressing the practical usefulness of their material. These are

a) the *Community care*/Gower Publishing 'Social work practice handbooks' series,

b) the BASW/Macmillan 'Practical social work' series.

8   Qualities of an effective carer

There are no 'golden rules' to learn in order to become an effective carer – we each do the job differently according to our own personalities. However, for the purpose of analysis it is useful to break down the task of caring into a number of basic elements. Each aspect of the carer's role can then be examined separately and its independent value be appreciated.

Let us start by examining some of the important characteristics present in a good caring relationship. While reading through this chapter, try to consider the relative value of each quality, whether it is present within yourself, and whether you feel you would want to work towards developing this or that particular quality.

Some of these qualities will seem to be similar, while others may overlap to some extent, and the list below is by no means exhaustive.

Personal qualities

Empathy
'Empathy' means appreciating a person's feelings from that person's own point of view and life situation. It requires understanding and an ability to 'stand in someone else's shoes'.

'Empathy' should not be confused with 'sympathy', which also implies understanding but coupled with feelings of pity. Action inspired by pity, however well-intentioned, can be harmful – for example, a mother may be overprotective to a fragile child and prevent his growth towards independence, or a carer may perform tasks for an elderly person which he could be encouraged to do himself.

Some people feel that empathy can be heightened by practical experience – that is to say that, by spending a day in a wheelchair or being toileted by another member of the caring staff, a carer can appreciate what it is like to be handicapped and dependent on others. However, not all conditions can be experienced in this way.

Others argue that it is not necessary to undergo artificial experiences of this nature: that people can rely on their intellectual capacity to put themselves in another's place.

Love
'Love' is an impossible word to define accurately. We all have our own individual interpretations; however, for the purpose of this analysis, it means having a warm affection, a strong fellow-feeling, towards other human beings.

It is likely that all social workers are attracted to the job initially because they feel a generalised 'love' for other people – particularly those less able to help themselves. Does this mean that all individuals cared for are loved by those who provide care, or is it possible for a professional carer to attend to peoples' needs without necessarily 'loving' them? This dilemma is highlighted if the people being cared for are unco-operative.

Sensitivity

In this context, 'sensitivity' refers to someone's ability to be aware of and responsive to the feelings of another person. All people are different and so need to be treated according to their individual requirements.

Some people may have difficulty expressing their needs and may attempt to conceal their true feelings. A sensitive carer will often pick these up without their having to be made explicit. For example, having one's intimate personal needs attended to by a stranger can be embarrassing for some people. Others, who may be more used to the situation, may be less concerned. It is therefore necessary to treat each person accordingly.

Being sensitive also requires a carer to anticipate a person's feelings – the bewilderment and confusion experienced by children first coming into care, or the grief and despair felt by anyone bereaved, for example.

Basic courtesies

An essential aspect of a carer's role is the need to observe basic courtesies – that is, to be respectful and polite.

Being respectful

To be respectful, a carer must have an awareness of a person's personal rights, dignity, and privacy and must show this at all times. It is particularly important to be respectful to clients when performing personal tasks (such as feeding, dressing, and toileting) – the clients are the ones who know how best these tasks can be performed, and it is essential that they retain as much control over the situation as possible.

Residential homes are in many cases the permanent homes of residents, and the way an establishment is run should reflect its respect for the people who live there. Residents should be able to influence the way the home is run and should be encouraged to participate and make decisions where this is possible.

Politeness

Politeness is the means by which we are able to demonstrate our respect for someone, and before we undertake to care for people it is important that we are aware of the value of good *manners*. This does not mean that caring relationships should be formal, only that there should be consideration on both sides. For example, do you think it is important for care staff to knock on the door of a person's room before entering? Are the residents of elderly persons' homes asked how they wish to be addressed? Should they be called 'Mr', 'Mrs', or 'Miss', or by their forename? Should this be decided to fit in with the policy of the home or be left to the individual client?

Communication and interpersonal skills

To be an effective carer, it is important that you are able to communicate. This means that you need to be able to receive and review information and to express yourself accurately. A caring relationship is a two-way process.

The ability to listen
An ability to listen properly goes beyond simply listening to what a person is saying. There is a distinction to be made between listening and hearing. We all listen but we do not always hear. Often this is because we are too preoccupied with our own affairs and things which are currently concerning us. Commmunication is further made difficult by people who – through shyness, embarrassment, or any other reason – are not always direct in expressing their needs and may feel disposed to obscure or hide them.

Sometimes a person's real needs are communicated not by what is said but by what is left unsaid. For example, a child in care may be unwilling to talk about his family because this brings back painful memories. It is important for the social worker to create an atmosphere of trust and security which will encourage direct expression.

Facial expressions, posture, and other forms of body language all give clues to a person's feelings. A good carer will be aware of these forms of *non-verbal communication*. It is thought that non-verbal messages reflect a person's mood or true desires far more accurately than does immediate verbal communication.

Liking people and showing it
Liking people we care for is important, and there are various ways in which this can be demonstrated. Smiling and touching are both simple reminders to people that we like and care for them. (Obviously, touching can sometimes be inappropriate — it is very personal, and we should not offend people. For example, the touching by a carer of an adolescent of the opposite sex would usually not be acceptable.) Of course it is much easier to like people who are pleasant and co-operative than those that are not, but the carer must make the effort to see the human being beyond difficult personality traits.

Warmth, friendliness, and cheerfulness
Warmth and friendliness are vital ingredients of a caring relationship because they help create a positive atmosphere.

Nobody wants to wake up to or be touched by a reluctant carer. It is important to be cheerful as you undertake routine tasks, but this should not be taken too far – superficial pleasantries can soon be seen through, so it is very important that cheerfulness is as genuine as possible.

Naturalness

Bearing in mind that the most valuable asset we bring to the job is ourselves, a good carer allows her natural personality to come through.

Naturalness reflects ease of manner, relaxation, and trust and is often contagious – thus it can encourage the client to be natural too, and this helps to eliminate any barriers that may exist. So, be yourself as much as possible.

Practical ability

Whatever the social-work setting, it is important that carers demonstrate competence in their work and encourage their clients to feel confident about their practical ability. If, say, a social worker is taking a group of children on an outdoor-pursuits weekend, it is essential that they trust in her ability. Similarly, the severely physically disabled person needs to have complete faith in the person lifting him into and out of the bath.

The client should feel safe when carers perform physical tasks like lifting or easing someone in bed.

Attitudes

A carer's attitudes are not always voiced, but they are nearly always conveyed. That is to say, a client will pick up how a carer thinks of him. Consequently, carers should strive to develop positive attitudes.

Acceptance
Acceptance involves recognising the human being in a person and taking the person as he is. It may be difficult for someone to inwardly warm to a bad-tempered old man whose face is disfigured or to a severely handicapped child who persistently coughs back food, but acceptance requires the carer to look beyond the handicap or any disruptive behaviour to care for the person.

Being non-judgemental
Related to the notion of acceptance is the principle of being non-judgemental. This means being open-minded and resisting the tendency to blame someone for his own or another's circumstances. Blame can only hinder any enabling process. For example, in a case of child abuse it may be difficult to accept, in an unbiased manner, the parents responsible for injuring a child, but how is a nursing officer or social worker going to be of any help to the child's parents until this is achieved?

Tolerance and patience
One requirement of a social worker is that she may at times have to 'soak up' other people's anger and frustration, and she must be prepared to do this. This is not to deny that the relationship is two-way and that a social worker can legitimately reject inappropriate anger.

At other times a social worker may see a way out of her client's difficulties but the client may not initially be receptive to any outside direction. The social worker should be patient and move at the client's own self-determined pace.

Knowledge

Knowledge derived from various sources is an essential component of an effective carer's resources.

Academic knowledge
It is important that social workers have some familiarity with basic psychology, sociology, and human growth and development, so that they can be more aware of a person's needs and the influence of his social environment. This means that the client will be viewed, not in isolation, but more comprehensively in his family and social setting. This fuller information will hopefully lead to the person being cared for more sensitively and his needs being more responsively catered for.

The carer should also have some knowledge of differing social-work theories and methods of working. This is dealt with more fully in chapter 7.

Awareness of other agencies
Part of a carer's duty is to be familiar with the role of other caring agencies and the way in which her clients can benefit from the resources

offered – for example, those who work with mentally handicapped adults need to be aware of what is offered at the local college of further education, both during the day and in the evening, to see if their clients could benefit from the courses or other facilities provided.

It is very important that all social workers have an up-to-date knowledge of the social-security benefits available to clients. It is also necessary to know whom to contact at the DHSS if difficulties arise in relation to this.

In addition, a carer needs to be aware of events and other happenings in the locality which may be of use to clients – for example, jumble sales, furniture auctions, and social and leisure events which may add to the enjoyment and enrichment of people's lives. Most of these events will be organised by informal or voluntary groups and organisations.

Minorities and other cultures in society
Insight into the needs of minority ethnic or cultural groups is essential in an increasingly varied and complex society like ours. This may range from an understanding of the traditional strength of the Asian or Chinese family, which may involve the 'arranged marriage' of a teenage girl born in this country, to the significance of diet to a member of the Rastafarian cult. This information, if accurate and sensitively used, can produce more effective and intelligent caring.

Life experience
Many people believe that life's experience is the best teacher. However, a great deal depends on how effectively and intelligently we use the experience that life offers us. In our caring for others, we will often gain insights from past experiences which increase our understanding and empathy.

We also learn a great deal from our own unhappiness and sorrow, and this should help us to identify with other people going through difficult or testing times. Similarly our joy can help and inform the way we work.

Self-awareness
We all receive clues from those around us as to how others feel about us – how they see us and what they think of us. It is important (but difficult) to be able to interpret these 'messages' accurately. In particular, it is useful to perceive what effect our behaviour has on other people, and for the carer this is essential if we are to be more effective.

There are many ways in which we can increase our self-awareness or 'self-knowledge'. Reading can help, and taking part in groups and corporate activities can be immensely useful. Finally, we must not forget that asking other people what they think of us (and our behaviour), whether on a one-to-one or group basis, can greatly enrich our understanding of ourselves if we really hear what is being said. Do not be afraid to ask, at appropriate times.

Political awareness

We could also call this 'political consciousness'. A great deal of what we do in our private or working lives is limited or controlled by constraints. These may stem from financial or political factors or both.

Caring for others can be a political activity in two ways. Firstly, making decisions about other people's lives and how they will live is a political activity – with a small 'p'. Caring for others often means that we are in a powerful position in regard to our clients. It is up to us not to abuse this power but to use it in a loving and sensitive way in the best interests of other people.

Secondly, the social and other caring services in our society receive a financial slice of a much larger cake – the total resources which central and local government decide will be spent on provision for defence, housing, education, etc. This necessarily involves the caring services in a struggle for more resources, and this again can involve us in political debate and activity.

A knowledge of political, social, and financial issues and questions is necessary because such knowledge helps to inform the way in which we work and enhances our knowledge of the world about us.

Conclusion

It is important to point out that the above qualities should be balanced (as well as interrelated) to a certain extent. For example, a brilliant academic knowledge without empathy or basic courtesies will be of no use. The ideal is a well-rounded or 'whole' person who has several areas of strength upon which to draw when caring for others. One area will complement another and lead to a situation of overall competence if not excellence.

A note of caution which may encourage you – the ability to be an effective carer does not depend on academic capability. Research conducted into the effectiveness of social work tends to point to three factors as being of overriding importance: empathy, non-possessive warmth, and genuineness. It is these qualities which produce positive results.

One final point needs to be stressed – caring for others effectively in a full-time capacity requires energy. This means that *you must find time and space for yourself* – time to relax, enjoy yourself, and 'lose yourself' in an activity which is completely different from work. Obviously your friends and family are a tremendously valuable resource in this regard. If you do not 'recharge your batteries', then you will become depleted and will be of little help to either yourself or others. Some people call this 'professional burn-out'. It is a serious state of affairs, but sadly many people in the caring professions experience it. The result is that social workers' relationships, marriages, and quality of life will suffer.

In order to help others we must help ourselves. There will be times when job satisfaction and the appreciation of clients will not be there, yet the job must continue to be done. It is therefore very important that we look after our own physical, mental, and emotional needs. We will each find our own particular ways of doing this. Generally, however, good food, regular exercise, and relaxing and interesting leisure activities will be of great benefit. Having fun and enjoying a sense of humour – whether our own or others' – will also prove restorative. In the end, not only we ourselves but also our clients will reap the benefits.

Exercise 1 – your personal qualities

Read through the chapter, write down the qualities you feel you already possess, and consider the areas you need to improve upon.

Exercise 2 – someone else's personal qualities

Choose a member of your group whom you know well and may have observed in a caring situation. Write down what you think his or her caring qualities are and assess which qualities you feel he or she needs to develop.

Exercise 3 – investigating personal feelings

Divide into pairs and each complete the following set of sentences as spontaneously as possible. Discuss your answers with each other. Finally, assess whether you think that this has been a useful way of investigating personal feelings.

1. One thing I really like about myself is. . .
2. I dislike people who. . .
3. When people ignore me, I. . .
4. When someone praises me, I. . .
5. When I relate to people, I. . .
6. Those who really know me,. . .
7. My moods. . .
8. I am at my very best with people when. . .
9. When I am in a group of strangers, I. . .
10. I feel lonely when. . .
11. I envy. . .
12. I think I have hurt others by. . .
13. Those who don't know me well. . .
14. What I am really looking for in my relationships is. . .
15. I get hurt when. . .
16. I am at my best with people when. . .
17. I like people who. . .
18. What I feel most guilty about in relationships is. . .
19 Few people know that I. . .
20. When I think about intimacy, I. . .
21. One thing I really dislike about myself is. . .
22. I get angry with. . .

23. One thing that makes me nervous with people is. . .
24. When I really feel good about myself, I. . .
25. When others put me down, I. . .
26. I feel awkward with others when. . .
27. I feel let down when. . .
28. In relationships, what I run away from most is. . .
29. I hate people to see that I am. . .
30. I feel most embarrassed when. . .
31. I. . .

Exercise 4 – guiding

a) The group is split into pairs. One of the partners in each pair is then blindfolded. Half the group then lead their blindfolded partners around the room, taking care to avoid contact with any of the other couples in the group. After five minutes the roles can be reversed.

   Consider how it feels to be totally reliant on somebody else. Did you feel secure and able to trust your partner?

   Conversely, did you feel confident as a guide?

b) The above exercise is repeated, this time with non-verbal instructions only.

Exercise 5 – feeding

(If it is possible, arrange with your college catering staff for the group to be served meals at two separate sittings.) Again the group is split into pairs. At the first sitting one partner assumes that he or she is disabled and unable to feed himself or herself and is fed by the partner. The roles are then reversed.

The aim of the exercise is to experience the dependency of having to be fed by someone else. How does this feel? At the same time, you might comment on the kind of feelings you experience while feeding someone else.

Exercise 6 – role-play – an incident in a children's home

Setting   A children's home

Roles

Terry
You are 14 and living in a children's home which is preparing you for a foster or an adoption placement. You have been at the home since your reception into care two years ago. Your parents divorced three years ago, and neither now has any contact with you. You experienced an unhappy family background characterised by much family violence, particularly

between your parents.

Earlier this afternoon, during a game of football, you were fouled badly as you were nearing the goal. You got up and hit the boy in the face. The boy you hit was your closest friend, and you haven't seen him since.

Nine months ago you were placed with foster parents, but the placement broke down – partly because they were too bossy, you think. They felt they were unable to control you. New foster parents have now been found for you and, having met them twice, you think you'll like them. You want to live in a family home and don't want to remain in a children's home, although you get on with the staff and some of the children.

You are concerned about your outbreak of temper and resorting to physical violence, which you thought you had learned to control. You are also sorry that you hit your friend and feel that he will now withdraw his friendship. You are concerned too that your behaviour might jeopardise your chances of being placed with new foster parents.

Keyworker
You are disappointed to learn that Terry has been involved in a fight but consider it to have been a spontaneous reaction rather than premeditated. You have talked to the other boy involved, who has returned from hospital with very bad bruising around the nose and eyes. He is still angry and resentful towards Terry.

You like Terry and feel that he desperately needs to be part of a family. He was disappointed that his other foster placement broke down and sometimes despairs at being unable to be placed with a family. You have high hopes that the current foster placement being considered for Terry could be successful – the new foster parents are younger than the previous ones, understanding, and have said that they like what they have seen of Terry. The couple have a son of their own, 18 months younger than Terry, and a younger daughter, aged seven. The family also like animals and have a dog and three cats. Terry is fond of animals.

Since he returned from playing football at 5 p.m., Terry has retired to his room and missed his evening meal. It is now 7.30, and you have called into his room half an hour ago to let him know that you will be coming to see him shortly. He mumbled that he did not want to see anyone.

Task
Role-play the keyworker visiting Terry in his room to 'talk out' the events of the day.

Questions for essays or discussion

1. How important do you think an academic knowledge is for someone working in the caring services?
2. If you were working as a professional carer, how would you unwind and prevent 'burn-out'?
3. How good is your knowledge of the life-style of members of minorities

(the elderly, other cultures, the handicapped, for example) who live in your community? How would you improve upon it?

4. Empathy is 'putting yourself in another's situation'. Think of someone you know who has some kind of problem and concentrate on viewing the world as that person sees it. Write up an account of a 'day in the life' of the person you have chosen, describing it from his or her perspective.

5. Should carers 'love' the people they care for, or is it possible to look after someone whom you do not particularly like?

6. All societies have rules and taboos about physical contact between people. Consider the situations where it might be appropriate for a carer to touch a client and how this might be done in an acceptable way.

Further reading

1. *Creative social work*, edited by David Brandon and Bill Jordan (Blackwell, 1979). A look at the practice of creative social work in a number of different settings.

2. *I never promised you a rose garden*, Hannah Green (Pan, 1964). A moving insider's account of the experience of mental illness, in novel form.

3. *Dibs in search of self*, Virginia Aixline (Penguin, 1964). A brief and enlightening account of psychotherapy with a small child originally classified as 'defective'.

4. *One flew over the cuckoo's nest*, Ken Kesey (Picador, 1973). A look at the large-scale psychiatric institution from the point of view of the patients.

5. *A view in winter: reflections on old age*, Ronald Blythe (Penguin, 1981). An interesting account of old age.

6. *Zen in the art of helping*, David Brandon (Routledge & Kegan Paul, 1976). An alternative look at the helping process.

9 Current developments in the caring services

Introduction

The quality of general social-services provision, which includes social work, reflects how much our society 'cares'. How we provide for children, the sick, the handicapped, the elderly, and offenders will be a good indication of how our society values the lives of the individuals within it.

One of the difficulties in summarising the current state of social work and the services it delivers to the public is the enormous diversity of provision – the quality and standard of services vary hugely from region to region. The picture is further confused by the changes which constantly occur within caring practices. Change in one area will bring about change in another – for example, development of 'community-care' policies will have ramifications within residential provision.

The effects of change are not always manifest until later – often many years later. For instance, the Seebohm-inspired development of social-services departments, inaugurated in 1971, was subsequently affected by both the local-government reorganisation and the restructuring of the National Health Service in 1974. Only in recent years have the effects of this innovation and reorganisation been noticed and an appraisal been made possible.

Similarly, changes brought about through new legislation may take time first to be implemented and then to percolate through the system. For example, aspects of the Children Act 1975 governing custodianship were not formally introduced until 1985, and the provisions of the Chronically Sick and Disabled Persons Act 1970 have not been made as extensive as was first envisaged.

However there are distinct developments within social work which have recently been put forward or have already been introduced and are in the process of being established, and we will discuss these in this chapter.

Community care

Since the 1950s it has increasingly been recognised that large-scale institutions tend to erode the independence and initiative of their residents. In response to this, policy-makers in the late 1970s and 1980s have been committed to a concept of community care. This term has three broad aspects:

i) The closure of large-scale institutions and the rehabilitation of current residents to enable them to live in their own homes within the community.

ii) Where they do not have their own homes or it is not possible for ex-residents to live independently, provision is made for clients to live in accommodation which more closely resembles ordinary housing. The establishment of small group homes with social-work or community support is a result of this philosophy.

iii) The third aspect stems from the general acceptance that people have a right to remain in their homes for as long as possible and should be supported by caring agencies in collaboration with the resources that are present within every community. The Barclay Report made the point that the majority of care is undertaken by families themselves and that this actual and potential source of support should be tapped and nurtured, assisted, and protected by caring services.

Applying an old Japanese Zen saying, it has been said that social work is like 'selling water by the river', illustrating the enormous capacity for self-help within the community. This is the preventive element of community care, aimed at helping people to function without recourse to permanent residential care.

Community care should not be seen as a panacea – it is open to criticism where it is not supported by enabling resources. There are many people within the community who are engaged in providing full-time care to a sick or elderly friend or relative. However willingly they undertake this role, it is not normally the result of a considered choice but rather a response to circumstances. Sudden illness or deterioration can render permanent care essential, and lack of appropriate community-care resources may leave one person – probably female – with the responsibility for providing care. This in itself may cause undue strain, followed by resentment which in time is likely to affect the caring relationship.

In 1981, a voluntary organisation – the Association of Carers – was formed to offer support to and focus attention on the plight of those who care for dependants in their own home. It has undertaken research in conjunction with the Equal Opportunities Commission. According to the Association, 'there are currently about 1¼ million people whose lives are very much restricted because of someone's disability or frailty', and 'there are now more women caring for an elderly or disabled person than there are rearing ordinary under-16-year-old children.' The Association points out that, at any one time, one in three women between the ages of 35 and 59 are caring for a dependant. This not only is seen to adversely affect the carer's physical health but also the average estimated cost (including loss of earnings) was calculated at £8500 p.a. in 1980. Support is therefore essential for these people.

One of the major assumptions underlying the viability of community care is that there is a community that wants to care. This is not always evident, but may need to be fostered and encouraged. Consider, for example, the initial reaction of residents of a road or street when it is proposed that one or two of the houses be converted for use by mentally handicapped adults, ex-offenders, or battered wives. Street residents may accept that this is a valuable and necessary community resource but may prefer that it is established elsewhere. Unfortunately, this has been known to happen.

Finally, despite the positive aspects of community-care philosophy and its representation as a worthwhile practice, there will always be a need for some kind of residential provision. Many people's problems are simply far too great to be handled effectively by members of the community, even with extensive social-work support.

Residential care

This has seen great changes in recent years, and residents themselves have been encouraged to retain greater independence and more control over their lives. Caring establishments have become more specialised, and the standard of care has risen. In many homes the staff have been encouraged to abandon residual paternalism – the 'we know best' attitude – and to engage in more of an enabling role, helping residents to act for themselves. Here there are opportunities for both residents and staff to have more responsibility for the way the service is run. The increased use of day care and short-stay admission has also enabled homes to develop a rehabilitative role.

Some local authorities have constructed well-thought-out building projects aimed at supporting people in the community – sheltered housing, elderly persons' group homes, support units, and core-and-cluster developments are examples of practical alternatives to large institutions.

Child-care legislation

Child-care legislation has developed in an ad-hoc and piecemeal fashion, reflecting the priorities of the time and responding to particular circumstances. In consequence it is now confusing and very complex, and in need of review. An additional complication is that, once an Act of Parliament is passed, local authorities need to interpret the new legislation and incorporate it into their procedures, and this naturally takes time. Also, because of the complexity of the changes proposed, separate parts of the Act may come into force at different times, in order to avoid disruption of services. Such partial implementation of such legislation as the Children and Young Persons Act 1969 and the Children Act 1975 has characterised a period when frustration and confusion have surrounded child-care law. The Children Act 1975 was an attempt to balance the rights of the child, the parents, and the substitute carers, but some of its provisions have yet to be implemented.

Parental rights
Social workers are aware of parental-rights issues and will advise parents

of their rights and actively encourage them to seek legal assistance. The 1984 DHSS circular LAL (84)5 was a directive to local authorities to consult parents carefully at each stage of procedures involving parental rights. The Association of Directors of Social Services (ADSS) recommends that the DHSS goes further and produces a booklet as a guide to parents involved in legal situations, in order to foster a better understanding between parents and the local authority.

Parents need to be aware of their rights and to be able to make a full contribution to care proceedings. Many may be anxious and frustrated at the time of the court hearing and, although all families can apply for legal aid, there is at present no appeal for those who are refused it.

The growth of NAYPIC (the National Association of Young People in Care) has helped children in care become more aware of their rights. This voluntary organisation also offers support to young people leaving care.

Voluntary care
Recent figures quoted by the Association of Directors of Social Services for children received into voluntary care under section 2 of the Child Care Act 1980 show that 60% of children remain in care for no more than eight weeks, some are readmitted to care later, and a small proportion of children remain in care for long periods. These figures highlight the continuing need for preventive intervention aimed at minimising short-term admissions and providing alternative forms of help.

Family courts

Family courts were first recommended in a 1965 Government White Paper *'The child, the family and the young offender'* as an alternative, less formal, and more informed way of dealing with young offenders than the juvenile court. They have not been introduced in England, Wales, and Northern Ireland, but, following the Social Work (Scotland) Act 1968, a children's hearing system was implemented along these lines in Scotland.

In 1974 the Finer Report on one-parent families again recommended family courts, to replace the family and domestic divisions of the High Court, county courts, and magistrates' courts. The idea was to have a single family court (in each area) to deal with divorce and separation, to move away from the need to legally establish a guilty partner (the 'advocacy' model) towards concentrating on deciding what is best for the child.

This recommendation has not yet been implemented. However the introduction of family courts now seems imminent, although their composition and the range of cases they will consider has not been decided on.

In 1984 a House of Commons social-services committee recommended that 'the Government now provide the House with a detailed and fully costed scheme for the establishment of family courts.' This select committee was impressed with the Scottish children's hearing system – particularly in the way 'the informal settings of the hearings enabled children and families to face up to problems in discussion and so help them to resolve them.' The Association of Directors of Social Services also welcomes proposals for a family-courts system and feels that this could be introduced to coincide with a comprehensive review of child-care legislation, adding that new child-care law should be 'spared a process of implementation in dribs and drabs'.

Both the National Association of Probation Officers (NAPO) and the British Association of Social Workers (BASW) are committed to the concept of family courts. BASW proposes that cases covering guardianship, custody, parental rights, access, affiliation, adoption, and care and control be transferred from magistrates' courts to family courts; but NAPO is opposed to the transfer of juvenile-crime matters to such courts.

Joint services

The interrelationship between social-care problems has demonstrated the need for collaboration between different agencies, and in some areas this has resulted in the provision of joint services. Nursery-centre provision, combining the advantages of social-services day nurseries with the educational benefits of nursery schools, is one outcome of this. So too is the work of community-health teams and the practice of social-work attachments to general practitioners and schools. Interdisciplinary training needs of professional carers are now manifest, and so joint training courses for social workers and nurses have been developed.

There is a need for housing departments to have more knowledge of social-work provision, and for social workers to have more understanding of housing matters. The voluntary organisation 'Shelter' has therefore encouraged social-worker training courses to devote more attention to matters of housing. Housing is seen as a central source of the problems of many families and a contributory one of others.

Decentralisation

As we have seen, many local social-service departments are trying to make their services more accessible and accountable to the community they serve. To achieve this, some SSDs have decentralised their workforce and now operate from patch-based or neighbourhood offices. In some instances this move has been made in conjunction with other local-authority services, such as housing, cleansing, and direct works.

Where local authorities have decentralised their services, there is the possibility of undertaking imaginative and purposeful community-based social work. However, as this development is still in an experimental stage, it is too soon to comment on any impact that it may have had.

Patch-based social work enables workers to be more accessible to members of the public.

Specialisation

Notwithstanding the Seebohm Report's recommendation of generic training, the subsequent increase in specific legislation concerning adoption, fostering, mental health, and other aspects of social work has made apparent the need for some social workers to specialise in certain areas of work. At the same time, all social workers need to have a comprehensive understanding of a whole range of available information and resources, both statutory and non-statutory. In addition, they will need an appreciation of the community and life-style of their clients, so that they may continue to assist them in overcoming difficulties and encourage patterns of self-help and self-determination within the community.

Minority groups

More attention has recently been paid to the needs of minority groups within the community and to their wider representation as either recipients or practitioners of social services.

Educational provision is being extended to reach those people who would not have had access in the past – married people who have brought up families, women isolated in the home, and the unemployed, for example. Community education seeks to enable members of communities to decide their own learning requirements and to participate in the sharing of knowledge.

Social-work organisations are creating posts which cater especially for the needs of ethnic minorities and are encouraging these posts to be filled by people from these groups – for example, 'section-11' funding from the Home Office can be used to enable black social workers to recruit black families to foster black children in care. However, it is not only to work with specific families that members of various ethnic minorities are appointed – there is a general aim to include working personnel from all minorities, so that services truly reflect the diversity of modern society.

Many authorities have declared themselves 'equal-opportunity employers', welcoming applications regardless of sex or ethnic origin and also encouraging applications from registered disabled persons. Others have gone further and have included awareness of racism and sexism in staff-development training and have made any racist practice the basis of a dismissible offence. Many organisations are engaged in eliminating all identifiable forms of institutional racism present in their practices. This involves an examination of the literature they use and a scrutiny of their recruitment policies. Various other procedures have been studied to make sure that no groups of people are discriminated against.

Change

Changes within the caring services do not necessarily stem from the ideas of planners: sometimes they occur following changes brought about by social workers themselves which eventually percolate upwards and become official policy. An example is where homes have introduced group living and have demonstrated its success. Experimental developments within the voluntary sector can also lead to their being adopted by social-services departments – family centres, for example. Change tends to occur in response to change in society at large, and sometimes a crisis is the spur. Notably, the findings of the Maria Colwell enquiry instigated developments in non-accidental-injury registration procedures, and these were subsequently refined following the findings of the enquiry into the death of Jasmine Beckford, in 1985.

Change within the caring services may best be described as being of an evolutionary nature, rather than an abrupt break with the past. It also ebbs and flows – for example, specialisation comes into fashion, then goes out, only to return. No-one is in overall control of change, but this may be a strength rather than a weakness – rich diversity offers an assurance that changes will not result in things going disastrously wrong, as they check and balance each other.

Conclusion

Those who have experienced working in the caring services in the mid-1980s can see that the SSDs are currently undergoing changes more profound than at any time since their inception in 1971. Social workers have a wide range of knowledge and skills and employ a wide range of social-work methods when working with families. The introduction of community-care programmes is offering a further challenge to social-work staff. In areas where resources are made available, this move is exciting and rewarding.

In the field of education, curriculum changes in schools are being developed in order to make the content more relevant to children's needs and their lives after school. Further and adult education – incorporated in community education – is being made accessible to many people who formerly would not have had this opportunity. Many housing departments are encouraging tenant consultation and participation, and community work generally is striving to engage more members of the community and to respond to felt needs.

The Probation Service is mindful of external pressure on it to become more coercive and is at pains to remain a caring social-work service. Meanwhile, innovative practices and developments are still taking place in the voluntary sector, setting its sights to the future. Finally, co-operation and mutual understanding of other carers' tasks is increasing, and there is now plenty of scope to undertake satisfying and rewarding work. Society cares, but does it care enough?

Questions for essays or discussion

1. What is meant by the phrase 'Community care should not be seen as a panacea'?
2. 'Residential care should always be a last resort for people in need.' Discuss this.
3. What do you think are the main advantages of a family-courts system?
4. Consider the social influences which deter young men from under-going training as nursery nurses. What would be the advantages to small children if there were more males employed as nursery nurses?
5. Do you think it is important that the composition of those who work in the caring services reflects that of wider society? How do you account for the under-representation of certain ethnic-minority groups?
6. In what ways can those who care for dependent relatives in their own homes be supported by the rest of society?

Further reading

1. *Kids at the door – a preventive project on a council estate*, Robert Holman (Blackwell, 1981). An account of a project funded by the Church of England Children's Society concerning a community-based approach to preventive social work. 'The author, from his own home on a council estate, works with delinquent, truanting, and unhappy teenagers in their own environment.'
2. *Caring – experiences of looking after disabled relatives*, Anne Briggs

and Judith Oliver (Routledge & Kegan Paul, 1985). Carers speak about their feelings, practical problems, and the response of the Welfare State to their plight.
3. *Mastering social welfare*, Pat Young (Macmillan, 1985). A wide-ranging introduction to social-welfare provision.
4. *Who cares for the carers? - opportunities for those caring for the elderly and handicapped* (Equal Opportunities Commission, 1982). An examination of the practical plight of carers, with recommendations for an improved support service.
5. *Parents of mentally handicapped children*, C. Hannan (Pelican, 1980). A sensitive account written by the parent of a mentally handicapped child.

10 Conclusion

From reading this book, you may have gained the impression that everybody's needs are catered for by the caring services and that these services are comprehensive and interlocking. This would be a false impression. We have been concerned to outline the roles and functions of people working within caring agencies and, in order to do this, we have of necessity ignored shortcomings in welfare provision.

Standards of social welfare vary a great deal from area to area, as they depend on the resources available – which are never unlimited – and the commitment to use those resources effectively. Some authorities have introduced innovative and imaginative work practices, while others have resisted change. Throughout the book we have focused on the positive developments in care practice, rather than on any shortcomings.

The previous chapter reviewed current developments within the caring services themselves. However, these services have their place within a larger setting governed by economic and political constraints. What follows is an explanation of some of these limitations.

Cuts

The present (1986) Government is concerned to reduce overall public expenditure, and this has led to fears that the Welfare State may be in danger of gradual erosion. For example the 1986 White Paper and bill on the reform of social security (following the Fowler Report of June 1985) proposed reductions in benefits, the phasing out of the State earnings-related pension scheme (SERPS), and means-testing for maternity and death grants. Furthermore, child benefit has not been protected against inflation. Organisations such as the Child Poverty Action Group and the Policy Studies Institute fear that such measures will mean increased hardship for many thousands of people.

As a result of cuts in services that have been made over the past ten years, social-work agencies have been greatly hampered in what they have attempted to do. Waiting lists grow for day-nursery places and for accommodation in residential homes for the elderly or special accommodation with community support. Proposed projects have had to be abandoned, such as plans for rehabilitating mentally handicapped people within the community. ('Mind' – the National Association for Mental Health – considers that the general support for the recovery of mentally ill people in the community is quite inadequate and that this could lead to an increase in psychiatric problems, as many of these individuals will almost certainly go from one crisis to another if they are denied the best possible opportunities for returning to normality.)

We assume that social workers have the wherewithal to do their jobs, but, because of the extra duties which have resulted from cuts in manpower and the tendency of large organisations to become increasingly bureaucratic – requiring a greater amount of time to be spent on form-filling etc. – many find that they are becoming more and more frustrated in their efforts to give good service. All too frequently the work gets done only because individual members of staff work well beyond their contractual requirements. The danger of this kind of situation is that it can lead to professional exhaustion, or 'burn-out' as it is sometimes called.

Privatisation

Privatisation is the selling off of State-owned property or the policy of contracting out to private (commercial) companies of work previously done by public employees (school or hospital laundry, for example) and allowing commercial use of State facilities (such as NHS hospital beds and medical equipment). In the belief that, in order to maximise profits, a commercial enterprise is likely to be motivated to operate more efficiently, the present Government has actively pursued such policies. However, there is concern that, once profit-making is the prime motive for the provision of services, some of the services may shrink or disappear if entrepreneurs find them less lucrative than expected; thus continuity – a hallmark of the Welfare State – might be lost for good.

Non-implementation

Legislation has increased the rights of individuals and increased the protection of those in care. Provision has been made for a wide range of client groups, yet – despite statutory requirements – policies are not always implemented. For example, the Chronically Sick and Disabled Persons Act 1970 required local authorities to register all such people within the community and to provide resources to improve the quality of their lives. Under this Act, housebound elderly and handicapped people are eligible for free telephone installation, assistance with television costs, and other services. In practice, local authorities cannot find the resources for such extensive provision; they install telephones in the homes of only a small number of eligible clients in each financial year; they have to make 'priorities out of priorities'.

Ratecapping

Local authorities have been further constrained in their efforts to maintain a high standard of public service by the 'ratecapping' procedures introduced by the Government in 1985. Under these procedures, those local authorities who were not prepared to make cuts in expenditure, and who anticipated raising the level of local rates in order to maintain services, were to be penalised by having central-government funding withdrawn.

Community care

It should be remembered that, while local-authority services may appear extensive, they do in fact meet the needs of only a small proportion of the population. Many people are cared for by relatives in their own homes at great personal cost, and, either through ignorance or inaccessibility of the available provision, they do not resort to local statutory services.

The idea of 'community care' is popular and represents good social-work practice, but the burden on individual carers can become intolerable if they are not supported. Most of the individuals who care for others in their own homes are women – a disproportionate amount of responsibility continues therefore to fall on females within society.

There are many poor, sick, and disabled people in our society who live alone. If statutory services fail to provide support, they will have nothing to fall back on – some of them will despair and will fail to survive.

Unemployment

Another consequence of economic decline over the past ten years has been the steep rise in unemployment. The number of unemployed is now over three million.

Unemployment is not only generally demoralising: it creates problems for the individual – feelings of frustration, inadequacy, uselessness, and desperation. It brings financial hardship which often causes friction within a family and sometimes leads to a broken marriage. It brings isolation which causes a decline in family and community life. For some, it brings the temptation to resort to crime. The destructive nature of all these interrelating factors cannot be overestimated. A survey commissioned by the Association of Metropolitan Authorities, published in 1985, showed that some 90% of people seeking help from social workers in cities are unemployed, and most come from households where no other adult has a job.

Law and order

Many are dissatisfied with the Government's response to increasing social unrest (to which unemployment seems to have contributed). Following the riots in the summer of 1981, there was some increase in urban spending, but the discontent and decline in some of the poorer inner-city area continues, and major trouble broke out again, in Birmingham and London, in 1985.

One of the Government's responses to the problems of crime and delin-quency has been to 'hit' offenders harder, in the hope that this will act as a deterrent. We now have the largest prison population of any European country except Turkey, and we appear to sentence people to longer terms of imprisonment than most other countries.

Despite evidence by the Home Office's Young Offender Psychology Unit that the 'short sharp shock' regime in selected detention centres does *not* affect the reconviction rates of young people, in 1985 the Government announced the extension of this regime to *all* detention centres.

The recent introduction of stricter conditions which may be inserted by courts into probation orders appears to indicate that the Government wishes the Probation Service to become more controlling and punitive. Those who view the Probation Service as a caring social-work service to offenders feel that such a development would not be compatible with compassionate ideals of practice.

Defending social work

Social work has plenty of detractors. It is easy to criticise it, especially when the media give mass coverage to the very rare occasions when something goes seriously wrong – for example, when a child who has been in the care of the local authority dies and a social worker is deemed to have been negligent. This 'bad news' is thought to be worth reporting, but the thousands of accounts of social-work intervention which make 'good news' are ignored.

It is easy to make negative criticisms, but those doing so often have little, if any, understanding of the demands and complexities of the social worker's job and the accompanying pressure of too much to do in too little time. Those making judgement stand detached from the situation and in some ways seek in the social worker a scapegoat for what has gone wrong. Against this often hostile media coverage and public opinion, social work should be defended – for the sake not only of its practitioners but also of their clients.

Many of the controversial issues mentioned in this chapter may fill those who wish or intend to become involved in social work with much concern. As we have already mentioned, cuts and reduced staffing levels often mean larger case-loads and a more demanding job.

The next few years certainly hold challenges for those in the caring services who are determined to defend welfare provision. However, despite reservations and fears about what the future holds, social work, in all its various settings, remains an interesting and rewarding job. Helping individuals or families to resolve their difficulties, and helping people achieve personal growth despite the difficulties and frustrations inherent in their situation, remains a very satisfying activity.

Annex 1   Training for work in the caring services

Introduction

Some people believe that effective social workers are 'born and not made'. The implication of this is that no amount of education, experience, and training will equip a person to function well if he does not have certain innate qualities. This may be considered an extreme view. Although individuals who earn their living working with people must have a liking for them and a wish to care for them, useful experience and relevant education on a training course are essential for effective caring. This chapter is concerned with the wide variety of training courses available to people who wish to pursue a career in caring. It does not cover social-work courses only – it also outlines the training that is available for those who wish to work in health, education, housing, and youth and community work.

A definite requirement for a professional carer is a degree of maturity. For this reason, no-one can practise as a professional *field* social worker (or probation officer) before the age of 22. However, there are various ways of gaining experience before then. Voluntary work provides one method, as does work as a trainee social worker or work in a residential or day-care setting.

Many people around the age of 16 have little, if any, idea of the kind of job or career they want to pursue. It is unreasonable to expect them all to be absolutely certain of what they want to do – individuals often need to have had some experience in a particular field of work before they can decide whether or not they will enjoy doing it. Those who go on from school into further or higher education have an advantage in that they can delay making a decision about a career. There are others who leave school at the age of 16 – often with no formal academic qualifications – who for various reasons are without, or who are denied, access to further education. These are in a less fortunate position.

The Central Council for Education and Training in Social Work (CCETSW)

This is the independent body, established in 1971 and financed by central government, which has a statutory authority, throughout the UK, to

a) promote education and training in the personal social services,
b) recognise courses of training in social work,
c) award qualifications for such courses as it recognises or approves.

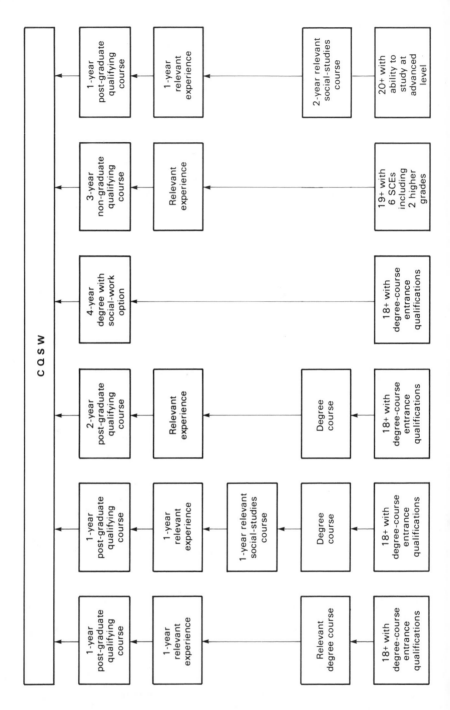

CQSW

1-year post-graduate qualifying course	← 1-year relevant experience	←	2-year relevant social-studies course	← 20+ with ability to study at advanced level
3-year non-graduate qualifying course	← Relevant experience	←		19+ with 6 SCEs including 2 higher grades
4-year degree with social-work option	←			18+ with degree-course entrance qualifications
2-year post-graduate qualifying course	← Relevant experience	← Degree course	←	18+ with degree-course entrance qualifications
1-year post-graduate qualifying course	← 1-year relevant experience	← 1-year relevant social-studies course	← Degree course	← 18+ with degree-course entrance qualifications
1-year post-graduate qualifying course	← 1-year relevant experience	←	Relevant degree course	← 18+ with degree-course entrance qualifications

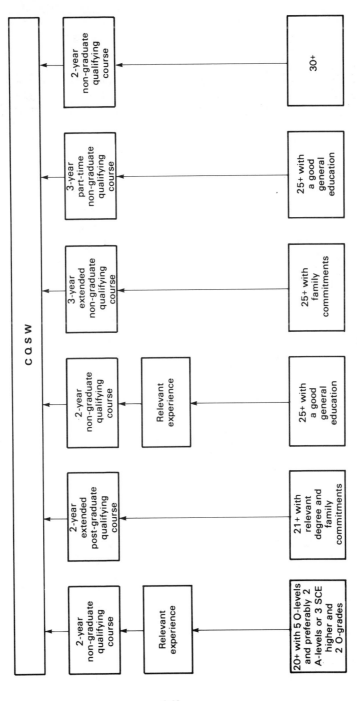

Routes to the CQSW

269

This will include training for social-services-department social workers; probation officers; and staff of day, domiciliary, and residential services – as well as those working for voluntary organisations. It also caters for those working in education departments, say as education welfare officers (EWOs).

Courses accredited (or recognised) by CCETSW provide preparatory or pre-training experience, training proper, and 'in-service' training for those already working in some kind of caring role. The most important courses are

  i) the Certificate of Qualification in Social Work (CQSW),
 ii) the Certificate in Social Service (CSS),
iii) the Preliminary Certificate in Social Care (PCSC – see page 276),
 iv) the In-service Course in Social Care (ICSC – see page 287).

CCETSW also has an *information service*, which publishes and distributes information about a wide range of training opportunities in social care. The addresses to write to for this service can be found at the end of this chapter.

The CQSW course
To become qualified as a social worker – in other words to be a *professional* social worker in the UK – one must successfully complete a course leading to the Certificate of Qualification in Social Work (the CQSW – introduced in 1972). It is accepted by all the major employers of people in social welfare, including the Probation Service. As a qualification, it currently has the highest status in social work. It is available through a degree course for undergraduates and through diploma courses for graduates and non-graduates, and these groups have separate courses.

No one can begin a CQSW course before the age of 20. (Many people are, of course, much older when they undertake training.) There is no formal upper age limit imposed by CCETSW, but some colleges and universities do not consider students over 45–50.

CQSW courses take place in universities, polytechnics, and colleges of higher education. The institution itself selects students, not the Council.

The diagram on pages 268–9 shows the various routes which can be taken to gain the CQSW, with the relevant qualifications needed.

Although all courses lead to the same qualification – the CQSW – there is no *nationally* set syllabus. Different courses can vary a great deal. Some may concentrate on social-work intervention with individuals and families, while others may look in more detail at community-work approaches. All courses should contain some details of social-work theory, social policy, the legal context of social work, and human growth and development. There should also be some understanding of political issues and constraints which face the social worker.

As well as academic study in college, great stress is placed on *practice placements* in a wide range of agencies that practise social work. The organisation of placements will vary a great deal, depending on which

The training of social workers increasingly involves technology and experiental learning techniques.

course is attended. General assessment procedures also vary greatly.

Note   CCETSW is currently reviewing the organisation of the CQSW course. For more details, see the conclusion to this chapter.

For information regarding CQSW courses and application forms, you should write to

The Clearing House for CQSW Courses,
Fourth Floor,
Myson House,
Railway Terrace,
Rugby,
Warwickshire CV21 3HT,

stating whether you require details of graduate or non-graduate courses.

The CSS course

The Certificate in Social Service, introduced in 1975, is an in-service qualifying training course. When first established by CCETSW, it was not regarded as a training course, but in recent years it has become one. It is now a nationally recognised qualification. To be accepted on the CSS course you must already be working in the field of social welfare. Courses take place in colleges of further or higher education.

There is some confusion about the difference between the CQSW and the CSS. The CQSW has the higher status and is regarded as a

271

'*professional*' qualification. It is not easy to define exactly what this means, but what it does is to qualify an individual to practise as a social worker. The CSS course does not do this: it is in-service training for staff employed by local-authority social-service departments or voluntary agencies, *other than field social workers*. Those taking a CSS course will usually be working in day care, residential care, domiciliary care, or other *direct service* to clients. They may be care assistants with elderly people or residential social workers working with children. They may be home-help organisers or adult-training-centre instructors.

Too clear a distinction should not be made between 'social work' and 'social service' – the two roles interrelate and the division between them is blurred. Many feel that it is unfortunate that there is a difference in status between the CQSW and CSS, and CCETSW is at present reviewing the two certificates with a view to combining them in one qualification.

If the CSS has always been the 'poor relation' of the CQSW, then, parallel with this, residential social work has traditionally been seen as inferior to field social work. Happily, this is changing. More students of the CQSW course are now choosing to enter residential work.

The CSS course aims to build on previous experience and training. It lasts not less than two years and not more than three years. Students leave their job for either one or two days a week, or sometimes for short 'blocks' of study, to attend a college that is fairly local. Students do not need to leave their homes or work to participate.

The CSS is divided into three locally devised *units of study*:

i) a *common unit* for all students, in which they study basic core subjects;
ii) a *standard unit* which focuses on the particular client group the student works with – for example, children, adolescents, the elderly, or handicapped adults;
iii) a *special unit* which deals with particular *practice skills* – for example, assessment, organisation, or management.

Students are selected for courses by agencies and colleges in co-operation. They must be 18 years or over and, if under 21, must have five O-levels or high grades in five other academic qualifications. They must also provide evidence of relevant work experience. The agency for which they work must provide a *study supervisor*, whose role it is to help the student combine college studies with her work experience in a relevant and meaningful way.

Further training opportunities.

CCETSW recognises a variety of courses of *post-qualifying studies* (PQS) for both CSS and CQSW holders. These are usually based in universities, polytechnics, or colleges of higher education. They make provision for a wide variety of subjects and client groups – for example, child care, work with the handicapped, and work with offenders. They lead to a variety of higher degrees, diplomas, or certificates, almost all of them particular to

272

the academic institution in which they are based. Information about PQS can be obtained from the CCETSW information service.

A note on generic training.
Before the introduction of the CQSW, those working or intending to work in the caring services were trained on particular courses designed to train the workers of specific agencies – for example, child-care, welfare, or probation officers. The coming of the CQSW introduced '*generic training*'. This can be contrasted with *specialist training*: it means being trained to deal with *any kind of problem in any kind of social-work setting*.

Generic training does not mean that social workers do not specialise later – many of them will, either by taking further training courses or because agencies will organise their work in a particular way.

How to fill the gap between school and social-work training

There are various alternatives open to you if you are 16. While at school, you will have to decide whether to leave and get a job, or whether to continue studying full-time or part-time. In the present situation of high unemployment, you may well be advised to continue studying. We will now look at four ways of spending your time after school.

i) You could seek a job which would enrich your life experience and which would, at the same time, provide a useful background for work in the caring services. A job need not be specifically relevant to caring in order to provide a good and a useful experience for you. If you do, however, want to be more directly involved, some clerical and other jobs for school-leavers in social-work agencies give you the opportunity to observe and learn more of what social workers actually do.

ii) You could take a one- or two-year foundation or pre-training course in social care. Such a course is usually based in a college of further education, but some you may be able to do at school. Examples are the one-year Certificate in Pre-vocational Education (CPVE) or the two-year City and Guilds Certificate in Home Economics for Family and Community Care. CCETSW awards the two-year Preliminary Certificate in Social Care (PCSC). These courses may give you the opportunity of gaining O-levels or even A-levels.

Although they are not training courses for a qualification and do not guarantee you a job afterwards, they will provide a good opportunity to gain some knowledge of what caring work may involve and will also alert you to available training and job prospects in the field. You will also be continuing your general education.

iii) You could undertake some *voluntary work*, whether or not you are in paid employment. There will be many local agencies (both statutory and voluntary) that would value your services, and for you it will be

273

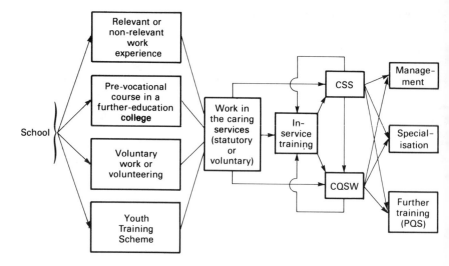

Alternatives after school towards a career in social work

useful experience – you will be broadening your knowledge of what caring involves. You could either make contact directly with a particular agency which interests you, or you could get in touch with the volunteer bureau of the local Council for Voluntary Service, which would give you details of what is available. A prolonged period of voluntary activity can be useful later on as relevant experience for a training course in social work – even for the CQSW itself.

iv) As a half-way stage between further training and work, a Youth Training Scheme (YTS) could usefully help you to combine work with study and at the same time provide you with a small income. (More of this below.)

If you are 18 or over, you need to start thinking about gaining the type of experience that is required by social-work training courses. Apart from a prolonged period of voluntary work, as mentioned above, you could consider working as a *social-work assistant* in a social-services area office or day centre, or as a *care assistant* in a residential setting. There are a few opportunities to work as an unqualified *Probation-Service ancillary* at this age.

If you are aged 20 or over, you may be able to find work as a *trainee* with a local-authority social-services department or the Probation Service. Unfortunately, owing to cutbacks in public spending, opportunities to be seconded as a trainee for training on a salary are becoming increasingly limited. It may well be a long time before this situation improves.

274

Preparatory or pre-training courses

These courses are also known as 'pre-vocational' or 'foundation' courses. There are several open to school-leavers at 16 or 17 years of age. Some are organised by *national* educational or training bodies, such as City and Guilds or CCETSW. Others are *regional*, administered by Regional Advisory Councils for Further Education. In addition, there are *local* courses run by, and particular to, individual colleges of further education.

National courses

The Certificate of Pre-vocational Education (CPVE) This is an important new qualification for those who are 16 (who have completed compulsory secondary education) and would like to spend a further year in full-time education but do not intend to study for A-levels and who have not yet decided on a job. At the start of the 1985/6 academic year, about 1000 schools and colleges were involved in the CPVE, and this number will increase. CPVE courses offer skills and studies in a wide range of vocational areas, including health and community care.

The certificate is issued by a Joint Board which combines two established examining bodies – the City and Guilds of London Institute (CGLI) and the Business & Technician Education Council (BTEC). The CPVE course replaces certain well known courses for students interested in caring skills, such as the Foundation Course in Community Care (CGLI course 689). It is intended to help prepare students for adult life and help them form a vocational interest by planned 'tasting' of what certain jobs involve, as well as actually developing vocational skills. It will also provide the opportunity to enter more specific vocational courses in further education or to proceed to A-levels and higher education.

The CPVE is an integrated programme, not a collection of separate subjects. The framework of study contains three elements:

i) *Core competences*, which include personal and career development, communication, social skills, numeracy, science and technology, creative development, and practical skills.
ii) *Vocational studies* are taken in three stages of *modules* (introductory, exploratory, and preparatory). Preparatory modules include child care, nutrition, human development, health studies, care of the handicapped, care of the elderly, first aid, and home and institutional management.
iii) *Additional studies* can take as much as 25% of the course time. They provide time for leisure, recreation, and community activities as well as for additional qualifications such as O-levels or CSEs, or remedial help with studying.

Work placements will be available to give opportunities to gain experience in a range of caring agencies.

The CPVE usually takes one year, full-time, but – as a result of a pilot

275

scheme in 1985 – part-time courses may be offered from autumn 1986. Although the 'core competences' are compulsory and are likely (in part) to be nationally tested, there are no specific requirements that state the range of vocational studies which individual schools and colleges may offer, so there will be variation. An increasing number of schools are running the CPVE. There has also been some discussion of a future link between the CPVE and the Youth Training Scheme.

After the CPVE, students could go on to YTS, other vocational courses, or actually start work.

The Certificate in Home Economics for Family and Community Care (CGLI course 331)   This is a two-year home-economics-based course for 16-year-olds who want to work in caring. The first year is the CPVE, discussed above, with students specialising in the second year in either food and nutrition or family and community care. There are no official entry requirements, but entrants should have had a 'good general education'. Subjects studied include human development and welfare, home and accommodation studies, craft studies, housekeeping and budgeting, child care, and general studies.

Assessment is continuous. External assessors interview the students at the end of the second year, and at this time the students also sit an examination. Successful students would be considered capable of working as assistants in any post that requires a knowledge of 'home-making', care of the family, and the elderly. Some use this course as a preparation for going into general nursing or psychiatric nursing or the care of the mentally handicapped.

The Preliminary Certificate in Social Care (PCSC)   This is not a qualification for work in the caring services, but a very useful preparation. The certificate is awarded by CCETSW – in fact it is the only pre-vocational course accredited by the Council.

It is a two-year full-time course. It will allow you to continue your general education and at the same time give you the opportunity to see what career opportunities in caring are available. It is intended for the 16–19-year-old. Some colleges require two or three O-levels from students as an entry qualification; others do not. On the course, there will be further opportunity to gain O-levels, and even A-levels. Over 100 colleges of further education in the UK offer the PCSC course, so there should be one near you.

Study will be both *general* and *vocational*. General subjects will include sociology, human biology, human growth and development, and social administration. Vocational studies will include home economics, practical caring skills, community studies, and communications.

Practical experience will be provided by placements in work settings, both one day a week and in 'block'. Most courses involve short residential courses where you go with your fellow-students and some members of staff to stay in a location away from home. These can prove very enjoyable

Residential courses aim to encourage co-operation and teamwork – essential ingredients for a future in caring.

and helpful indeed – they will give you the experience of living and working together in a more intense and intimate atmosphere.

Following the PCSC course, future career prospects are usually good. Most students who gain the certificate manage to find work in the caring services in a residential setting (with children or the elderly) or day care. Many also go on to take further training in caring skills, either full-time or while 'in-service'.

In April 1986, CCETSW announced that it proposed to cease to be involved with PCSC courses in Scotland after the 1986 intake and, subject to satisfactory negotiations with other validating bodies about alternative provision, it was willing to cease awarding the PCSC elsewhere in the UK by 1990.

Regional courses

There are several courses organised and certificated by Regional Advisory Councils for Further Education. One of the better-known courses is the Certificate of (or in) Further Education (Pre-nursing and Caring Services). This is usually a one-year full-time course for people who want to work in hospitals or other caring work. Studies may include English, mathematics for everyday life, human biology, caring skills, food and nutrition, first aid, home nursing, and life (or social) skills. The course will involve practical work placements. Most courses do not require formal academic qualifications for entry – instead, you will be expected to attend an interview and a college test.

The courses take place in colleges of further education – you should ask for a prospectus at your local college, which will provide details.

Local courses

Many colleges of further education offer pre-training courses in community care, at the end of which they award their own certificate or diploma. There is no point in giving details of these, as they are so diverse. Many of these courses provide good experience in caring skills and a preparatory theoretical foundation for work in the social services. For further information you should enquire at your local college.

The Youth Training Scheme (YTS)

The Youth Training Scheme (or Youth Training Programme – YTP – in Northern Ireland) is run by the Manpower Services Commission. It is a voluntary, work-based training scheme for 16-year-old school leavers, some 17-year-olds, and older disabled young people. The scheme, which applies nationally, lasts for two years and offers planned work experience and general training, including at least 20 weeks off-the-job training or further education. Trainees are paid a small allowance per week.

Some schemes are general – they offer experience of working with children or the elderly. Others are specific – they offer, for example, experience as a home help. Schemes are locally organised and vary a great deal. Some guarantee a job after successful completion, and other agencies who use trainees will offer permanent employment if they are pleased with the young person's performance.

Further details about local YTS/YTP can be obtained from careers teachers, careers offices, Jobcentres, employment offices, or colleges.

New BTEC National diplomas

In response to requests from some colleges experienced in running nursery and caring-skills courses, the Business & Technician Education Council has launched a pilot scheme for a new National-diploma programme in caring studies (nursery nursing) and hopes to pilot a more general National diploma in social care in the near future. These are two-year full-time assessed vocational courses, including practical work placements, and will allow students to enter both the statutory and voluntary caring fields. They are also designed to provide a passage through to higher education. Four O-levels (or their equivalents) are required for entry.

Training courses

The remainder of this chapter will deal with the whole range of training for work in the caring services, including nursery nursing, the health service, mental health, residential work, and day care.

Nursery nursing

Nursery nurses care for children up to seven years of age in a variety of settings – day or nursery centres, nursery (or infant) schools, hospitals, college or town-hall crèches, and as nannies in private houses.

The minimum age of entry to qualifying courses is 16. Successful students receive the certificate of the National Nursery Examination Board (NNEB). The course takes two years, full-time. The NNEB does not itself lay down entry requirements, but individual colleges often ask for one or more O-levels or grade-1 CSEs.

At least 11 colleges are currently offering courses for qualified nursery nurses. In these colleges, the NNEB offers a Certificate in Post-qualifying Studies. It involves college instruction, practical placements, private study, and project work. Applicants must have the NNEB certificate and at least two years in practice as a nursery nurse since training.

There are also pilot schemes for advanced training for nursery nurses.

The health service

About one million people work for the health service. Most are based in hospitals, some are in clinics and health centres, and others work in the community. Below are some details about various jobs in the health service.

Nursing

Nurses are the largest professional group in the National Health Service (NHS). They work in hospitals, health centres, and in people's own homes. They liaise with other members of the health team, such as doctors, physiotherapists, dieticians, and so on.

There are different categories of nurse: enrolled nurse, registered general nurse, and registered sick children's nurse.

The enrolled nurse (EN)   You can train as an enrolled nurse in general, mental, or mental-handicap nursing. The patients may be either adults or children – sometimes both are nursed in the same establishment. Training takes two years. You must be at least 18 years old and you will probably need to have one or two GCE O-levels or grade-1 CSEs or a wide range of grade-2 *and* grade-3 CSEs. Courses take place in schools of nursing, although there are plans to move all nursing training into colleges of further or higher education.

At the end of the course there is a qualifying examination. If you pass successfully, your name can be entered in the professional register. When they are training, enrolled nurses are in the employment of their local area health authority.

The registered general nurse (RGN)   General nurses are no longer called 'State registered nurses' (SRN) – they are now registered general nurses. The training course of a registered general nurse differs from that of the enrolled nurse – it is more detailed and includes more theory. The course takes three years. The statutory minimum educational entry requirements are five GCE O-levels (grades A, B, or C), which must include English language, English literature, or history. In addition, at least five other general-education subjects must have been studied. Some well known schools of nursing may give preference to students with A-levels, and many schools prefer the subjects to have been passed at one sitting.

Minimum age of entry for training is 18. Upon successful completion of the qualifying examination, individuals apply to have their name entered on the professional register.

The registered sick children's nurse (RSCN)   The sick children's nurse is trained to understand the special needs and problems of children from birth to adolescence. There are two ways of training:

i) you can first qualify as an RGN, then go on to take a separate RSCN course of about 56 weeks' duration;

ii) you can take an intensive combined RGN–RSCN course which takes about three years and eight months.

In either case you must be 18 before starting training.

The midwife
Midwives help women during childbirth. They give care and advice during pregnancy and labour and after the birth, and they also look after the new-born baby.

To start training as a midwife you must be 17 or older. The course takes three years, except for those already qualified as RGN (or the old SRN), in which case the period is 18 months. Minimum educational requirements are five GCE O-levels (grades A, B, or C), including English language and a science subject.

The district nurse
A district nurse (sometimes called a *'community nurse'*) provides nursing care for people in their own homes, and in so doing provides a very valuable service to the community. District nurses may be based in health centres, in local doctors' surgeries, or in their own homes.

Training to become a district nurse takes six months. The course is open to RGNs and takes place at a number of colleges in the UK. Upon qualifying, RGNs become district nursing sisters. Occasionally, some health authorities may provide in-service training for enrolled nurses.

The health visitor (HV)
A health visitor's job is to promote health and prevent mental, physical, and social ill-health in the community. This involves educating people in ways of healthy living.

To become a health visitor you must successfully complete a course leading to the award of the health visitor's certificate.

There are four types of course:

i) courses for qualified RGNs (or SRNs) who have had training in midwifery and obstetrics are run in about thirty polytechnics and colleges

of higher education in the UK;
ii) there are modified post-registration courses for nursing graduates in universities, polytechnics, and colleges of higher education;
iii) there are degree courses with a health-visiting option, open to RGNs;
iv) there is an integrated degree course which combines a degree in nursing with a certificate in health visiting.

Minimum educational requirements will be the same as are required for RGN training or for a degree course.

The physiotherapist
Physiotherapists use physical activity and exercise to help prevent and treat disease and injury. Most will work in the NHS, but some are employed in schools, clinics, sports clubs, industry, and private practice.

To train as a physiotherapist you must have a minimum of five GCE passes, two of which must be A-levels. They must include English and two science subjects. There is much competition for these courses, so you may be asked for more than the minimum requirements. The minimum age for entry is 18. Courses take three or four years and lead to the qualification of the Chartered Society of Physiotherapy. You can obtain more information from the Society at 14 Bedford Row, London WC1R 4ED.

The occupational therapist (OT)
Occupational therapy aims to treat mental and physical illness by occupation and activity. Therapists attempt to understand the causes and symptoms of illness and will treat it on a one-to-one basis, in group work, or with recreational activity. The overriding aim of therapy is to help the person to be as independent as possible. OTs work either in hospitals (general or mental) or for social-services departments (in the community) or for voluntary organisations who cater for the severely handicapped.

To train as an occupational therapist, you must be 18 and have at least five O-levels, including English and a science subject, and one A-level. Many courses will require you to have two A-levels. The course takes three years. Applications should be made to training schools through the College of Occupational Therapists (Clearing House), 20 Rede Place, London W2 4TU.

The speech therapist
Speech therapists help people with voice, speech, and language disorders. They work with people of all ages, in school and community clinics, but some are based in hospitals, treating people who have suffered an accident or illness that has caused speech difficulties.

You qualify by successfully completing a degree course recognised by the College of Speech Therapists. These courses are offered in universities and polytechnics, and entry requirements will vary from one institution to another. You can receive more information about these courses from the College of Speech Therapists, Harold Poster House, 6 Lechmere Road, London NW2 5BU.

The doctor or general practitioner (GP)

The role of a general practitioner is a very demanding one. General practitioners' tasks include advising, treating, and often reassuring patients. What people often need is time and attention, rather than medical treatment, so a GP will act as a counsellor – especially to people who would rather go to their doctor than to anyone else. However, the pressure of work may make it impossible for a doctor to perform this counselling function.

Doctors work in general practice, in hospitals, or in community medicine. They work either for the NHS or in private practice.

Entry requirements are high, and there is great competition for places. Training takes at least five years. Once qualified, the doctor has to spend one year (paid) as a resident house officer in an 'approved' hospital, before he can be fully registered.

Courses take place in universities, and applications should be made through the Universities Central Council on Admissions (UCCA) at PO Box 28, Cheltenham, GL50 1HY.

Mental health

The registered mental nurse (RMN) and the registered nurse for the mentally handicapped (RNMH)

Entry requirements for courses are the same as those for registered general nurses. Becoming an RMN means working either in a psychiatric hospital (or the psychiatric ward of a general hospital) or in the community as a *community (psychiatric) nurse*. The latter usually involves helping a patient to resettle in the community after a period in hospital, visiting her at home. This aspect of the work is encouraging, as policies of 'community care' mean that fewer people are spending long periods of time in mental hospitals.

Mental handicap – often present from birth or an early age – requires great skill and patience from the RNMH. This type of nurse will be part of a highly trained team of professionals, including psychologists and social workers. The aim is always to help the mentally handicapped person to become as independent as possible. It involves working in the community, as many mentally handicapped people live outside hospitals.

The psychologist

Psychology is really more of an academic discipline and a general qualification than a profession. Only about 10% of students who study psychology on degree courses actually become professional psychologists – the other 90% go into such areas as social work, nursing, market research, and advertising.

Psychologists study how people think, feel, and behave as single individuals and as individuals within groups. They are interested in the effect that people's behaviour has on others. They should not be confused with psychiatrists – the latter form a quite separate profession for which medical training is required.

Psychologists are interested in how we learn to read and write, solve problems, and gain new skills. They are concerned with 'normal' as well as abnormal behaviour.

A psychologist may work in various disciplines:

a) *Clinical psychologists* have completed a degree in psychology and have had further training over a period of three years part-time or two years full-time. There are about 1000 in the country as a whole. They are based mainly in hospitals, where they deal with the problems of people who appear to be suffering from mental disturbances. Work may involve helping the family of a newly disabled person to adjust to their new circumstances.

b) *Occupational psychologists* are concerned with people at work, or in work settings. They may devise tests and interviewing methods for recruiting staff, assist with training schemes and industrial relations, or work to improve the people's working environment. Some psychologists enter this field of work direct from their degree course; others undergo further training.

c) *Psychotherapists* are closely related to clinical psychologists, but they are more concerned with specific mental illness. Psychotherapy is a form of 'talking therapy' in which people are skilfully encouraged to explore their problems.

d) *Educational psychologists* are employed either by local-authority education departments or in child-guidance clinics. You will find more details about their work in the section on 'Education' below.

The psychiatrist

A psychiatrist is a qualified medical doctor who has specialised in the diagnosis and treatment of mental illness. It takes many years to qualify. Unlike a psychologist, a psychiatrist may prescribe drugs for the treatment of mental illness, and sometimes uses electroconvulsive therapy (ECT). Psychiatrists work either within the NHS or in private practice.

The psychiatric social worker

Psychiatric social workers are based in hospitals. They offer advice and assistance to patients in hospital, and also after patients have returned to the community. Part of their work is to help people to maintain links with the community, thus they may become involved with 'halfway-home' projects – houses where people live with both mutual and outside support for a certain period of time. This acts as a bridge to full community integration.

A psychiatric social worker has undergone generic training (the CQSW) and has subsequently specialised in mental health.

Education

We focus here on two specific professional groups – education welfare officers and educational psychologists.

The education welfare officer (EWO)
The education welfare service is as old as compulsory State education itself. In its early days, work focused on school non-attendance, but now EWOs have a wide range of duties which include acting in a supportive role, providing a link between a pupil's home and school, and liaising with other caring services.

In most localities, the education welfare service is a part of the education department, and EWOs work in teams on an area basis.

People who want to become EWOs are likely to be accepted if they have a good general education. There are no strict entrance requirements, but recently some areas have required candidates to have the CQSW. Some CQSW courses make particular provision for students who wish to work in the education welfare service.

The educational psychologist
There are about 1000 educational psychologists in the country. They have to gain a teacher's qualification as well as a degree. After at least two years' teaching experience, they then take a two-year post-graduate course. So, in total, it takes at least eight years to qualify.

Educational psychologists assess individual children who may have special educational needs and provide advice to schools and local authorities on provision in education. The Education Act 1981 increased their responsibilities – they are now professionally involved in the assessment of children who may need special education, not just those suffering from mental handicap.

Housing

Some of the larger local-authority housing departments have trainee posts for people wishing to embark on a career in housing. Normally applicants should have two A-levels. Part-time day release will be offered to allow trainees to study for the Institute of Housing examinations. Any employee can take the Institute's examinations, but these are difficult to pass when study is combined with full-time work. Better results are obtained by post-graduate students who study full-time over one year.

In the past it was quite usual for a person to start at the basic-grade level in a clerical post and gradually advance his career within the housing service. Nowadays there are degree courses in housing at three polytechnics. Graduates of other disciplines who have demonstrated an interest and commitment to housing may also be employed in housing – they may join homeless-family and single-homeless teams. This work requires qualities of maturity and sensitivity.

A useful point of entry for young people – particularly those who have undergone a preliminary social-work course at a further-education college – is the post of benefits clerk or clerk in an estate-management office. Although the work has administration responsibilities, there is a social-work element to the job which includes advising, interviewing, and helping families deal with rent repayments and other housing matters.

More information about careers in housing can be obtained from the Institute of Housing, 12A Upper Belgrave Street, London SW4 8BA.

Day care

Both local authorities and voluntary organisations (such as 'Age Concern') run day centres. There is a wide variety of centres that cater for the elderly, children, the handicapped, and those who have suffered some form of mental illness. Very often they provide medical treatment, chiropody, hairdressing, occupational therapy, and other services.

There is no one particular qualification for staff who work in day centres. Many staff will only have relevant experience, without formal qualifications. Others will have completed pre-training courses such as the PCSC. Some may hold the CSS, and some the CQSW. Sometimes day-centre staff attend courses of in-service training at colleges of further education. (See later in this annex for more details of this.)

Instructors in adult training centres will usually have had experience in a trade, handicrafts, or the professions. Some will have formal teaching qualifications. A specific qualification is the Certificate in the Further Education and Training of Mentally Handicapped People. A course of training for this certificate is offered at the South Glamorgan Institute of Higher Education and at Stockport College of Technology.

Residential work

Like day-care staff, staff in residential work come from a variety of backgrounds and have a variety of qualifications, or none. There is no specific qualification in residential work. Some will have completed a pre-training course, others will have undergone in-service training, and some will possess the CSS or the CQSW. Less than 4% of residential workers are professionally qualified; however, this situation is changing – an increasing number of CQSW students are choosing to go into residential work, especially residential work with children.

As we have said earlier, residential work can involve work with children, the elderly, the physically or mentally handicapped, the mentally ill, offenders, and those with specific problems such as alcohol or drug abuse.

Local authorities, voluntary organisations, and private concerns all provide residential care. The usual minimum age for entry is 18. If you enter a post without a qualification, you may be given the opportunity of doing in-service training later on, or you may be seconded to go on a full-time training course to qualify professionally. Some agencies offer more in-service training than others. The Probation Service has recently developed an in-service course that requires attendance at a college of further education for one day a week.

Youth and community work

The role of the youth and community worker is becoming more diverse. Sometimes the community comes to the worker (at a youth club or to a worker based in a community centre, for example); sometimes the worker needs to go to the community (for example the community or 'detached' youth worker); and sometimes the job involves a combination of both.

The section of the local authority responsible for youth and community work is usually the 'youth and community service', but in some areas it is still called the 'youth service'. It may be part of the education department or part of the recreation and leisure department. Youth workers are also employed by voluntary organisations, for example the YMCA, YWCA, National Association of Youth Clubs, and National Association of Boys Clubs. Often a percentage of the salary of these workers is provided by the local education authority. Career possibilities have improved in recent years, as there has been greater mobility between the statutory and voluntary sectors of the service.

Working with young people through the medium of informal leisure activities is still the most important part of the youth worker's role. However, youth workers are becoming involved in 'community education' – helping the young to cope with the pressures of life and to face problems – while also making the community more aware of the particular needs of young people. An increasing number of youth and community workers are employed by social-services departments, as *intermediate-treatment officers*. Their job is to develop schemes of community-based care for young people at risk. Others specialise in work with unemployed young people.

There has been a great expansion of the youth and community service over the past 25 years. There are now several ways of becoming a qualified youth and community worker:

a) Satisfactory completion of a two-year full-time diploma or certificate course. Several polytechnics and colleges offer this course of training for youth workers and/or community-centre wardens.
b) Satisfactory completion of a one-year full-time course of post-graduate training for youth workers and/or community-centre wardens. This course is offered by four colleges in the UK.
c) One college in England offers a part-time course of in-service training of three years' duration (Avery Hill College of Education, London).
d) Becoming a qualified teacher can be a sufficient means of entry to the work.

Some CQSW courses have community-work 'options'; therefore some students from these courses will go into youth and community work.

Applicants for specific youth- and community-work courses should normally be over 23, but a few courses will accept people under this age. You will need a minimum of five GCE O-levels (grades A, B, or C) or the equivalent.

More information can be obtained from the Council for Education and Training in Youth and Community Work (CETYCW), Wellington House, Wellington Street, Leicester LE1 6GD.

In-service courses

In-service courses (some regarded as training, others not) take place in all kinds of agencies and settings. It is not possible to go into specific details here. Some of these will be *induction* courses for newly-appointed employees; others will be *staff-development* courses, provided later in staff members' careers.

Outside the agencies, colleges – especially colleges of further education – provide in-service courses of varying lengths for a wide range of personnel in the caring services, such as home helps, care assistants, and EWOs.

In addition to this multiplicity of courses it is necessary to mention one course in some detail – the In-service Course in Social Care (ICSC).

The In-service Course in Social Care (ICSC)

Over 100 colleges in the UK run this course, in close co-operation with a wide range of agencies. The ICSC course is accredited by CCETSW, which issues a 'statement of completion' to each student who attends college for not less than 80% of the total course time and who satisfactorily completes work set by tutors. Most courses require attendance one full day a week over a period of three terms (one academic year).

CCETSW stipulates that applicants to the course should spend not less than two days a week providing social care. Students must have had at least six months' experience in their current job and should have already received some form of induction and basic job training from their agency. The Council makes clear that the course does *not* provide a qualification; nevertheless, it aims to help students in their work, to help them to develop as people, and to help them to think constructively about future training.

The course provides for a range of care workers – for example, those involved in day-care and residential work with children, the elderly, and the handicapped. As a result of a recent development, the course is also open to workers from the Probation Service – these may be ancillaries, working with a team of probation officers, or workers employed in probation hostels or day centres.

For too long, residential work has been regarded as the 'poor relation' of field-work. Lack of provision for the further training of 'unqualified' personnel in the residential sector has been partly responsible for this. It is therefore encouraging that the ICSC has been expanded to provide for students from a wider variety of social-care backgrounds.

Conclusion

This chapter has aimed to provide a comprehensive guide to courses for those intending to enter the caring services.

For 16-year-olds, the CPVE has been a major new development in pre-vocational education. It has replaced some of the more established community-care courses.

For older people seeking a professional qualification in social work, important new changes in the organisation of training were announced in September 1985 by CCETSW. As from the academic year starting in 1990, the CSS and CQSW will cease to exist as separate awards and a single qualifying award in social work will take their place. The usual period of training will be extended from two to three years, and all students will be assessed to a common standard. All students will undertake at least one period of supervised and assessed practice outside their day-to-day place of employment.

This is an encouraging development which should help to boost the traditionally inferior status of residential social work compared with field social work.

Appendix 1 – financial help during training

Funding will depend upon the type of course attended and upon various other factors such as the age of the student and the student's financial situation, or that of his parents.

Mandatory awards (or grants)
Sometimes these are referred to as *'duty awards'*. They are grants given to any eligible students for courses which are *designated* by the Department of Education and Science (DES) in England, Wales, and Northern Ireland or by the Scottish Education Department (SED). Designated courses are of a high academic standard and include degree courses, diplomas of higher education, initial teacher training (including the post-graduate certificate – PGCE), three-year courses leading to a university certificates or diplomas, and other specific courses agreed each year by the DES or SED. You can obtain the complete list from your local education authority (LEA). It includes several courses which lead to professional qualification. Mandatory awards are *not* available for students under 18 years old.

Application for a mandatory award should be made to your LEA (or to the SED in Scotland). Students who are refused a mandatory award can apply for a discretionary award.

Discretionary awards (or grants)
These are made at the 'discretion' of the local education authority. There are two types:

i) Awards for designated courses to students who have not qualified for a

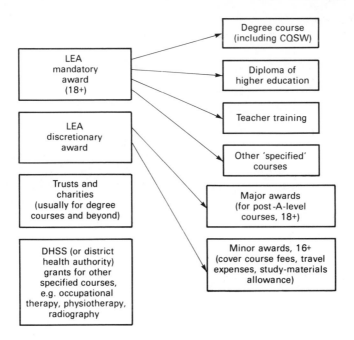

There are various sources of funding while training.

mandatory award (see above). They are paid at mandatory rates.

ii) Awards for any other course. The LEA has absolute freedom to decide whether or not to make these awards and to decide all rates and conditions. In general, LEA's make

a) *major* awards to students on advanced courses (i.e. higher than A-level) – these are paid at near-mandatory rates;

b) *minor* awards to younger students on non-advanced courses – these usually only cover course fees, travel expenses to and from the place of study, and an allowance for books and writing materials. It is this type of award that is allowed to students between 16 and 19 years of age who wish to take a pre-training course such as the CPVE or PCSC.

You should apply to your LEA if you want a discretionary award or to ask for further details about them.

Other sources of funding

A number of trusts and charities award grants to students in certain specific fields of study. Most of these are for initial degree courses and beyond, and there is often great competition for them. You can find out more about such grants from the following books, which should be in your local reference library:

a) *Charities digest*, published by the Family Welfare Association;
b) *Directory of grant-making trusts*, published by the Charities Aid Foundation;
c) *The grants register*, published by Macmillan.

Funding for specific courses

Paramedical courses   There are certain below-degree training courses for paramedical careers for which the DHSS will make a grant at mandatory-award rates. For occupational therapy, the DHSS pays the grant direct. For certain other courses – such as physiotherapy, radiography, remedial gymnastics, and dental hygiene – the DHSS makes an assessment of the grant, but the local district health authority actually pays it. Applications for these grants should be made through the training school that has accepted the student for a course.

Nursing courses   All nursing courses, except those which lead to a degree, are taken while the student is in the full-time paid employment of the local area health authority.

CQSW courses   For CQSW students resident in the UK, there are four sources of financial support from *public* funds:

i) The local education authority awards a mandatory grant where the course is a degree. Where it is not a degree, it may award a discretionary grant.
ii) CCETSW can award grants to students who wish to do a postgraduate course and who intend to work for a local-authority social-services department or voluntary organisation.
iii) The DES awards bursaries to students on a post-graduate course who are employed by a local education authority.
iv) The Home Office, or a local probation committee, can sponsor students who intend to work for the Probation Service, whether or not they are already graduates. (This does not apply in Scotland.)

A diminishing number of students are able to arrange *secondment* on salary from the local authority which employs them. This applies to both graduate and non-graduate courses.

Finally, those students who fail to get financial help from any statutory source can sometimes successfully apply to a charity or a trust fund. The total amount received is likely to be small.

CSS and in-service courses   Strictly speaking, the CSS course is in-service training. Employed students who are on in-service courses, based in a college, will continue to be paid by their agencies while they are training. In addition, course fees and travelling expenses are usually paid, and some agencies also meet the cost of books, writing materials, and subsistence.

Further information on grants

Students in England, Wales, and Northern Ireland should consult *Grants to students: a brief guide*, which is published each academic year and is available in late spring. You can find it in schools, colleges, careers advice centres, and local libraries. Otherwise you can obtain a copy from The Department of Education and Science, Elizabeth House, York Road, London SE1 7PH.

Students in Scotland should consult *Guide to student allowances*, which is available in similar places or from The Scottish Education Department, Awards Branch, Haymarket House, Clifton Terrace, Edinburgh EH12 2DT.

Appendix 2 – useful addresses for information

CCETSW information service

a) England:
   CCETSW Information Service,
   Derbyshire House,
   St Chad's Street,
   London WC1H 8AD.

b) Scotland:
   CCETSW Information Service,
   9 South St David Street,
   Edinburgh EH2 2BW.

c) Wales:
   CCETSW Information Service,
   West Wing,
   St David's House,
   Wood Street,
   Cardiff CF1 1ES.

d) Northern Ireland:
   CCETSW Information Service,
   14 Malone Road,
   Belfast BT9 5BN.

Health-service careers

a) The Nursing and Health Service Careers Centre,
   121–123 Edgware Road,
   London W2 2HX.

b) English National Board for Nursing, Midwifery and Health Visiting,
   Victory House,
   170 Tottenham Court Road,
   London W1P 0HA.

Appendix 3 – useful sources of information

Jobs
The most comprehensive annual guide to opportunities and trends in employment is *Occupations '86*, published by COIC (the Careers and Occupational Information Centre – part of the MSC). It is available in public libraries or careers-information or advisory-service offices.

Courses
A comprehensive guide to courses offered by colleges is the *Directory of further education* '86/'87. It is published annually, for each academic year, by CRAC (the Careers Research and Advisory Centre). It is available in schools, colleges, public libraries, and careers advice offices.

Nurse training
Information about training courses and schools of nursing can be found in the current issue of the *Directory of schools of nursing*, published by HMSO.

Exercise 1 – what a job involves

Having decided on a caring agency (whether statutory or voluntary) for which you would like to work, write a letter to the person with overall responsibility, asking if you can go and interview a member of staff who is doing a job which you yourself would like to do at some time in the future.

At the interview, find out

a) what qualifications (if any) you require to get the job;
b) the experience required before taking up the job;
c) what the job actually entails – such as particular duties and respon- sibilities;
d) the authority structure of the agency, and whom you would be directly responsible to;
e) any aspects of the job which give particular joy or satisfaction;
f) any aspects of the job which are particularly difficult or testing;
g) future promotion or career prospects.

Afterwards, ask yourself

i) how well do your personal qualities equip you to do the job?
ii) what experience do you need to gain in respect of the job?
iii) how might you go about getting this experience?

Exercise 2 – role-play – a college interview

In a group of three, you are to role-play an interview taking place in a college of further education.

Roles

1. A prospective student
2. A member of the college staff conducting the interview
3. An observer

Student
You are very keen to do a particular course (it can be one of your own choosing – pre-training, training, etc.) and feel that you have the ability, application, and commitment to do it. You are keen to convey to the interviewer your personal qualities, strengths, and capabilities. You also want to make it clear that you require certain things from the course in order to help you make progress in advancing your knowledge and skills. You want to find out a good deal about what the course can offer.

Interviewer
You want to find out if the student has the qualities that the college looks for in course members – persistence, concentration, a certain amount of maturity, and a serious commitment. You will also want to try to assess academic ability and some familiarity with study skills, or at least the student's wish to improve what capability she already has.

Observer
You should merely observe and take no part in the proceedings. You should observe very carefully, noting the content of what is said, the mood of the participants and how it changes, and how well they set about the task. Anything else of interest should be noted. At the close of the role-play, you should 'feed back' to the 'actors'.

Task
Allowing at least 20 minutes, role-play the interview. You will then need at least 10 minutes for feedback. Total time – 30 minutes.
Note   The roles can, of course, be reversed, until all three have had a chance to play each.

Following the role-play
A useful discussion could follow the role-play – around general issues in interviews, power and power relationships, the setting of 'agendas', who asks the questions, what questions were asked, etc. It will be useful to bring the whole group together to compare differing experiences.

Exercise 3 – course evaluation

Opinions vary a great deal as to whether training or experience is the more important in preparing for work in the caring services. Most agree that some form of training is essential but that it should of course be relevant to whatever the student intends to do in the future.

Examine a course you have completed in the past, or one you are currently undertaking, in respect to the following criteria:

a) How relevant have you found the different parts of the course to the work in the caring services which interests you?
b) How well were vocational and academic studies represented? Were they balanced or not?
c) How well do you think it has equipped you for any physical skills you will require?
d) Comment on different teaching styles on the course. Which have you found helpful and why?
e) How do you feel the course has contributed to your personal growth?
f) What improvements or innovations would you introduce to the course?

Questions for essays or discussion

1. The Central Council for Education and Training in Social Work has announced that it is to do away with the CQSW and CSS as separate social-work qualifications and is to have a unified system of training. Do you believe that there should be *one* qualification for social workers, both field-workers and residential workers? Give full reasons as to why/why not.
2. We live in a multi-racial society. Some teachers in social-work education believe that 'racism-awareness' training should be an essential ingredient of all courses. What do you think about this?
3. Do you think it is important for professionally qualified carers to have the opportunity to undergo further training, after they have been some time in a post? Give reasons for your answer.
4. Would it be beneficial for nurses, the police, and employees of housing departments to have a greater knowledge of social-care theories and practice? Could those in the caring services likewise gain from an experience of what these other areas of work involve? Explain your answer.
5. Many people feel strongly that our society and the way in which children are brought up encourage 'sex stereotyping' of male and female roles. They believe that we should actively do something about this. Do you think that 'sexism-awareness' training should be a part of the education of someone who intends to work in the caring services? What kinds of issues or topics would you introduce into a course curriculum if you felt strongly about this?
6. Why is it important that courses of training for nursery nurses include a social-studies core as a part of the curriculum?

Annex 2   Practical work placements

An essential ingredient of all social-work and community-care training courses, whether at a preparatory or professionally qualifying level, is the *practical placement*. The way in which placements are organised will depend on the nature of the course and the degree of involvement expected of the student. Most courses offer the student the chance to experience more than one placement.

Placements give students the chance to see the type of work they feel they would like to do and an opportunity to practise some of the skills learned in college.

Broad aims of a practical placement

a) To provide students with learning experiences within a practical setting which will help enhance personal characteristics such as reliability, sensitivity, practical ability, confidence, and initiative.
b) To enable students to link theory and practice through practical work experience in a variety of placements.
c) To develop skills in communication and collaboration with staff and clients.
d) To give students an awareness of the work and range of the caring services.
e) To encourage the development of a critical capacity within the student, so that she may evaluate the standard of care.

Observational placements

Many students beginning social-work preparatory courses may have had no experience of any working environment, let alone a social-work setting. Other students may have done some voluntary work, or have friends or relations who are social workers, or they may have visited friends or relations who live in residential-care establishments. Students on professionally qualifying courses are likely to have worked in only one particular setting.

Taking into account these mixed degrees of experience, the initial placement may be a short introductory one involving the student in an *observational* capacity, aimed at helping her to adjust to the working situation and to begin to learn what can be expected of her in the future. Students will be able to watch carers at their work, observe the daily routine of the agency, and learn to detect the needs of the people being cared for.

Types of placement

Placements may be undertaken within a whole range of social-work and caring agencies. Initially it is more appropriate for students to be placed in practical work situations which are more familiar, where there is more structure and the student is not likely to be given too much responsibility, and where the roles of the workers and the organisation are more easily comprehended.

Where possible, beginners are usually placed in day nurseries, play-groups, or even special schools. Subsequent placements may take place in hospitals, probation hostels, public-health authorities, children's homes, elderly persons' homes, homes for mentally or physically handicapped people, and other voluntary organisations. Some students may be placed with the Probation Service, the education welfare department, social services, or the health service and may accompany professionals as they go about their daily tasks.

Students who are undergoing professional qualifying training will be given actual cases to work on by themselves, but students on preliminary courses will not have this opportunity.

Organisation of placements

Depending on the duration and level of the training course, practical placements may be undertaken on one or more days during the week, which may form part of a *block* experience of one or a number of consecutive weeks. A block placement enables the student to become more fully involved, and it consolidates the experience gained over previous work visits. She will feel a more integrated member of the establishment and may appreciate more fully the day-to-day events and more easily observe the continuity of care. Furthermore, the student will have the opportunity to commit herself more deeply and also respond spontaneously to circumstances.

There now follows an outline of some important aspects of social-work placements. Many of these may perhaps seem obvious to some students – particularly to those who have worked in other settings and have an idea of what is expected from them – but these aspects are mentioned in order to help those who have had little adult life experience outside home and school.

A guide to practical placements

Introductory visits
The idea of an introductory visit is to allow you – the student – to make contact with the agency and to be introduced to the member of staff who will be supervising you during the placement. On your pre-placement visit,

you will be able to establish the expected hours of attendance, familiarise yourself with the social-work setting, and be informed of any special requirements of the agency. (For example, you may be required to wear a uniform – your course tutor should be able to provide the appropriate garment.)

First day of placement
You will probably be given an opportunity to meet other members of staff and be shown round the establishment. You may be allocated specific tasks or be expected to work alongside a particular member of staff. You will be made aware of fire-drill and other safety procedures.

Keeping a diary
Not all courses insist on this practice, but keeping a diary of your day-to-day involvement can be a useful way of focusing and reflecting on your experience. You will also find the diary helpful as a source of reference when you are preparing the assignment which may be expected from you on completion of your placement. You may find it interesting to compare your initial impression with how you feel at the end of your placement.

Practical assistance on observational placements
There is a limit to the amount of time that can be spent simply observing others, so even when you are on an observational visit you may have the opportunity to assist in a practical way. The offer of help is always welcome in any work situation, and observation can of course continue.

Practical placements
There is often a great deal of practical work to be carried out in a residential, day-care, or hospital setting, and routine physical tasks form a high proportion of the carer's role.

Students should be prepared for *lifting*. In order to lift or raise a person in bed, you need to have been properly instructed – some people have seriously damaged their backs straining to move an adult on their own. Lifting takes two people – you will not be expected to lift anyone by yourself, and nobody will mind helping you.

Time-keeping
Residential establishments involve shift work and staff change-overs – all activities are based on rotas. While on placement, although you will not actually be a member of staff, activities will be planned with you in mind. If you are late, organised events may have to be delayed or even postponed – taking a group of elderly residents on a local outing will be more difficult if only one adult is able to supervise. Time-keeping is important for any placement, because social workers will have appointments to keep.

Shift work
Normally your hours of attendance at a placement will be from 9 a.m. to 4

p.m. This is equivalent to the time you usually spend in college. However, in order to fit into the requirements of a residential placement, you may be expected to do shift work. Being available for the hours of a normal college day will be of no use in, say, a children's home or a probation hostel, as most of the residents will be out during this time. Obviously it is important to be around when the clients are there, so you could be asked to start work early in the morning (6 or 7 a.m.) or attend the later shift (from 1 or 2 p.m. until 9 or 10 p.m.).

The late shift may pose problems for some people – for example, older students with young families of their own and students who are unhappy at the prospect of making their own way home late at night. If you have such an objection, do not be afraid to express it – arrangements may be made to accommodate you. At the same time, it is as well to remember that shift work is an essential aspect of residential work – it is something you need to prepare for if you want to do this kind of work.

Attendance
Once you have been accepted by an establishment for whatever duration, you will be included in work plans and provision will be made for you. If you are ill or cannot attend for some reason, it is important to inform your placement supervisor and college tutor as early as possible. Even though your involvement is limited by the length of the placement, residents will be used to seeing you on a particular day of the week and may be disappointed if you fail to turn up – particularly if you have promised to do something for them or with them.

Being respectful
If you are placed in a residential establishment, it is important to remember that you are in someone's home. Naturally you need to observe basic politeness and to spend time learning how things are generally done in the home. At any place of work there will be accepted ways of behaving, and it is important for you to try to be aware of them.

Being co-operative
Being somewhere on placement involves your being a member of a team, albeit in a restricted capacity. Team-work involves sharing, supporting, and co-operating with others, so naturally you should take your part in this process. There may be a number of tedious and routine jobs to perform, but you should be willing to undertake them. Similarly, doing your share of tea-making and washing-up for other staff members is part of being a team member.

Asking questions
People are generally willing to share their knowledge and expertise, especially if you express an interest, but they need to know what it is you do not understand or what you would like to know more about. Obviously you have to select an appropriate time to ask. At the same time, you need

Staffrooms can often provide an ideal setting for relaxed informal discussion.

to be thoughtful about your enquiries and make sure that they are relevant. If you do not ask questions, it may give rise to doubts from the agency as to your degree of involvement.

Confidentiality

In most social-work settings, you are likely to have access to clients' records – particularly those of the clients whom you deal with. You may come across information of a very sensitive nature, and it is important to remember that such information is *strictly confidential*. You may know personally some of the families whose records you are reading, but it is vital that you use this information only to increase your understanding of a person's background.

Under no circumstances must you ever divulge confidential material to anyone other than those with whom you work. It is sometimes appropriate to describe circumstances of case histories to colleagues for academic reasons, but you should avoid mentioning any names, as this could cause embarrassment or suffering. Throughout a career in social work, as in any other life situation, you will be exposed to information which will require your judgement alone to help you decide whether or not you should be silent about it.

Representing your course and the college

Placements form a valuable aspect of any student training. They are made available through the co-operation of the agencies concerned. They take time and effort to set up, and they can be used regularly thereafter by a series of students. Agencies will be keen to take interested and committed students, but a succession of poor students will discourage any organisation from making placements available for other students in the future. It is.important to remember that during your time on placement you are contributing to the reputation of your course and the college you are attending.

The importance of reading

In order to increase your understanding of the work of the agency with whom you are placed, it will be beneficial to back up your experience with relevant reading. You may obtain some written information from the agency itself, which may have its own library or a stock of professional magazines and journals. Otherwise, you should be able to find sources of information about the particular agency or the service in general within your college library. You should do some reading on the special needs of clients with whom you are working or about different play or recreational activities which you might be able to put into practice. Information gained from reading will help you get more from your placement experience.

Placement supervision

Most agencies encourage students to be actively involved as much as possible, but there may be occasions when you will be preferred to be 'seen and not heard'. During your placement, you should receive regular supervision from a member of staff in order to obtain some direction and some feedback about the progress you are making. You will have an opportunity to express any anxieties you may have and to ask questions about the policy and practice of the organisation. For example, you may wish to establish the level of participation expected of students during agency staff meetings. Your supervisor may at some time ask you how you would run a residential home and what changes you would introduce. Your answer will be an indication to her of your commitment and interest in the work.

The standard and availability of supervision and the length of time devoted to it will vary according to the type and duration of the placement. A good supervisor will provide a student with time for considered reflection on social-work policies and practices, will help her to see the relationship between theory and practice, and will generally provide support and encouragement. If any difficulties have arisen during the placement, the supervisor may contact the tutor from college.

Visits from college tutors

College tutors normally visit students once during their placement, but some will visit more often. Ideally they would like to have the opportunity of observing you working with clients, but this is not always possible – for example, when you are accompanying an education welfare officer who is visiting a family, or when you are engaged in bathing a resident in a home for physically disabled people. Tutors will have other college responsibilities and will be free to visit you only on certain days, but they will give you and your supervisor advance notice of their intention to come and see you.

The tutor will be concerned to observe how you manage to put into practice the skills and knowledge you have gained during time spent at college. She will be interested in your understanding of the agency and its involvement with the rest of the community. A placement visit gives the tutor an opportunity to learn more about you as a person, your needs and your ambitions, and a chance to consider appropriate future placements with you.

You may have the opportunity of showing your tutor around the establishment. This will be instructive and interesting for the tutor and will give you the chance to reverse your usual roles – you will be providing the information instead of being the recipient.

At some stage during the tutor's visit, she will spend some time talking to the head of the establishment, or your supervisor, about your attitude and involvement, in order to consider the progress you have made.

Assessment

At the end of the placement, students will usually be assessed by the supervisor and the college tutor. This assessment will have been going on throughout the placement, and the views and opinions of other members of staff will have been sought and taken into account. Additionally, the student will be expected to contribute to the formal assessment.

Assessments made after initial placements will be regarded as tentative, but the final-placement reports will more accurately reflect a student's suitability for the work and readiness to be considered for full-time employment.

Assessment forms vary according to the level of the course. The example on page 302 has been devised to illustrate some of the basic aspects that assessors will be looking for. Some colleges will require a fuller assessment and reports, particularly for students completing final placements.

Comments

Placement supervisor's comments   Susan has been on placement for one day each week for ten weeks and has spent the last two weeks on block practice. She has been an outstanding student. She was very reticent at first and a little uncertain, but has since become very involved and has worked enthusiastically. She has shown a great deal of interest in and

Name of College

Name of student: Susan McIntosh

Duration of placement: Dates from Jan. 19— to April 19—

Name of organisation: Thomas Lottie elderly persons' home

Key to assessment: 1. Excellent.   2. Very good.   3. Good.
4. Below expectations.   5. Poor.   6. Very poor.

Please tick appropriate box.

	Tutor assessment						Supervisor assessment						Self assessment					
	1	2	3	4	5	6	1	2	3	4	5	6	1	2	3	4	5	6
1. Attendance	√						√						√					
2. Punctuality		√						√						√				
3. Initiative	√						√								√			
4. Reliability		√					√								√			
5. Manner and appearance			√					√							√			
6. General attitude		√					√								√			
7. Willingness and ability to help	√						√								√			
8. Understanding of situation	√						√							√				
9. Identification of clients' needs	√							√						√				
10. Ability to relate to clients	√						√							√				
11. Relationship with staff		√						√							√			
12. Practical development	√						√								√			
13. Communication skills	√						√							√				
14. Practical caring skills		√						√							√			
15. Response to guidance		√					√							√				

A placement assessment form

understanding of residents. I think they will miss her.
Signed: *W. Cross*

College tutor's report   Susan has matured during this, her second, placement. She has overcome her tendency to stand back and await instruction and has involved herself fully and enthusiastically. I think she has enjoyed the setting and responded to the support given to her by various members of the home's staff.
Signed: *J. Brock*

Student's comments   I have enjoyed the placement and liked the atmosphere of the elderly persons' home. I enjoyed working with the residents. I feel I am suited to this kind of work. This has been my best placement so far.
Signed: *S. McIntosh*

When they make their final assessment, the tutor and supervisor will be looking at how well you have managed to fit into the work placement. They will have considered your relationships both with clients and with members of staff and how you have used your time when not engaged in a specific task or activity. They will have observed whether or not you have gone about your job in a cheerful and co-operative manner, and your reliability will have been judged by your punctuality and degree of efficiency in carrying out instructions. Above all, they will have gauged the interest you have shown and the commitment you have demonstrated.

The assessment reports can be a valuable source of information about how others see you – of points of weakness and areas of strength. You can compare these with your own thoughts and feelings about your experience.

Conclusion

Each placement experience is unique and contributes importantly to the student's development and understanding of the work. However, the organisations themselves also can benefit from a student being placed with them, even though it makes added work – particularly for the supervisor.

Having somebody new around can be refreshing for both staff and residents alike. A new person has the opportunity to see the situation from an outside point of view, before she gets used to the routine, and this may produce some new ideas. At the highest level, a student may be able to highlight redundant practices or make constructive suggestions for change. Essentially, though, the value of a student to an establishment is that she provides an extra 'pair of hands' and assistance which eases the work-load of existing staff.

Tutors too can benefit from a student's practical placement. Visits to and discussions with students can inform the tutor of current practices and of any changes that are being made. In this way, tutors can be more up-to-date in their knowledge about the practical social-work situation.

Finally, you may not always be able to be placed with the agency of your choice but you will often be given an opportunity to express a preference. It is not always practicable to arrange placements to suit each individual's choice. Sometimes a tutor will place a student in an agency distinctly not of the student's choosing, where the tutor feels that maturity and understanding could be gained. Sometimes students welcome the chance of an early placement in a field where they would not normally wish to work but where they can get experience and extend their knowledge of the caring agencies. It is normal, however, for students to undergo their final or major placement within an agency of their chosen field, so students undergoing professional training who have chosen community work, or, alternatively, who have selected the probation option, will be placed in those fields. Wherever a student is placed, she always has an opportunity to develop skills and understanding of a kind which may be generalised to any social-work setting.

Appendix 1 – an account of a typical day's work for a student in an infant school

School begins at 8.55 with morning assembly – usually prayers and a hymn. The nursery nurse's first duty of the day is to usher the children into the hall and try to form some kind of orderly line with them. However, if the nursery nurse has strong convictions against attending the assembly, then she does not have to be present.

After assembly, the children promptly walk to their appropriate classrooms and take off their coats and bags. The time is about 9.10, and the teacher does the register and various administrative tasks while the nursery nurse prepares for whatever activity the children are doing that day, such as painting/printing or modelling.

She usually has a small group of children to work with when they have finished their reading or mathematics, as the class works the integrated day.

If the children have any difficulties with their mathematics or English/reading, she will often break off from the creative activity to help alleviate the teacher's work-load of hearing readers etc. The nursery nurse also works with the teacher to organise the displays around the room and is often given the opportunity to do displays on her own while the teacher is occupied with the children's lessons.

The days are always varied, according to the class curriculum, and the nursery nurse generally helps with all activities such as dance, physical exercise, and reading stories. She is able to take on as much responsibility as the teacher feels she can cope with and is necessary at any particular time.

Typical school day

8.55 Assembly
9.10 Mathematics/painting
10.30 Break
10.45 Painting/constructive
play

12.00 Dinner
1.30 Musical movement
2.45 Break
3–3.30 Storytime/prayer

Appendix 2 – account of a typical day's work for a student in a day nursery

9.00–10.00 The room has previously been set out as follows:

Basic play – sand, water, paint;
Constructive play – e.g. octagons;
Imaginative play – home corner;
Manipulative play – dough;
Creative play – collage;
Fine movements – puzzle, crayons;
Book corner.

'Free' play is the predominant theme of the first hour, and during this time the student is expected to generally integrate with the children and encourage them to participate, but giving them freedom of choice.

There are intermittent chores such as changing children, cleaning up any mess in the room, taking soiled clothes to the laundry, as well as looking out for the general safety of the children.

9.30 Breakfast is served in the room.

10.00–10.15 Coffee break.

10.15–10.50 The children play outside with bicycles, scooters, baby trucks, etc. The student is expected to mix with the children and talk to them, pick up any who fall over, and take any child inside who needs changing. She should be alert and able to cope with any accident or conflict.

10.50 Prepare the room for lunch – put away toys etc., clean the floor, and set tables.

11.00 Continue outside supervision.

11.20 Take children to the bathroom.
Bathroom routine: toilet (undress any children who cannot manage); encourage each child to get his own facecloth, to wash, and to hang up his towel on the appropriate hook.

11.30 Sit down to lunch. Serve food. Ensure that children eat as much as possible. Eat own lunch with them.

12.00 Clean up room. Put children to bed. Set out toys (alternative choice to morning). For children who don't sleep – story-time.

12.30–1.15 Lunch break. (This is in fact 'time away from the children'.

305

The student is expected not to leave the establishment without permission.) During lunch break, any preparation for afternoon must be done. One day a week the student undergoes a supervision session with her nursery nurse, when she is told of her negative and positive attributes and areas she must concentrate on.

1.15–2.00 Continue outside supervision.

2.00–2.30 Family time. The groups of children (known as 'families') are separate, and the student supervises this time maybe two or three times a week, having chosen and prepared the topic beforehand – creative work, for instance. There are usually six to eight children and, while taking them alone, the student is in fact being herself observed by the training nursery nurse.

2.30–3.00 Clean up the room, set tables for tea, take children to the bathroom.

3.00–3.15 Tea.

3.15–4.00 Outside supervision.

In bad weather, outside play is replaced by continued free play with inside toys.

During the day the student is often asked to sing or read stories to the children. She is also expected to show interest in the children's background and to talk to their parents.

Exercise – role-play – introductory placement visit

Situation
An initial visit to a placement in order for a student to introduce herself and find out more about the agency and what is to be expected of her during the placement.

Roles

1. A member of staff of the agency
2. A student
3. An observer

Member of staff
You are the member of staff responsible for the student who is about to be placed with you. Your task is to explain the function of the agency and what will be expected from the student.

Student
You are about to undertake a placement with the agency or organisation. You need to ask pertinent questions and be able to explain about the course you are on and what you expect from the placement.

Observer
Observe the meeting between the member of staff and the student and make any relevant comments.

Task
Role-play the meeting. All the roles can then be interchanged.

Questions for essays or discussion

1. You are placed with an organisation and you observe a member of the care staff being short and abusive to one of the residents. This is the second time you have seen this, and you wonder whether you should mention the matter to your superior. What do you do?

2. If you had six termly placements during a two-year course, what type of placements would you choose for yourself and why would you choose them? In what order would you prefer to experience them?

3. What do you expect from visits from your college tutor? Does the tutor visit the placement often enough and stay long enough, or does the tutor call too frequently?

4. Write up a week's placement. Categorise time you spent doing various things. How much time did you spend talking to clients? Was this enough?

5. Write up a case study of one of the people you have met on your placement.

6. How important is it to keep a diary during your placement? In what ways have you found the practice useful?

7. What is the value of supervision, and why is it important that supervision should be made available at regular times?

Index